PRACTICES OF COMPASSION

Practices of Compassion

AN EXPLORATION AND EXPERIENCE

Edited by
M. DARROL BRYANT
LAMA DOBOOM TULKU
YANNI MANIATES

WORLD BUDDHIST CULTURE TRUST

MANOHAR
2018

First published 2018

ISBN 978-93-5098-193-1

Published by
Ajay Kumar Jain *for*
Manohar Publishers & Distributors
4753/23 Ansari Road, Daryaganj
New Delhi 110 002

Printed at
Shri Ganpati Enterprises
Delhi 110 052

Contents

Acknowledgements

EVERY PROJECT REQUIRES a host of people making varied contributions to achieve the project's desired goals. Our project was, from the beginning, intended to be a contemplative seminar as well as a publication that would share with a wider audience the fruits of our coming together for five solid days of silence, spiritual practice, lively exchange and dialogue, graced with the bonds of appreciation, even friendships that emerged.

We want to begin by thanking the Venerable Doboom Tulku for initiating, funding, and convening the contemplative seminar on the Practices of Compassion. His words of welcome set the perfect tone, and his contributions throughout were wise and to the point. The whole event exceeded all of our expectations and we are immensely grateful. And we are especially thankful to Doboom Tulku's assistant Ms. Chungkey. Her ever-present smile, her helpfulness, and her good humor made everything run smoothly.

We also want to acknowledge the assistance of the Rev. Packiam Samuel, the Director of the Henry Martyn Institute. His facilities along with the lovely garden and its outdoor dome made this a very apt place for our meeting. And the food if we may add was excellent.

This seminar began with a 'seed idea' from Professor Anne C. Klein that emerged two years before our actual meeting in Hyderabad. Prof. Klein had earlier been a student with Doboom Tulku in India. He and Prof. Klein renewed their connection when Doboom came to the USA. It was subsequently discussed with Professor M. Darrol Bryant, when he met Doboom in Trenton, Ontario, Canada, where it achieved its final form. Darrol then assumed responsibility for gathering the written contributions and distributing them to all the participants through the modern miracle we call the internet.

Some scholars contributed papers but were not able to join us in Hyderabad. Thank you. While many of your contributions were discussed in Hyderabad, we missed your presence. But they have enhanced this volume.

It is finally the participants themselves at our contemplative seminar that we must acknowledge. The best laid plans come to nothing if the right people don't show up. You were the right people. You came from many different religious/spiritual backgrounds. You were well grounded in those traditions – yet you were all open to listening to each other and were respectful of diverse views. Often, meetings of scholars are marred by an academic competitiveness, but we saw none of that here. Perhaps it's because we were not all professional academics. Or, more likely, that we were all well-grounded in our own spiritual paths and thus able to relate openly to others. Or, it may have been that we first met and connected with each other in silence and the right spirit. Whatever the reason, the bonds of goodwill and friendship that marked our goodbyes to one another at the end of our meeting in Hyderabad continued to inspire us as we put together this volume. Our world is always, but especially now, in need of practices of compassion.

THE EDITORS

Introduction

IN LATE JANUARY 2016, sixteen participants gathered in Hyderabad in Telangana, south India. We had come to participate in a Contemplative Seminar on Practices of Compassion. Our host was the Venerable Doboom Tulku, the long-time head of Tibet House in New Delhi, but now the Managing Trustee of the World Buddhist Cultural Trust. We were meeting in the facilities of the Henry Martyn Institute, a centre established in Lahore in the 1940s to engage in dialogue with the Muslim world. The Institute had finally come to settle in Hyderabad following partition. We were a group of scholars, practitioners, and lay persons from Buddhist, Christian, Hindu, Jain, Muslim, Sikh and other spiritual traditions. Another ten people had sent written contributions but were unable to join us in India.

Hyderabad was long at the heart of the Muslim community in southern India – and it remains so today. It is home to the iconic Charminar, a remarkable masjid from the sixteenth century, and to the nearby Golkonda citadel/fort/palace that was the centre of a vibrant fifteenth century Muslim state. But even earlier there was an important Buddhist centre nearby. Nagarjuna, a second century Buddhist, had established Nagarjunakonda, that became the location of several Buddhist monasteries and universities. It is there that the Venerable Doboom Tulku hopes to establish a Centre. Echoes of this multi-faith history and the centuries' old exchange between Muslims and Hindus permeated our gathering.

We called it a 'contemplative seminar' because we did not want it to be a conventional conference. We felt it was imperative to meet in silence and meditation before we turned to the exchange of words. So each day we began with a half-hour of a spiritual exercise led by the members of our gathering. They decided if we would meet in silent meditation or prayer or movement. We also closed each day with another half-hour of silence and/or a spiritual practice. This proved to have a significant impact on our seminar.

Then, over the five days of our gathering, we turned to discuss the papers that had been written on practices of compassion – not theories, but practices. Notice that we gathered to discuss the papers, not hear them read. We had circulated all the papers to the participants in the months leading up to our gathering in Hyderabad. They were sent out with the reminder that we would not be reading papers, but only discussing papers, sharing our questions and our responses. Prof. Bryant, who had worked with Lama Doboom Tulku and Prof. Anne Klein in shaping this seminar, had insisted on this format. His argument was that endless reading of papers undercut the purpose of our gathering: to engage and learn from one another. While it took some getting used to, we found it to be a useful strategy. It enhanced the vitality and tone of our exchange and dialogue.

Now when we move from the immediacy of the living encounter that is a contemplative seminar to a volume containing the written contributions, we lose all the moments of insight, the immediate yeas and nays of discussion, the dynamics of dialogue, and the wonder of shared silence. We simply have to ask the reader to imagine everything that is happening in the give and take of discussion.

In the volume you now hold in your hands, we have put the papers into categories, largely by tradition. But here we will introduce you to what you will read by introducing the papers in the order in which they were discussed in Hyderabad. And we will also mention the periods of silence and meditation that framed each day. This may give the reader a more lively portrayal of how things unfolded for the participants in Hyderabad.

We began in the late afternoon of 27 January 2016 with 'Mangalacharan' or 'Verses of Auspiciousness' by Swami Chidananda, Ven. Olande Ananda Thera, and Mohammed Fayyazuddin. We were then welcomed by the Venerable Doboom Tulku and Rev. Packiam Samuel, the Director of the Henry Martyn Institute. Professor M. Darrol Bryant outlined the schedule of papers to be discussed and the meditative sessions for the coming days.

Yanni Maniates then led us in our first contemplative/meditative session. It was deeply moving and a different way to begin our encounter with one another.

The following morning, we met in our second contemplative session. It was led by Swami Chidananda and drew upon Hindu spiritual practices.

We began our discussion by turning to a fascinating paper by Yanni Maniates entitled 'May You Be Free from Suffering, May You Be At Peace. . . ,' Director of Eco-Ministry and Event Coordinator for the Interspiritual Network, he has been a spiritual teacher for more than thirty years. Here, Maniates shares with the reader his experience of what he calls 'the Embrace'. It is, he continues, this 'unitive experience' that awakens us to compassion for ourselves, others, and the earth. It also grounds our quest to free ourselves and others from suffering and the quest for peace. Its emphasis on transformative experience rather than theory struck an important first note for our discussion.

It was followed by two papers by Shiv Talwar, an engineer who is also the founder of the Spiritual Heritage Education Network (SHEN) in Canada, entitled 'Breathe Deeply for Health, Wellness, and Compassion: A Summary' and 'Breathe Deeply for Health, Wellness and Compassion'. Darrol Bryant has known Shiv for decades and has seen the growth of SHEN. It hosts an annual conference that brings together a global cast of spiritual teachers from diverse traditions, sciences, and professions. Here, Shiv explores the physiology of meditation, arguing that it is 'deep breathing' that 'opens our minds to higher emotions of selfless love and compassion'. It was another angle of vision on the meditative experience.

We also drew some links between Talwar's contributions and a contribution by Brenden Ozawa-de Silva entitled 'Compassion at the Core.' Brendan is a Professor of Psychology at Life University in Georgia in the USA. He has been involved in a decade-long programme that has developed a science based Cognitively Based Compassion Training (CBCT). This is a programme that draws on Tibetan Buddhist traditions but employs them in a non-religious way. It has been successfully tested with different groups. Brenden says that he has learned that 'self-centeredness is the single source of all our woe…' and that this programme 'shifts our understanding of who we are as human beings'. It also includes some material on recent scientific research on meditation.

In our second session that morning, we considered the contribution of Zuleikha on 'Awareness, Art and Service'. Zuleikha is an international performer and educator who explores 'ancient spiritual and movement technologies of the sacred'. Some of us would call her a dancer, but she quickly allowed us to see how she combines movement and spirituality in ways that both educate and heal. Rather than talking about her contribution, she performed it. It was very moving, and she also shared with us some of her practices for making a more compassionate world.

We also considered the excellent contribution of Professor James Gollnick on 'Dreamwork as a Practice of Compassion'. Gollnick has been recording his dreams since the late 1960s while pursuing formal and informal study of psychology, especially the work of Carl Gustave Jung. He has been offering courses on dreams and on Jung at the Universities of Toronto and Waterloo since the 1970s. Here he recounts his own experience with dreams, the shifting story of the interpretation of dreams, and current developments in dreamwork that underscores its compassionate nature. Although he was unable to attend our seminar, his paper brought forth another dimension – dreamwork – concerning practices of compassion.

In the afternoon session we began our discussion of Buddhist traditions and practices of compassion with Prof. Anne Klein's account of 'The Four Immeasurables'. A notable Buddhist scholar at Rice University in Texas, she focuses her attention on 'equanimity (*upekkha*), love (*metta*), compassion (*karuna*) and joy (*mudita*)'. These are the qualities that mark the Awakened One and can transform the practitioner of the Buddhist Way. She draws upon several Buddhist teachers in outlining the meaning of each of these terms, beginning with equanimity. Tsongkhapa, the fifteenth century founder of the Gelug order of Tibetan Buddhist, defined equanimity as 'freedom from reactions, positive or negative' and 'the ability to be even-minded toward everyone'. It is on this foundation that we see the emergence of the other three qualities that 'deepen our connection with others'. Klein notes that it is 'with practice – lots of practice! – of the four boundless states' that we 'gain access to the wisdom of our real nature'. It is a dense piece but one that certainly rewards our attention.

'Compassion from the Buddhist Perspective' by Venerable Wangchuk Negi furthers the discussion on one of the 'four immeasurables': compassion/*karuna*. A Professor of Buddhist Philosophy at the Central University of Tibetan Studies in Sarnath, India, the place of the Awakened One's first sermon following his enlightenment 2500 years ago, Negi opens his piece by reminding us that 'genuine happiness does not come from external forms or through objects, it is obtained within'. He then leads us through the philosophically rich and multifaceted understandings of compassion found in the Buddhist traditions. Yet Negi continually reminds us that our compassion for others is empty if it is not the centre of our actual practice and daily life. Is there any other tradition that has given us as rich and deep an understanding of compassion as we find in Buddhism?

Our next session turned to Swami Chidananda's 'Interwoven into the Way of Life: Compassion Practiced in the Hindu Tradition'. Swamiji opened his contribution by recounting an incident from his school days involving a teacher of sports, a confiscated ball, and the intervention of another teacher. His point was that compassion is woven into the daily life of Hindus; it is part of ethos of Hindu India. He then recounts many examples of 'compassion in action' in Indian life, ranging from the actions of Mahatma Gandhi to compassion for animals and in family life. He also distinguishes those acts of compassion that grow out of one's religious commitments and those that come from other sources. It was a good reminder for a group of largely religious practitioners.

M.P. Mathai's contribution on 'Gandhi and Compassion' came after our meeting in Hyderabad but should be mentioned here. Born in Gujarat in 1869, Mohandas Karamchand Gandhi became the leader in a struggle for the Indian community in South Africa and the struggle for independence from Great Britain in India. He was known to the world as Mahatma (great soul) Gandhi. Here Mathai explores the twin issues of Gandhi's own practices of compassion and the compassion embedded in his way of *satyagraha/truth force* and *sarvodaya/social well-being for all.* It enlarges the scope of compassion.

At the end of the day, we moved outside to the dome-covered structure in the middle of a garden for a period of contemplation in movement and dance led by Zuleikha. She also taught us some of the exercises developed for working with palliative cancer patients and homecare patients.

The following morning our contemplative session was led by the Venerable Wangchuck Negi. It involved some Tibetan chants and silence.

Our discussion focused on 'A Bouquet of Quotations on Compassion and Loving Kindness' that had been gathered for us by the Venerable Olande Thera. Originally from the Netherlands, he came to India in search of spirituality. He encountered Buddhism and has been in Sri Lanka for decades. He has obviously been gathering spiritual flowers along the way. His contribution provoked a lot of discussion concerning compassion as we considered his bouquet with quotations from HH the Dalai Lama, Thich Nhat Hanh, and many others.

We continued with Buddhism when we turned to Prof. Tashi Paljor's paper on the 'The Need of Compassion for the Attainment of Buddhahood'. A long-time professor of Buddhism in Ladakh, Dr. Paljor's paper emphasized the necessity of compassion for achieving higher states of consciousness. He emphasized the importance of the Buddha's teaching and reminded his readers of the 'rarity of birth as a human being'. Thus, the importance of taking advantage of this lifetime to study the teachings and gain merit.

In the midst of these more philosophical discussions, we recalled another paper that shifted the focus of our conversation. Author of *Living Religions*, a leading introductory textbook to the world's religions in North America, Mary Pat Fisher introduces us to 'Gobind Sadan's Practices of Compassion.' Gobind Sadan is a remarkable farm/centre on the outskirts of New Delhi. It was initiated by Baba Virsa Singh (*c.* 1934-2007), a Sikh holy man who acknowledged the authenticity of all prophets/religious founders, in the late 1960s. Gobind Sadan (*The House of God without Walls*) is dedicated to serving others. Baba Virsa Singh, along with his followers and local people, transformed some barren ground into a successful farm. It attracted local people: Sikhs, Muslims, Hindus, and others. It has become an interfaith community of over 250 people with shrines dedicated to Jesus, Mahavira, Buddha, Hindu deities, a Jewish wailing wall and there is also now a Muslim mosque. Mary Pat is now the resident director of Gobind Sadan, which is an important example of compassion in practice.

Coming back to our seminar, the afternoon discussion focused on the Muslim Way. Mohammed Fayyazuddin's informative paper on 'Namaz: A Practice of Compassion' led us into an important discussion of Islam. *Namaz* is the Urdu word for prayer. Fayyazuddin reminded us that Muslims are obligated to pray five times a day, and every prayer begins '…in the name of Allah, the most merciful, the most Compassionate…'. It is prayer that structures and shapes the life of a Muslim. This insight also informed the contribution of Seyed Azmayesh on 'Compassion according to the Sufi Masters'. He speaks of the 'applied compassion' found in the stories and poetry of Sufis, the mystics of the Muslim world. Both of them emphasize the centrality of the transformed and healed heart; it is the gift of the One who is most Merciful, most Compassionate.

Our closing contemplative session that day was led by Fayyazuddin and a couple of friends who had joined us that day. They showed us the way that Muslims pray, as we all stood shoulder to shoulder, as Muslims would when they go to the mosque. It was a fitting conclusion to our day and one that for many was their first encounter with this living faith. It was an antidote to the popular image of Islam that dominates the mass media the world over these days.

Following our meeting in Hyderabad, we added two further contributions that address practices of compassion in the Muslim world. During our contemplative seminar we learned of Maulana Wahiduddin Khan, author of more than 200 books on the teachings of Islam, wisdom, prophecy, and peaceful co-existence. He lives in New Delhi, and following our seminar Darrol Bryant and Yanni Maniatis went to see him. They met him in his modest home in Nizamuddin, New Delhi, where he graciously and wisely spoke about his understanding of compassion in Islam. We invited him to make a contribution to the volume and 'Zakat: A Practice of Compassion' is the result. Here, Maulana underscores the centrality of compassion in Islam. Allah is 'merciful and compassionate' as the Koran repeatedly proclaims. This is exemplified in *zakat* or alms-giving/charity, one of the means of 'instilling compassion for our fellow-beings' in Islam. Zakat is obligatory on all Muslims. It is a religious obligation – 2½ per cent of one's wealth 'to public welfare'. But there is also a voluntary charity/*sadagat* in Islam. It is a manifestation of the 'spirit of helping others' exemplified in the field of education. Even every little gesture – a smile, a helping hand – is a good deed/*sadaga*. We learned much from his paper.

Idrisa Pandit, the Director of the Studies in Islam programme at the University of Waterloo – and Darrol Bryant's colleague – provides an insightful contribution for 'our troubled world' in 'Compassion in Islam: Kindness in Action'. Ours is a time in which some seek to hijack Islam and fail to grasp that 'compassion in Islam encompasses the love and mercy of God'. Idrisa guides us into compassion in Islam by looking to the Koran and Muhammad. It was fascinating to discover that *rahma*, the Koranic term for compassion, has as its root/*rahm* meaning 'the womb source of motherly love'. It is 'part of our primordial being'. She also discusses Muhammad as example and presents some remembrances of his compassionate actions. She then provides a moving account of the guiding principles of 'Muslim Social Services in Kitchener/Waterloo', a local initiative that now involves volunteers from all faith communities.

On the following morning, the Venerable Olande Ananda Thera led our contemplative session, drawing on his Buddhist tradition. What kind of communion occurs when we meet in silence?

We then turned to the contribution of Darrol Bryant's 'Practices of Compassion: The Way of the Heart in Christianity.' Bryant introduces his paper by acknowledging how pervasive the discourse of compassion has become. He didn't say, but should have, that we need less discourse and more practices of compassion. So after reviewing the meaning of compassion in the Christian scripture and the world religions, he gives us three examples of compassion in Christianity. One is drawn from the Protestant traditions – he calls it institutional compassion – and cites the programme of Lutheran World Service and SODEPAX at the World Council of Churches. The second is the renewal of contemplative prayer in the Catholic Church, but opening out to other Christian groupings and beyond. Here, it is compassion as spirituality. And the third is the *Way of the Pilgrim* from the Orthodox tradition. It involves integrating the Jesus Prayer (Lord Jesus Christ have mercy on me!) into one's breathing so that it becomes one's interior that manifests in love and compassion for one's fellows. As in other traditions, compassion is manifest in a variety of practices.

There are two other contributions to the volume on practices of compassion in Christianity that were written after our meeting in Hyderabad. The first is by Vic Froese, a former student of Professor Bryant and now the Librarian at the Canadian Mennonite University in Winnipeg, Manitoba, Canada. It is entitled 'Practices of Compassion among Anabaptists'. Anabaptists emerged in the time of the Reformation in Western Christianity. They were Christians who practiced adult baptism, refused to take oaths other than to God, and refused to fight in wars. They formed a separate community of those who were first 'baptized in the spirit, then with water, and took up the Cross to follow Jesus'. They came to have different names like Mennonites, Amish, and Hutterites. Today, there are roughly 1.8 million Anabaptists of all stripes, the largest group being the Mennonite Brethren who have churches like other Protestant Christians. Other Mennonites like Old Order or horse-and-buggy Mennonites have separated communities. Here, as Froese notes 'Jesus is their common measuring stick for Christian compassion'. For them, compassion is not a concept, but a life lived in obedience to Jesus.

The second contribution by David J. Goa, the Founder/Director of the Chester Ronning Centre for Religion in Public Life in Alberta, is entitled 'Passions and the Disciplines of Compassion: Christian Orthodoxy and the Spiritual Life'. Goa takes a different route to compassion. He argues that in the Orthodox traditions, compassion is not a virtue to exercise, but emerges out of the disciplines of 'self-emptying that opens . . . our capacity to be present . . . '. to ourselves and others. 'Co-suffering love, compassion,' Goa sees, 'bubbles up when our own struggles, passions, are no longer front and centre.' It is a view of compassion that merits considerable reflection.

A further contribution by Bob Chodos, 'To be Holy is to Practice Compassion', came after our meeting in Hyderabad, and leads us into the Jewish world. In the Holiness Code of the Bible are found many commandments including the commandment that 'you shall love your neighbour as yourself.' It emphasizes the fact that 'to be holy you need to practice compassion'. This lies at the very heart of Jewish teaching. Chodos acknowledges that Jews, like other communities, have a mixed record on this front, but he also sees faithfulness to this teaching. He recounts some stories from the Bible, especially the Book of Ruth, but then turns his focus on the Jewish communities he has known. His parents were among those who founded community institutions to 'care for those in need' in Montreal, Quebec. And he notes the hospitals and other institutions that Jews established. Already in 1863, a 'Young Men's Hebrew

Benevolent Society' was established and the first hospital when there were only 500 Jews in the area. 'Compassion in personal relations is,' he observes, 'at the core of Rabbinic teaching.' He concludes with an account of the synagogue in Waterloo, Ontario, Canada, struggling with the question of sponsoring a Syrian refugee. There was divergent opinion, but they finally remembered the command 'to love the stranger' and voted to sponsor a refugee. It was compassion practiced.

Again our day ended with some silent contemplation led by Darrol Bryant. But as we began, we turned to watch Jiahua Zhu, a Chinese student that Doboom Tulku had invited to our seminar, create a Chinese calligraphy for our meeting. As the brush flew across the white paper and Chinese characters appeared we were entranced. It was a saying of Lao-tzu, the Old Master (a Daoist), it read: 'I have three treasures, guard and treasure them. The first is compassion; the second, frugality; the third, refusal to be 'foremost of the world'. We then sat in silence to heed the 'still small voice' within.

On the final day we again began in silence led by one of the Buddhist monks.

It was fitting as we turned to 'The Silence of Compassion: The Practices in Words' written by Sudhamahi Regunathan, formerly the Vice-Chancellor of Jain Vishva Bharati University. It eloquently presents a Jain perspective on compassion. She writes that 'the removal of all fear, known as *abhayadanam,* is the highest . . . action . . . the supreme manifestation of compassion' in the Jain Way. It is fear that blocks the development and manifestation of compassion. So the Jain renunciate (monk/nun) follows the 5 principles of *ahimsa* (non-violence), *aparigraha* (non-possessiveness), *achavtya* (no stealing, no coveting), *brahmacharya* (overcoming lust), and *asatya* (no speaking untruths). As one incorporates these principles into one's life, they lead to 'right perspective, right knowledge, and right conduct'. Jains see all life forms as endowed with soul. And this is why *ahimsa* extends to all living things. Jains are known for their compassion to animals and the establishment of bird hospitals.

We then moved into a new area when we considered 'Interspirituality and the Practice of Compassion', the joint offering of Kurt Johnson, Swami Shraddhananda and Yanni Maniates. While earlier contributions moved in an interfaith context, this contribution explored the practice of compassion in the context of 'interspirituality'. What is that? As the authors note: 'interspirituality takes many forms'. It is an emergent phenomenon found largely in the West among those who are exploring spirituality 'across religious boundaries' and outside traditional structures of authority. Some talk about 'multiple belonging' or being 'trans-traditional', while others identify as being 'spiritual but not religious', still others adopt a 'worldly or feminist or eco-centered spirituality' and some reject any limiting title and create virtual communities on the internet. It is an important aspect of contemporary life. To learn more of interspirituality, get Kurt Johnson and David R. Ord's award winning *The Coming Interspiritual Age* (2013).

Here they explore three expressions of this emerging interspiritual world. First, there is the 'Community of the Mystic Heart'. This is an initiative that grew out of the writings of Brother Wayne Teasdale, a Catholic monk, teacher and author, and his friendship with Kurt Johnson. Shraddananda and Maniates are also involved in this initiative that rests on a 'vision of the inner and outer practice of compassion', the merging of being and doing, both as individuals and as a part of a community. Secondly, there is the nurturing of compassion through virtual communities on the internet. These groups are exploding on the internet, linking individuals and building connections and communities. They also lead to the practice of compassion in the wider world of politics and policy. Whether or not they will sustain themselves over time we will have to see. But there is an energy there that is promising.

Another post-Hyderabad contribution entitled 'Compassion as "Living for the Sake of Others"' by Thomas Walsh moves us into that wider world. Walsh tells the story of the Universal Peace Federation (UPF), an NGO at the United Nations. Here, compassion is understood as 'living for the sake of others'. Following a brief survey of compassion in the world religions, Walsh notes three aspects of compassion: it originates in God, it is a relational virtue, and it is exemplified in the family. It is compassion that is, Walsh argues, the 'foundation for the transformation of the world.'

We then gathered for our final session of contemplative silence. It was followed by many hugs as we said goodbye to one another.

This volume ends on another note: a poetic version of Geshe Lhabu

Thundup's 'Importance of Compassion for Mahayana Meditation'. We hope it touches you as it touched us.

This is perhaps a fitting place to end this introduction. It is now time to turn to the contributions included in this volume. They will lead readers to see many things and to discover that compassion is not only an interior sensibility, or an empathetic feeling, but it is also an action in the world. It is action that moves us beyond ourselves towards enhancing the lives of others and transforming the world.

Welcome Address

LAMA DOBOOM TULKU

I WELCOME EVERYONE who has come here from far, not so far and near places. Some travelled from as far as North America and Beijing and we have a Buddhist monk from Sri Lanka. From within India, participants from Himachal Pradesh, Uttar Pradesh, Karnataka, Haryana, and Kerala have gathered.

More than welcoming, I wish to express my joyful appreciation for the fact that though this seminar is not a big gathering – it was never meant to be – yet it has the presence of a rich representation of scholars and practitioners from a wide range of religious traditions. That is significant.

This is not a regular seminar where papers are read. It is more a seminar of sharing one's knowledge and experiences on our selected theme: Practices of Compassion.

The reason for convening this contemplative seminar is because now a days not many people talk about spirituality. Few people talk in terms of its inner quality, and even fewer bother to think about or discuss compassion. We, as followers of spiritual traditions, recognize compassion as a virtuous quality. Therefore, we talk in terms of *karunasagar, karunaswaroop, al-Rahman,* etc. It is imperative in our world to talk more on this topic.

Allow me to share a few thoughts on the subject of the seminar.

The opposite of compassion is a careless attitude towards others. We don't care what happens to others. It's not only that we don't care about others, but when we ourselves face an undesirable situation, our natural tendency is to find fault in others and blame others. We tend to think we are blameless. In my tradition, this attitude is called self-centred behaviour.

This kind of attitude leads us, as individuals, societies, and nations to a really very dangerous situation.

But compassion is a noble quality of mind. One has to cultivate it. There is no readily available product or pill for compassion. Not as yet. However, the seed of compassion is there in the stream of everybody's mind. I wonder how many people have observed how the ferocious looking animals, such as tigers or pythons take care of their offspring. Even these ferocious creatures seem to have some basic sense of altruism, or empathy. It shows us that there is a seed of compassion in each and every sentient being. However, to make it manifest, the self-centred motivation or self-cherishing mind has to be abolished. Then, one can become a compassionate person.

Self-centred thinking normally works against compassion. We have to find a way to foster compassion gradually, sometimes using self-cherishing thought as a tool. In this way compassion can gain strength. Empathy – entering another's feelings – is, in my opinion, a bridge between the two.

The thought of compassion should be followed by acts of compassion. Engaging in acts beneficial to others, and being ready to forgo one's own benefit, is the noble act.

Does it make much of a difference whether there are visible beneficiaries or not? As far as gaining merit to the doer is concerned, I would say that it does not make much difference. For example Tibetans are good in creating invisible imaginative recipients and giving food and water to them. But, it would be more satisfying and practical if you see for yourself that your act is reaching needy human beneficiaries.

Now, I would like to offer a few words about the origins of the idea for this seminar. The seeds of this seminar were sown two years ago during my meetings and discussions with Professors Anne Klein and Darrol Bryant. I then requested them to be the co-conveners of this seminar with my input as the organizing overseer. However, Professor Klein was not able to make it to this gathering due to personal reasons. Professor Bryant then took sole responsibility for all the details of the programme, contacting the participants and inspiring them and others to write papers. The result is this gathering here in Hyderabad.

The main idea is that this seminar could be helpful for people from different traditions, religions, countries, backgrounds, and races to realize that they share many values in common. Everyone knows this is true, but it has not so far been put forward in a scholarly way, as far as my knowledge goes.

H.H. the Dalai Lama once said 'when you talk, you are sharing what you know, but when you listen, you are learning something new'. So I will stop talking and listen. We are all here to share and to learn from each other. So, let's do that!

PART I

EXPERIENCING, CULTIVATING AND RESEARCHING COMPASSION

CHAPTER 1

May You Be Free from Suffering, May You Be at Peace …

YANNI MANIATES

Be kind whenever possible.
It is always possible.

DALAI LAMA

Begin each day with a grateful heart.

ABOUT THREE DECADES ago I was in meditation and had a deeply moving, profound experience of being enveloped in 'The Embrace'. It was unlike anything I had had before. The only way I have been able to describe it over the years is that I felt totally at One with All That Is. There was no separation; there was no 'other'. There just – 'was'. And that 'was' was a deep 'knowing' of being totally loved, of 'being' Love itself, and of loving All beings/things without condition. It was a deep sense of all-enveloping compassion for myself, for the 'other' and for All. From top to bottom, inside and out and all around I was in a heartfelt, compassionate Embrace.

When I currently feel connected with this 'Embrace', there is a sense of being totally present with my Self and of being whole and held in the most loving and tender arms ever imagined. It is simultaneously a physical, visceral, emotional, mental and spiritual experience and yet it goes beyond all of those, too. It is simply a 'knowing' or a 'state of being' or an 'Oneness.'

Ultimately, it cannot be named; it is a state of Grace. The more I choose to surrender to it, the more I end up being in its Grace and Embrace. It comes in like a gentle, cooling summer breeze and refreshes and fills me to overflowing with a peace that 'passeth all understanding'.

As a result, if anyone asks me nowadays how I would describe

God/Goddess, this attempt at an explanation above is how I do. Not that describing the ineffable, Unnamed and Unknown can ever be done with mere three dimensional language.

So, it is within this state of non-dual, compassionate 'Embrace' that I feel that true compassion is birthed. A state where no longer is there 'other', no longer is there just 'me'; instead there is 'Us'.

And, I believe, that this state of 'Us' or unity or unitive consciousness is the starting point and end point of all inter-acting and inter-being – of all true communication/community – in a civil society. It is the Ground of our collective Being. It is the Alpha and the Omega; the beginning and completion of the full circle. It is our collective Coming Home.

It is the foundation of true compassion and it is from this place of consciousness/awareness that we can most clearly live as the Buddhists say with 'right' view, 'right' intention, 'right' speech, 'right' action, 'right' livelihood, 'right' effort, 'right' mindfulness and 'right' concentration.

For only from this place of oneness can we truly be fully compassionate, can we truly see all 'others' as 'us' and truly hold them as we wish, also, to be held in the 'Embrace'. As Jesus said, 'Love your neighbour as yourself'.

One of the gifts of living in compassion is this realization that there is no 'other' and that there is only One. This allows us to truly 'listen' to and to be really present for each other.

When with your mind you judge and analyse someone or some object as 'an'-'other', by doing so you separate yourself out from them and thus experience them as 'other' than you, when, in fact, they are not 'other'.

This 'separating out' is what creates all the conflict within ourselves, with 'others', with nature and also all the conflict in the world. We see people and things as 'other'. But really, how can anything or anyone be 'other' if we come from an awareness of the compassionate, non-dual 'Embrace?'

And so it is from this consciousness of the 'Embrace' that we then can go out into the world, not to prove our worth or find our value, – that is, to build our fortresses or 'make our mark' – but instead to deepen and spread this 'Embrace'/Compassion to others by our example of being a compassionate caregiver through the sacred service and care that we provide for each 'other' as well as the heart-felt stewardship with which we care for our Earth.

As we deepen our connection with the 'Embrace', we are called more and more to serve 'others' and the Earth and it is through doing this that our real value is revealed.

So, compassion is a state of being and becoming; it is a state of the heart. It is not an emotion; it is not a behaviour. It is the 'Embrace' in action.

Compassion from the ego has emotions attached to it. Compassion from the soul, does not. Compassion is learning how to develop the open heart. The heart and mind that are free from the fears, judgements, illusions and the false beliefs that distort and cause separation.

Many equate the word compassion with the human emotion that many mistake as and for love. Yet compassion is a stable, harmonious and balanced state through which there can be no fear, no indecision, and no uncertainty.

Compassion is not a state that judges, compares or analyses. It is simply a state of 'being', a state of silence, openness, appreciation, receptivity, embrace and allowing.

It is quiet and still and does not pay attention to words or appearances; instead it senses the 'essence' of things. It looks into the Soul of people and experiences.

It is a state of simply being present and just 'knowing'. It is a receptive state, a surrender, a merging with, a communion; it is just being present with no agenda. And the action(s) that it does take are inspired ones that come from the heart and not from the machinations of the detached, separated ego mind.

So, this is all good and an experience like this is truly personally life-transforming and deeply profound, but then what? Having experienced this profound state of 'Embrace' and compassion, what does one do with it other than savouring, enjoying and continuing to deepen it?

For myself, I initially decided that I wanted to share my experience with others, so I started to teach meditation, intuitive development and perennial and hermetic wisdom to others and made the experience of the 'Embrace' as the starting and ending point of whatever practices and technologies I was teaching. I, of course, could not really teach anyone any one particular way to get there, i.e. to have the experience of the 'Embrace' – but what I taught did 'point' to the experience and it helped many to find it for themselves in their own unique way. It was truly gratifying to see the continuing transformation in myself as I kept deepening my practice as well as seeing others 'get it', too.

Probably the meditation that is my most favourite to teach and to practice is the one that most embodies this feeling/experience of the 'Embrace' and helps one to keep that feeling running in the foreground of their life rather than just in the background or not at all. It is the 'Loving Kindness' meditation taught by the Buddha which is best practiced and recited as a mantra all day long:

May I be free from suffering; may I be at Peace.
May you be free from suffering; may you be at Peace.
May all beings be free from suffering; may all beings be at Peace.

This simple meditation and its daily practice is the embodiment of the experience of the 'Embrace' that I had almost thirty years ago. It helps me to 'quiet my mind and open my heart' to the infinite experience of Oneness, 'Embrace' and Compassion that awaits me every moment I chose to be mindful of it. As well, it guides the actions that I take or do not take in a day.

When I find myself lost in discordant thoughts or emotions, I remember and repeat over and over to myself: *May I be free from suffering; may I be at Peace.*

When I see someone else as 'other' than me or suffering, I whisper over and over in my heart to them: *May you be free from suffering; may* you *be at Peace.*

And when I see the world in chaos or the Earth being ravaged, I softly pray: *May all beings be free from suffering; may all beings be at Peace.*

This becomes my heartfelt prayer that All may be free from suffering and that All may be at Peace and hence they may all experience the profound Oneness and 'Embrace' that is their essence and birthright.

It has been very gratifying to see, over the years, how many of my students have come back and expressed to me how much this meditation has meant to them. And, also, how it has inspired them to not only deepen their sense of compassion and the 'Embrace' for themselves, but as well to share it with others both in teaching them how to access it and also in going out into the world from a place of deep compassionate 'Embrace' and becoming of real service to 'others'.

The following brief dialogue from Theophane the Monk's, *Tales of a Magic Monastery* I feel best sums this up:

'"Father, could you tell us something about yourself?"
The Monk leaned back.
"Myself?" he mused.
There was a long pause.
"My name ... used to be ... Me ... but now ... it's You."'

Everyone and everything is the divine, immortal 'You'. There is no 'other'. If we could learn how to 'quiet our minds and open our hearts' to the 'Embrace', we all could re-enter the Garden again and 'see' each 'other' and our Selves as One.

And to reinforce this a bit further, the Dalai Lama writes in his foreword to Wayne Teasdale's *The Mystic Heart* (xiv-xv):

> If ... you were to spend a few minutes every day thinking about and trying to develop compassion, eventually compassion, the essence of spiritual practice, will become part of your life. When that happens I am convinced that not only will your life be happier but also you will make a direct contribution to peace and happiness in the world as a whole.

In conclusion, over time as I deepened my practice and my connection with the 'Embrace', it became clear to me that this experience also needed to get out to the wider world and not just to a few people in my immediate vicinity.

Ken Wilber speaks of this when he writes that we first need to 'Wake Up' to the experience of the Transcendent and then 'Grow Up' by taking the richness and depth of this experience and applying it in our daily interactions, relationships and in what we 'do' in the world.

In effect, after a unitive, non-dual experience we are called to then 'grow up' and become a spiritual adult by integrating the experience deep within us and then in our own unique way embodying it in the world in some form that grounds it more and more into the collective psyche in some form of service that supports the inter-relatedness and inter-dependency we all share as co-inhabitants of Mother Earth.

For myself, most recently, this has led me to get deeply involved in a couple of networks of people who are actively working to facilitate the birth of a new inter-spiritual age that both honours, respects and shares each other's rich heritage and technologies for awakening as well as is dynamically out there 'in the world' doing 'good' deeds and spreading the 'good' news that we are all One.

So, recently, on a volunteer basis, I have gotten involved in the following networks that all encourage a deep spiritual life/practice combined with a sincere commitment to compassionate service and action in the real world:

The Interspirituality Network comprises organizations and individuals who are exploring and embracing the emerging Interspiritual paradigm. It brings together and supports individuals and organizations that are deeply committed to authentic understanding, cooperation and practice among all peoples. It provides opportunities to develop and deepen relationships, friendships, networks, community and collaborations that further the vision of a world of compassion, activism, peace and the celebration of the unity and diversity among all peoples of the world. It includes all and excludes none.

The Interspirituality Network website provides an online resource for articles, discussions, resources, individuals, organizations and events concerning the emerging interspiritual paradigm. Its goal is to help the global community share and cross-pollinate many diverse perspectives, practices, rituals, visions and ideals; experience the profound contemplative wisdom practices at the heart of the world's spiritual and secular traditions; celebrate the unity within the diversity of the world's spiritual traditions; experience a new consciousness that can guide us towards a sustainable, healthy world and peaceful earth for all humans and all living beings; and explore ways to take conscious compassionate 'action' in the world.

It enables communities and individuals to find organizations and activities that they can participate in that help them deepen their spiritual practice. As well, it connects them with activities that help them to perform service to their communities and the world.

I am helping to build the website content, newsletter and its other outreach initiatives. As well, I am going out locally and educating the public about it. http://interspirituality.com/

The From Self-Care to Earth-Care website and programmes provide space for the leading voices and activists across the interspiritual, eco-spiritual, sustainability and other transformative movements to dialogue, network and to vision and effectuate future programmes, events and initiatives across these areas. It has held a number of major conferences with numerous international experts participating and is planning more.

It seeks to find a common ground for all people to both openly and deeply communicate with each other as well as to join in service for the common good of all, based not just on ideologies of the mind, but also on ancient technologies of the heart. Technologies and inner 'knowings' that have been practiced, preserved and honed over the millennia in and through the great spiritual wisdom traditions of the world. Technologies with a 'heart' intelligence.

I have organized and given talks at a couple of its events and I have written articles for its outreach. As well, I am the co-editor of its online newsletter: *The Eco-Activist: Eco-Spirituality and Eco-Ministry.* http://www.selfcaretoearthcare.com/

The Forum 21 Institute mission is to catalyse transformative change in lifestyles, communities, organizations and policies through educational programmes and collaborative advocacy. Its vision is to realize a harmonious, peaceful and environmentally sustainable world based on ethical and spiritual values. I am Director of its Eco-Ministry programmes. http://www.forum21.co/

The New Altruism Paradigm: Evolution, Consciousness and Altruism – Tracking the Growth of Mainstream Science's Shift to Altruistic Evolution. I have been organizing events and editing material to help spread mainstream's science's discovery that we have an altruistic gene and how that can and will have a major impact on our future economic, political, religious and social systems. http://www.insideoutjourneys.com/the-new-altruism-paradigm/

The Community of the Mystic Heart offers a welcoming space for mystics and contemplatives of all faith traditions, or none – free of divisive doctrinal differences – to practice, to dialogue, to deepen, to expand, and to seek the commonality, while respecting the diversity, of the world's great mystical teachings.

As well, it is in the process of creating a leading-edge web-based platform that will allow it to interact virtually with people from all over the world. This virtual community will share spiritual resources with each other as well as ideas and projects for serving those in need and for pre-serving the Earth. I am helping to create content for this web-based platform. http://communityofthemysticheart.org/

These projects help me to connect and work together with a diverse and inspiring group of people, both locally and internationally, who are committed to helping to bring about a worldwide culture based on mutual respect and 'sacred service'.

The internet is enabling us to bring together so many different kinds of people who are looking for a way to serve. As well, it is helping us to identify some of those who are suffering in the world today and it is making it possible for people from all over the world to support them to find peace and sufficient sustenance in their lives.

The work I am involved in is one of the many embodiments of the compassionate 'Embrace' in action that is serving our world today. I am grateful to be a part of it.

May we all be free of suffering; may we all be at peace.

CHAPTER 2

Breathe Deeply for Health, Wellness, and Compassion: A Summary

SHIV TALWAR

THERE IS A form of breathing that occurs naturally in mammals in a relaxed state. It can be described as deep, diaphragmatic abdominal or rhythmic breathing.

Human beings are no exception to this natural breathing rhythm. Just notice how the abdomen of a baby rises on inhalation and falls on exhalation as it lies on its back relaxed.

Ever present stresses and strains of life make us lose this natural relaxed rhythm and adopt a habit of shallow chest breathing. This habit of breathing becomes our ordinary breath.

Breath is vital to life. Deep diaphragmatic breath is quality breath. Ordinary breath leads to ordinary lives and quality breath leads to quality lives. Ordinary breathing may sustain life, quality breath also enhances it.

Ordinary breathing is one of the many autonomous processes that sustain life. In addition, there are autonomous mental processes that

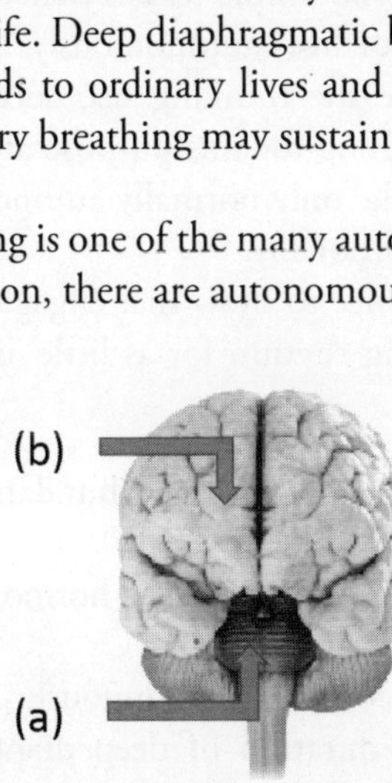

FIGURE SHOWING (A) THE BRAIN STEM THAT RUNS AUTONOMIC BODY MIND BEHAVIOUR AND (B) THE NEO-CORTEX WHICH RUNS OUR VOLITIONAL BEHAVIOUR

drive reactive behaviour. All autonomous body mind processes, including ordinary breathing, are run by the brain stem in accordance with our emotional states.

In addition to the brain stem, mammalian brains, human included, have another part called the neo-cortex. The role of the neo-cortex is to run volitional acts and behaviour. Relaxed breathing, which occurs in mammals in the absence of an external threat, is a volitional act run by the neo-cortex.

A fundamental requirement of acting volitionally is being aware and knowing that something specific needs to be and can be done. Thus, awareness, consciousness, knowledge, thinking, discerning, considering alternatives, deciding, willing, the generation of a volitional response to an external stimulus, etc., are all the functions of the neo-cortex. In addition, the neo-cortex is the seat of higher emotions of selfless love and compassion whereas the limbic brain is limited to base self-centred emotions that function largely in an autonomous manner.

Of all the mammals, human beings have the most developed neo-cortex. The human condition is such that we let this valuable resource sit idle and unused for the simple reason that we can survive letting the limbic brain run our lives autonomously. We must volitionally train our brains to use the thinking neo-cortex. We can practice volitional relaxed breathing for this purpose at any time of the day or night. Breathing is the only normally autonomic life process that we can at times run volitionally.

There is ample evidence to show that engaging in volitional deep diaphragmatic breathing rhythm for as little as 15-20 minutes can lead to quality lives:

1. It is the most efficient way to supply abundant oxygen to the body to enhance physical health,
2. It calms the nerves and balances related hormones for better physical and mental health,
3. It requires the neo-cortex to continuously attend to breathing; thus increasing the duration of deep diaphragmatic breathing amounts to an increased attention span,
4. Training of the neo-cortex to pay attention to breathing also trains

it to pay attention in general including to our behaviour thus making it thoughtful,

5. Training of the neo-cortex to pay attention to breathing also trains it to pay attention to the workings of our own mind thus increasing emotional intelligence, self-awareness and acceptance of the other,
6. Training of the neo-cortex to pay attention to breathing also trains it to pay attention and solve life problems such as poverty, habits, addictions, relationships, etc.,
7. Involvement of the neo-cortex in regular practice of deep breathing opens our minds to higher emotions of selfless love and compassion, and
8. It makes us the master of our own lives rather than being swept away in the tide of autonomic mind body behaviour.

CHAPTER 3

Breathe Deeply: Cultivate Compassion Naturally

SHIV TALWAR

Introduction

THE PROCESS OF cultivation starts with the preparation of the ground, planting the seed and then nurturing the saplings that sprout to become full grown plants and then trees. Surely, the cultivation of compassion is different than that of produce.

Is it similar to the cultivation of the taste of honey? That is easy. All you need is exposure to it; the first experience! It acts as the seed, sapling and the sprout at the same time ready to become a plant. The result of the first experience is always sweet and pleasant. But you can have too much honey for then your mouth stays too sweet too much of the time. You get tired of it. You may also develop diabetes.

Is it then similar to the cultivation of the taste of alcohol or coffee? The first experience of both of them is invariably that of bitterness. If you do not turn away from it after the first experience and try it again, you may start liking it. If you do not like it the second time, you may start liking it the third time. There is a good probability that you will never return to tasting either if you do not like it the first time, or the second time, or the third time. When you start liking it, you want to have it over and over; the pleasantness of the resulting feeling pulls you towards it again and again. If you are not careful and lack the discipline to moderate consumption, the consequential pleasantness loses the sheen of the transitory high in the face of the unpleasantness of hangovers and/or addictiveness which start to hurt and hurt real bad. Then you wish that you had never tasted it.

Cultivating compassion is the cultivation of the taste of compassion. It is both like and unlike cultivation of the taste of honey, coffee or alcohol. The first experience may be sweet like that of honey or it may be bitter like that of coffee or alcohol.

If the first taste is pleasant and sweet like that of honey, you want to keep experiencing it over and over. The taste of compassion, unlike that of honey, stays sweet and pleasant for ever without the unpleasantness of being too sweet. And it does not cause diabetes. It is unlike that of honey in its negative long term effects.

The first taste of compassion can be bitter like that of alcohol. Being compassionate may accompanied by an unpleasant feeling of sacrificing something you like for yourself on the negative side. On the positive side, it is accompanied by a feeling of self-fulfilment. The overall taste of bitterness or sweetness depends upon the relativity of the two opposing feelings. Once the feeling of self-fulfilment over powers the feeling of self-sacrifice, you are hooked to it. You want to repeat that experience over and over. Compassion is addictive like alcohol in its high but without its temporariness, hangovers and harmfulness.

Honey, coffee and alcohol are things. What is compassion? Compassion is a heartfelt feeling that seeks expression. Love too is a heartfelt feeling. Love and compassion are compatriots: one leading to the other. They both result from an implicit feeling of connectedness or oneness through a common ground of the parties involved. Universal love and compassion are the results arising from the feeling of connectedness and the oneness of all beings in the universe, through an explicit realization of the common ground of the whole universe.

Is compassion cultivable? It comes at the cost of selfishness, is it practical to willingly overcome selfishness? Some might say that we really cannot be selfless yet when we realize our connection with the others, we come to realize an expansion of our self. One then begins to include the self of the others as well. Our selfishness then begins to lie in the wellbeing of all to whom we feel connected. Is the connectedness with the others real or are we being fed a myth?

What and where are we? How do we function? How are we connected? Why can't we see that we are connected? What and where is the heart where compassion originates? These are some of the questions that we consider here.

My essay is presented in two sections. The first section presents the science of our oneness through our connection through a common ground and how it expresses in our being human. The second section presents how this science can be used in practice to cultivate compassion. Doesn't the value of the knowledge of science lie in its use in developing technology for the benefit of humanity?

I. Theory

Us: What are We?

Let us begin by looking at ourselves, the ground for the cultivation of compassion. The ground is a human being and the cultivator is the same human being. Cultivation of compassion is a matter of self-cultivation for the well-being of the universe.

What is a human being and how she/he functions? What is the heart, what is a feeling, what is a heartfelt feeling? To understand the cultivation of compassion, we have to understand what a human being is and how she/he can prepare her/himself for compassion to germinate and grow.

We human beings, like all existents in the universe, have an outer and an inner existence. Every animate being or an inanimate one, everything that exists has a gross outer existence and a world of subtle inner existence. There is the outer and inner of the being and there is the external world in which the being exists and interacts. The interactions of all beings with their external environment are driven by the inner existence of the being. For the material world, the inner existence comprises molecules, atoms, and the sub-atomic particles.

Similarly, our behaviour in the external world may appear to be acted out through our outer existence, it is in fact being driven by our inner existence. On the outside, we have five organs of perception and five motor organs of action. The organs of perception collect the information about what happens in the external world and transmits it inwards to our inner existence. This movement of information inwards comprise the stimuli to which we must respond because we are built that way.

Our life experience is proof enough to know that we must respond to every bit of information called stimulus fed inwards from the outside by our organs of perception.

Relationship of the Outer with the Inner

Our outer façade is gross. Gross is what is sense perceptible. Our inner on the other side is hidden, we need to expose it to sense perception as is the case with our anatomy and its function, or it may only be felt by our feeling mind: mind feels itself, it knows that it exists. Things that cannot be perceived by the senses but can only be felt by the mind are subtle. Some of the things cannot even be felt by the mind; they are simply too subtle.

At our very core is the infinitely subtle and totally imperceptible ground of our being which concretizes into an infinite number of principles successively more and more concrete until our fully gross bodies appear as our outer existence. The principles in the immediate neighbourhood of the gross body comprise our outer existence and the rest of subtle principles comprise the inner existence. We in fact are an integral whole comprised of all the principles from the infinitely subtle ground of our being to the fully concrete gross body. The division between the outer and the inner is rather arbitrary.

It should then be understood that we humans are an integrated whole comprised of an infinite number of successively gross principles starting from the totally imperceptible common ground within to the perceptible gross body on the outside.

If we consider any two adjacent principles, one is gross in relation to the other and one subtle. The gross principle is the outer of the two and the subtle the inner. Outer and inner are thus relative terms. A principle which is outer compared to those subtler than it is inner compared to those more concrete or grosser than it.

The ground of being at the very core of our existence is shared by every other existent in the universe and therefore, we are connected with the whole universe through it. On the contrary, our gross outer body being finite gives a sense of our separation from everything else. Thus, behaviour which is driven by considerations of the outer gross self is divisive in nature. Such behaviour may be considered narrowly selfish. On the contrary, behaviour driven by the deep inner, in our core around the common ground, is unitive in nature. Such behaviour may be considered as selfless in the wider sense or truly selfless. Love and compassion underlie such behaviour. Cultivation of compassion then is merely shifting the identification of a human being from the outer to the inner: from the body towards the mind, from the mind towards the very central core comprised by the common ground of the entire universe.

The inner core of our being where such a unifying behaviour originates is called the heart. We are either unaware of this heart or only faintly aware of it. It must be distinguished from the physical heart organ of which we are very aware. The former lies subtly at the core of the totality of our being while the latter lies physically at the core of our physical being.

Identifiable Categories of Principles

For the sake of understanding, we group the large number of principles in three categories:

- Body as the concrete outer,
- Mind is the relatively grosser part of the inner. It is neither perceptibly gross nor totally imperceptible. It can be felt by itself. Mind is said to be self-aware, and
- Spirit in the innermost core around the totally imperceptible common ground. Mind may be totally unaware of it or at times it may be faintly aware.

Some of us don't believe in the spirit? Why waste time and energy over things you can't even feel? Whether you believe in the spirit or not is immaterial to the current discussion. Facts do not change with faith, belief and acceptance.

The grouping of principles called the mind is further classified into the following successive groupings called the faculties of the mind:

- Sensory faculty located immediately inside the body. Its function is to transmit stimuli information inwards and response information outwards. It may be called our input output system,
- Ego is the set of principles subtler than those of the sensory faculty.

It may be defined as the system of ready logic based upon the experience of the senses. It is said to define a person's individual identity that sets a person apart from the others because of the specificity of the individual's sensory experience, and

- Intellect is the subtlest set of inner principles called the mind of which we are self-aware. It is the faculty of the mind which generally thinks and decides. It is called into action only when a considered decision is warranted in which case the ready logic of the ego yields to it.

Each of the five groups of principles called the body, sensory faculty, ego, intellect and the spirit, with their discreet names may give the impression of not being homogenous. In fact, their subtlety as an integrated whole increases progressively from the outer to the inner.

Each of the faculties of the mind except the intellect communicates in two ways. The sensory faculty communicates the sensory information from the body to the ego and the response information to the body. The ego may communicate the sensory information to the intellect. It communicates the response information to the sensory faculty. When the ego yields to the intellect, the intellect decides the response and communicates it to the ego.

Although the subtle can and does generally control the gross, the principles that comprise a human being enjoy a degree of autonomy or freedom of choice to be controlled by the subtle or to act otherwise.

The heart where compassion originates is the part of the spirit closest to the intellect. Being next to the intellect, it communicates with the intellect but the intellect does not communicate with it.

Every response generates a feeling of pleasantness or unpleasantness. The resulting feeling, the associated stimulus and response comprise a record stored in the database in our memory. This database predisposes us to a certain mode of behaviour.

Provenance of the Structure of Being Human

The mind, body and spirit and the three faculties of the mind as the constituents defining the structure of being human is our inheritance from the ancient wisdom traditions of the world. All of them agree that the universe and all its beings including the humans emerge from a common ground of being which is totally imperceptible thus unknowable and ineffable.

In the modern age, the concept of an ineffable common ground as the source of the material world is hailed as the utmost achievement of physical sciences. Science calls the common ground of all matter, energy. We know energy only when it has taken forms in terms of matter or in terms of wave like forms identifiable as heat energy, light energy, etc. The energy that takes identifiable forms is a total mystery. Besides being the source of all subatomic particles, it inheres in every atom. Without it no atom can sustain its integrity.

This is what the ancient wisdom traditions have been saying about everything in the universe. Spirit, just another name for the common ground, is all pervasive. It is the most fundamental constituent of everything whether animate or inanimate.

Philosophers have talked about the faculties of the mind as:

- Sensory faculty as the creaturely soul. All animate beings from single cell amoeba to human beings have a faculty of sensing its environment,
- Ego as the animal soul because animals essentially live by their natural instincts. It is shared by all complex animals developed along the path of evolution including humans, and
- Intellect as the human soul because it is present in its most developed form only in humans.

Living by the senses is a creaturely characteristic, life by the ego is that of the animal world, and life by the intellect characterizes human beings. To be fully human, we must fully exercise our intellect as we go through our lives.

Individual Differences

We are all built the same, then why do we behave differently? Given a set of conditions, one person behaves in one way and another in the exact same conditions behaves in yet another way. The answer lies in our predisposition at any given time.

We are born with a given disposition. Does that mean that we are forever subject to it? Can we change the disposition with which we are born? Can we change our disposition at any time, if we so choose?

Who decides that we will ever be disposed to change our disposition at all?

The answer seems to lie in our understanding that the human intellect is called into action only when a considered decision is warranted in which case the ready logic of the ego yields to it. In different people, the ego is more disposed to such yielding than in the others.

Physiological Correlates

In today's scientific understanding, our central nervous system is the physiological correlate of our mind with the individual faculties of the mind having their physiological correlates in it. The brain is a part of the central nervous system and so it is our nervous system that spreads its network all over our bodies including the external organs of cognition and action. The brain is structured in two functional parts: the limbic brain and the neo-cortex. The limbic brain springs into action in behaviour generally related to natural instincts and base emotions demanding fast and ready response while the neo-cortex waits and deliberates a considered response when needed.

Thus, the faculties of the mind work through their physiological counterparts as follows:

- The nervous system is the physiological correlate of the nervous system which works through it. All creatures have a nervous system howsoever rudimentary it may be,
- The limbic brain being instinctive in function is the physiological correlate of the ego. The limbic brain characterizes all developed animals; and
- The neo-cortex is the physiological correlate of intellect. Only mammals are blessed with a neo-cortex and humans have it in its most developed form. Mammals suckle their offspring while other animals do not. Suckling of the off-spring is a manifestation of love. The capacity of love and compassion develops with the development of the neo-cortex.

The Brain

1. *Anatomy:* The brain runs our entire life in the outer as well as inner world using the nervous system to obtain as well as to send information.

   The extensive nervous system connects with the brain through the nervous highways located in the spinal column. The limbic functions are physically located in neural structures on top of the spinal column causing the nervous system to connect directly with the limbic brain.

   The neo-cortex is comprised of a thin layer of neurons located physically apart from and around the limbic structures below the skull and connects with the nervous system only indirectly through the limbic structures.

2. *Function:* The anatomy of the connection of the nervous system with the functional parts of the brain favours the activity of the limbic function over that of the neo-cortex. The anatomy generally explains why the limbic brain representing the human ego, dominates over the neo-cortex, the thinking brain, in running human lives.

   The function of the neo-cortex is to be aware or conscious, know, understand, deliberate, to be aware of deeper feelings of the heart, consider in general, consider alternatives, consider related issues, consider consequences, think, discern, determine, decide and will a response appropriate to the stimulus in its prevailing context. Its function generally is time consuming. Depending upon the profundity of the situation, the more time it spends in deliberations, the better the quality of the response.

   Since awareness, consciousness, knowing, understanding and decision making, etc., are the functions of the neo-cortex, the purpose of the limbic brain is to respond where such things as awareness, consciousness, knowing, understanding, and decision-making are of no or little importance. There are many things going on in life that are more or less autonomic in nature. The limbic brain is meant to respond to such subliminal stimuli of which we are either totally unconscious or at best partially conscious.

Specifically the limbic matters include matters of inbuilt instincts of the body and the mind; threats to survival; intense appetites, fears; self-related base emotions related with matters of often repeated sense experience, etc., in connection with which ready experiential logic is available and desirable where other considerations and deliberation may neither be necessary nor desirable.

The Nervous System

The function of the sensory faculty is performed by the nervous system. Every part of the body and every bodily organ is connected with a vast network of nerves that connect to the central nervous pathways up and down our spines communicating back and forth between the brain and every part or we can say every cell of our physical existence.

1. *Sensory and Motor Nerves:* Nerves are of two types: the sensory nerves and the motor nerves. The sensory nerves perform the function of the cognitive senses in sending information inwards to the brain and the motor nerves perform the function of the active senses in taking the response signals outwards from the brain to their destination. The classification of sensory and motor nerves is based upon whether the nerves are input inwards or output outwards.
2. *Somatic and Autonomous Nerves:* The nervous system relays two types of information. Some information is somatic or conscious in nature. On the other hand, some information is autonomic or unconscious in nature. An example of former is our perception of what is happening in the outside world and our response to it while that of the latter is the information of our heart being sent to our brain and the brain responding to it by commanding the heart to pulse.

   The autonomic responses are generated by the brain in answer to the information sent from our physiological support organs. We are completely unaware of the physiological stimuli to which our brain must respond in order to exercise proper control of our life support systems for us to survive. It can easily be understood that the work load of the nervous system to transmit the large amount of autonomic control signals to keep various parts and functions of the body function on a 24/7 basis is by no means light.

Nerves that carry control signals for the life support functions of the body are called autonomic nervous systems. They connect the brain with the physiological organs responsible for supporting life. On the other hand, the nerves that connect the brain with the organs of our behaviour in the external world are called somatic nerves. This classification of nerves is based upon whether the signals they carry are unconscious or conscious.

3. *Direct and Indirect Somatic Activity:* As we live our lives, we perceive and we respond to our perceptions. This is direct somatic activity. Our brains are connected with our bodily organs that come in contact with objects of sense perceptions through the somatic sensory nerves and they respond through the somatic motor nerves sending signals to our physical motor organs. This is normal life. To enhance life, we must ensure the optimum functioning of related physical organs and the integrity of sensory and motor signals relayed by the somatic nerves.

   In addition to the direct somatic activity related with the external world, there is indirect activity generated by our memory of the past experience of the senses. Our memory can generate a large amount of indirect somatic activity within us which works in a manner remarkably similar to that of the direct somatic activity. Let us have a look at its sources.

   Our sense experience of the external world leaves their impressions in the memory. The impressions may be of pleasantness, unpleasantness, or of fear. This storehouse of impressions leads to sensory traffic in the following ways:

   (a) If an impression happens to be pleasant, the urge to repeat and relive the associated experience sends the signal of phantom stimuli through the somatic nerves seeking a response. If the conditions are favourable, the repetition of the experience may actually materialize otherwise the urge remains unfulfilled and we keep on hankering for it. Our hankerings comprise our appetites continually seeking satiation. The trouble is that the more we satiate them, the more they increase in their intensity.

In fact, the repetitions of pleasant experiences increase the need to repeat them. Perpetually in their state of un-fulfilment, our appetites keep generating phantom stimuli on and on leading to destructive mental disorders such as cravings, obsessions, habits, addictions, frustration, anger and delusion unless effective mitigating measures are taken.

(b) If a memory impression happens to be unpleasant, the urge to avoid the associated experience keeps on sending phantom warning signals through the sensory faculty of a real or imaginary threat of the associated experience or its likes. Such urges define our dislikes, which can become indifferences, apathy, revulsions, horrors, hatreds, anxieties, worries and nightmares preventing sleep at night.

(c) We are all afraid of death; death is our biggest fear. Survive we must. In addition to the threats to survival, we are afraid of getting what we want to avoid, and not getting what we want to get. Our fears keep generating phantom stimuli through our somatic nerves seeking responses in terms of avoidance of unwanted, hostile and threatening situations. Intense fears can lead to disorders of the mind such as distrust, loneliness, anxiety, depression, etc.

Our perpetual appetites, dislikes and fears generate so much noise in the somatic nerves that it begins to interfere with our normal lives threatening the integrity of direct somatic activity. We begin to miss out on what is in fact happening in the external world leading to unreal perceptions and responses inconsistent with reality. Our mental health issues are largely related with our indirect somatic activity of which we may either be fully conscious or partially conscious. In its subconscious state, it tends to become like autonomous activity and it keeps us involved in mindless activity depleting our physical as well mental energies and keeping us in states of mental as well as physical disorders. No one is free of the agitation caused by our appetites, aversions and fears.

4. *Urgency and Time Sensitivity of the Somatic Activity:* Somatic activity originates in many ways. There is the activity related to curiosity leading to the desire to know and understand. There is the activity related to ethics and moral behaviour originating in our desire for

social acceptance. There is the activity originating from the desire for economic security. There is the activity originating from our desire for pleasure and quality of life. There is the activity in the service of our likes, dislikes and fears. In addition, there may also be transcending activity originating from the desire for self-actualization or human perfection in order to be free from slavery to our appetites, aversions, and fears.

Lasting feelings of selfless love and compassion are the results of somatic activities of a self-transcending nature, although at times, these feelings may also arise at random from our implicit, inbuilt or instinctive knowledge of our underlying oneness.

It is easy to understand why those somatic matters that are survival oriented and those oriented towards persistent habits, addictions aversions and fears have a high degree of immediacy requiring unconsidered limbic response. It is also easy to understand that selfless matters of transcendence, knowing, understanding have the least degree of urgency and are meant for the neo-cortex. Only the other matters somatic activity can either be dealt with by the neo-cortex or by the limbic brain depending upon the neural circuitry of the brain deciding the likelihood of the limbic brain to yield to the neo-cortex.

5. *Two Divisions of the Autonomous Nervous System:* Autonomous nervous system has two divisions called sympathetic and para-sympathetic. The sympathetic division is activated when the information to be relayed is time sensitive and must be relayed in an urgent mode whereas the parasympathetic division is activated when the information is not time sensitive. Sympathetic activation is usually compared with the gas pedal which you push when you want the car to go fast and the parasympathetic activation to the brakes which you push when you want the car to slow down.
6. *Hormones Related with the Autonomous Nervous System:* The activity of the sympathetic division of the autonomic nervous system is accompanied by the release of a class of hormones called the stress hormones. Cortisol is a prime stress hormone. On the contrary, the activity of the parasympathetic division of the autonomic nervous system is accompanied by the release of a class of hormones called the rest and digest hormones classified as DHEA. The relative

amount of these hormones expressed as the cortisol/DHEA ratio is a number crucial to our physical health, mental health and behaviour in life.

7. *Work Load of our Nervous System:* Our behaviour in the external world is determined by the totality of our nervous traffic, termed sensory load, comprised of (a) the direct stimulus and response behaviour in the external world, (b) indirect stimulus and response behaviour in the internal world of our memories of the external experiences and (c) autonomic control traffic generated by and for the internal life support functions of the body running 24/7.

   It may be noted that the direct nervous traffic related to what is happening now at any instant in life in the external world is slight in comparison with the total nervous traffic including that generated consciously or sub-consciously by our memories and the unconscious traffic in relation to our mere physical survival.

8. *Relationship between the Somatic and the Autonomous Nerves:* The somatic and the autonomic nerves are not independent of one another. Their activities go hand in hand. The higher the activity of the somatic nerves, the higher the activity of the autonomic nerves and vice versa. The lower the activity of the autonomic nerves, the lower the activity of the somatic nerves and vice versa. The strategy to reduce the sensory load lies in the reduction of the autonomic load which in turn reduces the somatic load. One may think of this as a part of the mind body connection.

Our Disposition

How we behave depends upon how our brains are disposed to response to the various stimuli of life. Whether we choose to change the disposition of the brain depends upon us because we are more than our brain which is merely a tool that we use. The proof of this statement lies in the fact that we can in fact change the disposition of our brains by our conscious will to do so.

It was noticed above that the activity of the sympathetic division of the autonomic nervous system causes our glands to produce hormones classified as stress hormones and the activity of the para-sympathetic division is accompanied by the release of the calming rest and digest hormones in our blood stream. It was also noted that the relative proportion of these hormones expressed as a ratio is a number which is very crucial for our wellbeing. We can get ourselves tested in a biochemical laboratory for a determination of this number.

High values of this critical ratio correlates with mindless activity of the body with consequential high energy demand, faster and chaotic functioning of the autonomous life support functions of the body, and the low rate of our metabolic function producing low energy production. Such physical activity leads to physical fatigue and stress. High values of this ratio also are related with high mental coincidences of psychological disorders all the way to despair, despondency, nervous breakdowns and suicidal tendencies.

Low values of the ratio of stress hormones to rest and digest hormones configure the neural connections of the brain predisposing it for high activity of the neo-cortex resulting in considered behaviour.

Considered behaviour is what is called emotional intelligence. At first, consideration may be limited to selfish matters only, but it soon leads to a realization that our selfish interests are dependent upon the wellbeing of the others. And to be truly selfish is to care for the well-being of the others upon whom our selfishness depends. With continued consideration and the involvement of the neo-cortex in running our lives, an insight into the underlying oneness of all existence begins to dawn. That is the beginning of the knowledge and understanding of oneness leading to lasting feelings of selfless love and compassion.

Until recently, our brains were considered to lack flexibility and plasticity; neural circuits in the brain once structured were thought to be unchangeable. But recent research in neurology has conclusively shown that inflexibility is not the case. On the contrary, our brains are plastic and can be moulded with certain practices and neo-cortical activity to transform our behaviour as long as we continue with the transformative practices and activity.

Disposition at Birth

What is it that determines our dispositions at the beginning of our lives when we have no stimulus and response experience of life? The answer becomes easy if we consider the fact that our birth is not when our biological life begins. We spend over nine months prenatally in a hormonal environment. At our births, we inherit the crucial hormonal ratio of our mother which determines the circuitry of the brain determining not only our state of mental and physical health through our early lives but also our style of behaviour and learning capacity and discipline at school. Thus, most of us need help with our dispositions even before we are born on this earth.

II. The Practice of Cultivation

Generation of Behaviour

We have noticed that the anatomy of the connection of the nervous system with the functional parts of the brain favours the activity of the limbic function over that of the neo-cortex. As the direct recipient of the sensory information, the limbic brain may respond by itself or step aside and wait for response generated by the neo-cortex.

In view of the fast and ready nature of the limbic response and slow rate of considered response by the neo-cortex, it is easy to understand why, in general, high sensory load tends to demand ready limbic activity while low sensory demands can put up with the slow activity of the neo-cortex.

It is easily understandable then that the autonomic functions of physiological importance must be dealt with by the limbic brain.

Of the somatic functions, stimuli of emergent nature including threats to survival must also be dealt with immediately by the limbic brain. Time consuming deliberations by the neo-cortex may risk our very survival.

Of the somatic functions, those related with intense appetites, aversions and fears and hormone driven sense gratification tend to work subliminally not unlike our autonomic body functions. They too are largely handled by the limbic brain, although we humans can learn to bring them increasingly under the conscious control of the neo-cortex.

The question of the limbic brain involving the neo-cortex clearly arises only in the case of fully conscious somatic activity in relation to the external world of direct sense perception or the internal world of the memory. Whether the limbic brain indeed involves the neo-cortex in deliberating a response or deals with the stimuli by itself on the instinctive and emotional basis depends upon the neural circuitry of the brain determining the predisposition of the limbic brain to get into action or to yield to the neo-cortex.

Analogy of Two Competitors

We may consider the limbic brain and the neo-cortex as two competitors in a business. Of the two competitors, the limbic brain is the aggressive one actively pursuing the market while the neo-cortex is the laid back one who waits for any business yielded to it. The market they serve comprises of the work of our senses; the total volume of the market consists of the total sensory load. Part of that market is monopolized solely by the limbic brain and that is the load generated by the running of the autonomic body functions supporting our life.

Only the somatic load can be shared by the two competitors. Part of the somatic load related with threats to existence and intense appetites, aversions and fears is also monopolized by the limbic brain. The rest of the market may be serviced either by the limbic brain or by the neo-cortex. Only that part of the market in which the limbic brain is not interested or is only partially interested is yielded to be serviced by the laid back neo-cortex. Even there, the limbic brain pokes its dirty nose and meddles in or hijacks the service provided by the neo-cortex. The neural circuitry of the brain determining the predisposition of the limbic brain can only adjust its aggression as a competitor by increasing or decreasing its activity to a certain extent.

Human perfection is said to lay in completely stilling the limbic brain so that the entire sensory load is handled by the laid back neo-cortex.

Cultivation through Deep Diaphragmatic Breathing

It is a matter of simple observation to note that deep diaphragmatic breathing induces a sense of calm characteristic of parasympathetic activity. This sense of calm may be short lived but it leaves an effect which is of longer duration. The parasympathetic activity resulting from deep-breathing causes the release of the rest and digest hormones reducing the value of the hormonal ratio that restructures the brain circuitry with a corresponding reduction in the activity of the limbic brain and an increase in that of neo-cortex.

Regular practice of deep breathing for a few minutes per day over a period as brief as a few weeks can result in a significant restructuring of brain to change the course of one's life. However the restructuring achieved can reverse itself in just as brief a period as a few weeks when we stop the practice.

The stopping of deep breathing will result in an increase in the activity of the sympathetic division of the autonomic nervous system which causes the release of the stress hormones increasing the value of the hormonal ratio that restructures the brain circuitry increasing the activity of the limbic brain and decreasing that of neo-cortex. That takes us back to where we were in the first instance.

The strategy then is to keep the transformation caused by the restructuring the brain in favour of higher activity of the neo-cortex forever. That is if we keep deep-breathing regularly, hopefully forever.

How does It Work?

Normally or ordinarily, breathing is an autonomic process; we breathe and we are not aware that we are breathing. Breathing deep changes the breathing process from an autonomic to a conscious process. As an autonomic process, breathing is run on fast by our limbic brain and as a conscious process it is run at a slower rate by our laid back neo-cortex. Deep-breathing works by a reduction of sensory load in the following ways:

1. All autonomic life sustaining processes are linked together. By bringing breathing under our conscious control, we in fact indirectly are running all autonomic processes with the exception of our metabolic system, at a slower rate. What does it do to the sensory load? Of course, the sensory load is reduced.
2. If we engage in deep breathing practice with our eyes closed in a quiet place, we reduce the sensory load further by eliminating or minimizing the sensory load due to direct sense perception.
3. The neo-cortex can attend to only one thing at a time. If it is focused in the deep breathing process by attentively inhaling as

much air through the nostrils as possible and then exhaling as much air as possible, there is no time left for any somatic distractions from the memory of the individual. This eliminates any sensory load arising out of our appetites, aversions and fears.

4. Regular practice of deep breathing for a sufficient amount of time reduces the rate of ordinary breathing and that of other autonomic functions of the body running 24/7 day in and day out. That in itself keeps the critical hormonal ration at a low level for the disposition of the brain favourable to the activity of the neo-cortex and unfavourable to the activity of the limbic brain. We have noted that a reduction in the sensory load of the autonomic processes leads to a reduction in the somatic sensory demands of our memory.
5. Significant reductions in sensory demands caused by deep breathing and the consequential higher activity of human intellect (neo-cortex) opens us to feeling the activity of the heart. Remember that metaphysically the heart, where self-transcending feelings such as love and compassion originate, is immediately next to the intellect, and communicates directly only with the intellect. It can affect our daily lives only when the ego (limbic brain) yields to it.

Fruits of Cultivation

Deep breathing makes our lives fully human by keeping the intellect fully engaged in running our lives. It is beneficial for the practitioner individually, the family of the individual, the community and humanity as a whole in the following successive ways:

1. A low value on the critical hormonal ratio lowers the possibility of many stress related physical diseases.
2. Sustenance of low sensory load due to human memory makes for mental health.
3. Sustenance of focus on the breath for a period of time enhances our attention span, increasing focus thus leading to better learning ability.
4. Cultivation of considered behaviour replacing mindless reactive behaviour.
5. Focused, self-managed and energetic lives without unnecessary physical and mental activity.

6. Cultivation of emotional intelligence.
7. Cultivation of connectedness discovering that our happiness lies in the happiness of others.
8. Transcending selfish likes, dislikes and fears for family, community and humanity.
9. Cultivation of a sense of belonging to family, community and humanity.
10. Lives open to heart-felt feelings of love and compassion.
11. Cultivation of not only a feeling but certain knowledge and understanding of our underlying oneness and incidental love and compassion.
12. Living practical lives in the light of oneness, love and compassion.

Therefore, cultivate the habit of breathing deeply and start prenatally!

CHAPTER 4

Compassion at the Core

BRENDAN OZAWA-DE SILVA

MY INTEREST IN the study of compassion and in particular the scientific study of compassion began over ten years ago. In 2005 my mentor, Geshe Lobsang Tenzin Negi, a former Tibetan Buddhist monk who now teaches at Emory University and directs the Emory-Tibet Partnership, developed a protocol called Cognitively-Based Compassion Training (CBCT). That same year, Geshe Lobsang and I had been at a conference organized by the Mind and Life Institute in Washington, DC, on the clinical and scientific applications of meditation. At that conference, His Holiness the Dalai Lama listened as scientists and meditation experts extolled the virtues of mindfulness meditation and the ways it could promote health and wellbeing. Then at one point, His Holiness interjected, 'What about analytical meditation? In my view, this can be even more beneficial.'

I may be imagining this, but my recollection is that there was a bit of a stunned silence in the room after that comment. I would love to go back and look at the video to see if that is true. Certainly, I don't think anyone knew exactly what to say in reply. No one at the time was engaged in the scientific study of analytical meditation, and my guess is that a reasonable number of people in the hall had never even heard of the term.

CBCT was developed by Geshe Lobsang specifically to address a few things that were missing at the time in the scientific study of meditation. One of those was analytical meditation: the use of a (relatively) stabilized mind to investigate a phenomenon through meditation. Analytical or investigative meditation (*dpyadsgom* in Tibetan), isn't just thinking about something, because it requires a degree of stabilization that comes from non-analytical, or stabilizing meditation (*'jog sgom*). In fact, in his excellent work *Meditation on*

Emptiness, Jeffrey Hopkins suggests that *dpyadsgom* is only truly possible after attaining the third stage of training in calm abiding, or *zhignas* – a certain level of having developed concentration of mind.

A second purpose for creating CBCT was to show that there was a great richness of teachings on meditation that could be drawn from in the Tibetan 'Mind Training' or 'Lojong' (*blosbyong*) tradition. The Mind Training tradition is a remarkable spiritual tradition dating back a thousand years, and can certainly be considered one of the great treasures of world spirituality for its clear and direct methods for transforming selfishness and self-centeredness into altruism and compassion. For example, one verse from the beloved text 'Seven Point Mind Training' summarizes the essence of mind training when it instructs practitioners to:

Banish all blame to the single source,
And towards all beings, contemplate their great kindness.

This verse indicates that self-centredness is the single source of all our woe, and that when one realizes this, one will stop blaming others, instead recognizing that the harms that befall one in fact come from the enemy of self-centredness. For example, if another person is causing harm, they are doing so because of being blinded by the 'demon' of self-centredness. If they were freed from this ignorance, they would realize that such actions are wrong and self-destructive, and would cease then. When one recognizes this deeply, according to the Mind Training tradition, one becomes free to see others as only kind, and by reflecting on the infinite ways one is benefited by others, one will develop a deep sense of gratitude, which will lead to endearment, empathy and compassion.

CBCT contained eight steps in its original version, now condensed to six, that draw on a significant amount of material found in this tradition. In fact, the analytical portions of the meditation are all drawn from the Lojong tradition, and while considering what to name CBCT, Geshe Lobsang Tenzin even considered calling it 'Lojong-Based Compassion Training'. That name would have pointed to the heritage in the Tibetan Mind Training tradition. Its final name, 'Cognitively-Based Compassion Training', points to the use of cognitive, analytical meditation as the tool for transforming the mind and expanding compassion.

CBCT begins with the training of attention, which is a precondition for the practice of analytical meditation. It then moves to using this increased attentional stability to investigate the nature of mind and emotions. Here, the practitioner becomes aware that thoughts and feelings are transient and can be observed. Recognizing this can lead to a sense of empowerment, since one can learn to catch one's thoughts and emotions rather than being swept up by them. The practitioner also recognizes that underlying all thoughts and emotions is a basic orientation towards happiness and well-being, and away from suffering. When the practitioner recognizes that internal conditions lead to happiness and suffering just as much, if not more, than external conditions like wealth, power, fame, praise, status and sense-dependent pleasures, and when the practitioner generates a sense of enthusiasm for cultivating the inner sources of happiness and diminishing the inner sources of suffering, this mental state is called 'self-compassion' in CBCT. The practitioner now has a stable basis for expanding compassion for others: first through the weakening of bias and the cultivation of equanimity or impartiality; then through the practice of gratitude, which leads to endearment; and finally through the strengthening of empathy and compassion.

A further way in which CBCT contributed to the emerging field of contemplative science is that it focuses explicitly on the cultivation of compassion and associated mental states. Unlike mindfulness as taught in mindfulness-based interventions, compassion is explicitly interpersonal and pro-social. It is about the suffering of others. The final level of compassion taught in CBCT, engaged compassion, involves taking personal responsibility for the welfare of others. It is an attitude of becoming their protector. This supreme attitude has been lauded by His Holiness the Dalai Lama for decades now in his teachings and his public talks, because its cultivation leads to happiness for oneself and others, and ultimately leads to transformation in society and the alleviation of so many of the ills that currently plague us. Since CBCT also includes the factors that support compassion, such as gratitude, mindfulness, empathy and so on, it can therefore be seen as a practice for the cultivation of what His Holiness the Dalai Lama calls 'universal human values' and 'secular ethics'. His Holiness has written extensively and eloquently on this in his recent works, especially *Beyond Religion: Ethics for a Whole World*.

Recent years have seen a quickly growing interest in the study of contemplative practices, including the study of such practices within neuroscience (Fox et al., 2014; Klimecki et al., 2012; Lutz et al., 2008), psychology (Galante et al., 2014; Goyal, 2014), and the health sciences (Kok et al., 2013; Pace et al., 2008, 2010, 2013). This has resulted in recent developments such as a special issue of the *Annals of the New York Academy of Sciences* in 2014 dedicated to 'Advances in Meditation Research: Neuroscience and Clinical Applications' (Sequeira, 2014) and several new journals over the past six years including *Mindfulness,* the *Journal of Compassionate Healthcare*, and the *Journal of Contemplative Inquiry*. Although much of this work has dealt primarily with 'mindfulness' practices, recently increasing attention is being paid to styles of meditation that aim explicitly at the cultivation of compassion.

There is a small but growing body of evidence supporting the view that compassion is of great importance for our physical and psychological health and well-being on an individual level. Furthermore, compassion may be of even greater importance with regard to how we relate to one another on a social level, since compassion and its cultivation have ethical and social dimensions that may be just as, if not more, important as the dimension of individual health and well-being.

The creation of CBCT in 2005 allowed for the scientific study of compassion and analytical meditation in a new way. Research on compassion and compassion meditation had existed before that, such as the seminal work of Dr. Richie Davidson at the University of Wisconsin in Madison (Lutz et al., 2004, 2008), which suggested that compassion had significant and measurable changes in brain function and also suggested that compassion could be trained through meditation. The creation of CBCT, however, represented the first time someone had developed a comprehensive protocol for systematically cultivating compassion for beginners in a secular way and drawing from the Lojong tradition, and had done it specifically for scientific research. Since then, over ten years of scientific study have taken place on CBCT, and other compassion training protocols have been developed and studied scientifically (Ozawa-de Silva et al., 2012). This research suggests increasingly that compassion can be taught and trained in, with measurable changes in brain structure and function, and corresponding benefits such as improved immune response to psychosocial stress.

In one study that I was involved in, participants who had engaged in compassion training for less than two months showed lower inflammation as measured by the biomarker interleukin-6 (IL-6) when presented with a stressful situation compared to controls and those who had taken the compassion meditation classes but not practiced much (Pace et al., 2008, 2010). Similar results were found in a subsequent study with foster children, who were taught CBCT by my colleagues and myself (Reddy et al., 2013). Much more research needs to be done in this area, and we should be cautious about concluding too much from the available scientific evidence regarding the effects of compassion training. Nevertheless, these initial findings are promising and at least suggest that further research is warranted.

In addition to CBCT, other protocols have also been developed for the cultivation of compassion, and in some have been used for scientific research, including Stanford's Compassion Cultivation Training (CCT), and methods by Prof. John Makransky and also Wilson Hurley. There are also newly developed approaches in clinical psychology and psychotherapy that focus on or incorporate compassion, such as Paul Gilbert's Compassion-Focused Therapy (CFT) and Kristen Neff's work on self-compassion. Leading scientists, such as the affective neuroscientist Richard Davidson, the psychologist Paul Ekman, and the social neuroscientist and Max Planck director Tania Singer, have made the scientific study of compassion one of their central areas of focus over the past decade. As a result of their and others' efforts, the study of compassion has become a topic for major national and international conferences, and last November, Stanford University's Center for Compassion and Altruism Research and Education (CCARE) hosted their second conference on 'The Science of Compassion'. This is remarkable, as only a decade ago, any talk of a 'science of compassion' would likely have been regarded as extremely premature.

One of the important aspects of these developments is the fact that compassion is being seen as something that can be studied, cultivated, and deployed for therapeutic aims independent of a particular religious context. The importance of compassion is not new to religious traditions; it *is* rather new to psychology, psychotherapy, and science. And the idea that compassion can be cultivated and taught in a way that is independent of religion – with measurable benefits – is also quite new.

Perhaps the most beneficial thing to come from the scientific study of compassion is the way it shifts our understanding of who we are as human beings. This is not a trivial matter. One of the perennial questions we humans have asked ourselves since recorded history is who we really are; what our place in the universe is; what the meaning of our life is.

These questions might appear to have nothing to do with compassion. In fact, throughout much of Western philosophy, great thinkers have tried to address these questions and have often largely or completely ignored the issue of compassion. Yet as our planet becomes smaller and even more interdependent, trends in society and in science are moving us towards a new way of thinking. Part of that thinking involves understanding ourselves as beings who have compassion at the core – not the periphery – of who we are.

Part of the reason for this is that as human beings, we are dependent on each other for survival. Without maternal care, for example, our species could not survive for even one generation. And even with maternal care, if we had no support from others beyond our mothers, we would still not survive or thrive as we should. This in fact is something that we share with all mammalian and bird species, and from this, as the primatologist Frans de Waal has pointed out, we can see that compassion and care are quite old in our evolutionary history. It should come as no surprise therefore that our physiology and psychology are structured in such a way that we respond very positively to care, and do not develop properly if we are deprived of it. In fact, the developmental psychologist Philippe Rochat, has argued eloquently in his book *Others in Mind* that our basic need to affiliate with others is absolutely fundamental to our psychology, and results in our greatest fear: that of social exclusion and isolation. The research of the social neuroscientist Tania Singer is also doing much to show the fundamental importance of compassion in our lives – with implications even for areas such as economics.

The work of these prominent scientists is slowly pushing us towards recognition of the importance of compassion in our lives – for our physical health, for our psychological well-being, and for a flourishing society and world. This is something that His Holiness the Dalai Lama has argued for quite some time. In fact, His Holiness has pointed out if we were not dependent on each other, we would not need love and compassion. But the fact is, we are dependent – even on the level of our very survival.

Over the past ten years I have had the great privilege to study and learn CBCT for myself. Despite it being a secular practice, I have found it enormously beneficial to my spiritual life. I also engage in Buddhist meditation, and have done so for about sixteen years, but I would not say that this practice makes CBCT superfluous. The secular practice of CBCT has shown me more than anything else that compassion is a universal spiritual quality that can be cultivated in anyone regardless of their faith or lack thereof. It has shown me that the religious methods for cultivating compassion tap into deeper and more universally human roots. There is no longer any doubt in my mind that one can cultivate an extraordinarily rich and expansive compassion without relying on a particular religious tradition. This is not something that I might have said a decade ago. This is not to discredit religious traditions in any way, however. I have deep respect for them and believe they contain tremendous resources for spiritual development on an individual and collective level. But I now no longer see religious traditions as the sole means through which spiritual qualities like compassion can be cultivated.

Accompanying this conviction, which has developed slowly and over time, I have sought along with my colleagues to teach CBCT in a variety of settings and for a variety of populations. In addition to a general population of healthy adults, we have taught CBCT to foster children, to elementary school children as young as five years old, to undergraduates, to women working at a domestic violence organization, and to incarcerated women. Additionally, some of my colleagues (but not I) have taught CBCT to veterans of war, to individuals with early-onset Alzheimer's, to nurses, to medical school students, to the parents of children with autism, and to other populations. Many of these courses were part of scientific studies that have been published and are available through the Emory-Tibet Partnership website. The personal experience of teaching CBCT in such a wide variety of settings, and the results of these scientific studies, suggest that CBCT is a deeply meaningful spiritual practice that can lead to positive changes in psychological and physical well-being.

My experience in teaching incarcerated women has been especially powerful. The majority of these incarcerated women are already religious and hence have access to religious teachings and religious practices. Yet when presented with secular practices like CBCT, they respond very powerfully. Many of the women I have taught inside the prison have been incarcerated for murder. They therefore feel a tremendous burden – a number of burdens, really. Despite their religious faith, CBCT offered them something more: a series of techniques for approaching what they were trying to achieve. For example, where some of the women wanted to forgive, CBCT helped them reach a place of being able to forgive. I believe this is one of the great assets of analytical meditation. It is not enough to tell someone, 'It is better to forgive', or 'One must be compassionate', but one must be able to show the person *how* to gradually reach forgiveness and *how* to expand one's compassion, step by step.

The Mind Training tradition attempts to do just this. It tries to show practitioners that it is simply illogical and unproductive to hold on to anger and resentment; to think only of one's own well-being as if it existed independently of others; to believe that one is a self-sufficient person; to act as if no one has ever benefited oneself; to reject the existential truths of interdependence and impermanence. Being illogical has consequences: sooner or later, life sets you right. And when that happens, nothing other than suffering and pain ensue. The analytical meditation presented in the Mind Training tradition offers individuals a way to gradually replace that illogicality with clarity and understanding. The fact that it can be presented in a secular way makes it, to me at least, all the more appealing.

People often ask: if compassion is at the core of who we are, then why do we need to work so hard to cultivate it? There are two types of compassion. One is innate. We see it in the behaviour of loving parents, even non-human parents, like the meticulous care a mother cat gives to her kittens, even months after they are born. We see it in our natural aversion to gratuitous violence, and we see it in the fact that even a wrong-doer, someone we might call a psychopath, wants to be treated well – not betrayed, cheated, or hurt. But this innate compassion, which we do not need to generate, is limited to our in group: our family, our friends, our nation, our religion. The compassion that one seeks to cultivate in CBCT, or in the Mind Training tradition more generally, is an expansive compassion that includes all living beings equally, and that shows compassion to others based on who they are from their own side – not who they are to me. It is this expansive compassion that, if cultivated, could lead to the protection and flourishing of our societies and our world. And it is this expansive compassion, I believe, of which even a glimpse, once generated, begins to show us who we truly are.

References

Fox, K.C. et al. (2014). 'Is Meditation Associated with Altered Brain Structure? A Systematic Review and Meta-Analysis of Morphometric Neuroimaging in Meditation Practitioners.' *Neuroscience & Biobehavioral Reviews* 43, 48-73.

Galante, J. et al. (2014). 'Effect of Kindness-Based Meditation on Health and Well-Being: A Systematic Review and Meta-Analysis.' *Journal of Consulting and Clinical Psychology* 82(6), 1101.

Goyal, M. et al. (2014). 'Meditation Programs for Psychological Stress and Well-Being: A Systematic Review and Meta-Analysis.' *JAMA Internal Medicine* 174(3), 357-68.

Klimecki, O.M. et al. (2012). 'Functional Neural Plasticity and Associated Changes in Positive Affect After Compassion Training.' *Cerebral Cortex*, bhs142.

Kok, B.E., C.E. Waugh and B.L. Fredrickson (2013). 'Meditation and Health: The Search for Mechanisms of Action.' *Social and Personality Psychology Compass* 7(1), 27-39.

Lutz, A. et al. (2008). 'Regulation of the Neural Circuitry of Emotion by Compassion Meditation: Effects of Meditative Expertise.' *PloS one* 3(3), e1897.

——— (2004). 'Long-term Meditators Self-induce High-amplitude Gamma Synchrony During Mental Practice.' *Proceedings of the National Academy of Sciences of the United States of America*, 101(46), 16369-73.

Ozawa-de Silva, Brendan et al. (2012). 'Compassion and Ethics: Scientific and

Practical Approaches to the Cultivation of Compassion as a Foundation for Ethical Subjectivity and Well-Being.' *Journal of Healthcare, Science and the Humanities.*

Pace, T.W.W. et al. (2008). 'Effect of Compassion Meditation on Neuroendocrine, Innate Immune and Behavioral Responses to Psychosocial Stress', *Psychoneuroendocrinology* 34(1), 87-98.

——— (2013). 'Engagement with Cognitively-Based Compassion Training is Associated with Reduced Salivary C-Reactive Protein from Before to After Training in Foster Care Program Adolescents.' *Psychoneuroendocrinology*, 38(2), 294-9.

Pace, T. (2010). 'Innate Immune, Neuroendocrine and Behavioral Responses to Psychosocial Stress do not Predict Subsequent Compassion Meditation Practice time.' *Psychoneuroendocrinology* 35(2), 310-15.

Reddy, S.D. et al. 2013). 'Cognitive-Based Compassion Training: A Promising Prevention Strategy for At-Risk Adolescents.' *Journal of Child and Family Studies*, 22(2), 219-30.

Sequeira, S. (2014). 'Foreword to Advances in Meditation Research: Neuroscience and Clinical Applications.' *Annals of the New York Academy of Sciences*, 1307(1), v-vi.

PART II

PRACTICES OF COMPASSION IN SIKHISM, JUDAISM AND IN DREAMS

CHAPTER 5

Gobind Sadan's Practices of Compassion

MARY PAT FISHER

THE COMPASSIONATE PRACTICES of Gobind Sadan are based on the teachings of Guru Nanak, the First Sikh Guru, and also on the *Guru Granth Sahib*, the holy scripture which Guru Gobind Singh (the Tenth Guru) set as the Eternal Guru for Sikhs. Guru Nanak taught a simple threefold path to God: Work hard to support yourself by honest means, from what you earn share with others, and always remember God. He sang,

> Nanak seeks the company of those who are of low caste
> Among the lowly, nay, rather, the lowest of the low
> Why should he rival the lofty?
> Where the poor are looked after
> There does rain the look of thy grace, O Lord![1]

Guru Granth Sahib, the great compilation of inspired hymns of Sikh Gurus and also Hindu and Muslim saints, teaches us to live in the world, helping others, but to be inwardly detached from worldly things and attached only to God. Without self-interest, we are to be concerned for others' needs and difficulties. '*Chintaparai* – Worry for others', taught the Gurus.

Early in his life, Baba Virsa Singh, founder of Gobind Sadan, became imbued with these teachings and began to develop practical means of supporting himself and his followers and sharing with others. Being from a family of farmers, he took a small piece of seemingly worthless barren land on the outskirts of Delhi and began trying to turn it into a productive farm. With very hard work and great faith in God, he and his followers pulled out rocks and dug a well by hand, leveled fields, developed gravity-fed irrigation channels, built a dairy, and began planting crops. They themselves lived very simply in bare shelters and ate and shared from their own produce. From that base, Babaji then developed other larger farms in the state of Uttar Pradesh. The largest of these, Shiv Sadan, arose on a huge alkaline, flood-prone wasteland on the banks of the Ganges River. Again the extreme hard work and faith in God of Babaji and his devotees turned that poor area into flourishing fields whose income helped to provide food, medical services, and education for the poor people of the surrounding area. Seeing that the land was being productively developed, the government at last began to provide some basic services, too, including brick roads to replace the old mud cart-tracks, bus service five times a day, and telephone connections. Babaji explained,

> People have to eat. If you look at an area which is barren, an alkaline wasteland, and you see that the people of the area are poor and hungry, if that land can be farmed, then people will have food, and if they come and work they will receive an income as well. We look at it as a way to serve those in need, not just as development. If we cultivate the land, then people will be fed. We will give the poor fees for school and also help them come closer to God.
>
> Working for people is a great thing. We feel that all we have is for the poor, for the weak. Then we can feed whoever comes. We don't expect people to give us anything in order to stay with us. We say, 'Even if you have nothing, we will feed you and give you a place to sleep.' This also plays a role in Dharma: serving people, feeding people, giving people clothes and medicine. But you are only able to give if you have earned the money yourself. So we have been very successful cultivating wasteland and using the income to help others.[2]

Babaji taught that 'Compassion is the mother of Dharma'. Without compassion, he said, there is no foundation for spiritual practices. But he did not approve of giving to people who sit idle and beg. He always said that we should help those who work hard but still cannot meet their basic needs.

Gobind Sadan continues its dedication to serving those in need, without resort to fund-raising or government aid. Although Baba Virsa Singh left his physical body in 2007, the compassionate services he inspired are ongoing, with help from voluntary donations by devotees from their own hard work. A free school for poor children has been created in Babaji's name in Gobind Sadan's Delhi campus.

It now serves 102 students from pre-nursery to fifth grade. Although the children's parents are mostly illiterate in any language, the children are getting high-quality instruction in English to prepare them for good jobs. Since the parents cannot help them with their homework, most are also receiving supplementary tuition so that they can handle the challenging curriculum. The teachers take a loving, supportive approach, trying sincerely to help the children learn. Poor children of older grades are also given financial assistance with school fees, uniforms, books, transportation, and tutoring so that they can do well in higher-level schools. The children are highly motivated to learn so that someday they can earn an income and help to support their parents, most of whom are manual workers. Educational counseling and motivational sessions with older children and their parents are organized to help them move toward a better material future, with aid in accessing government-subsidized educational and medical support programmes for those below the poverty line or of minority communities.

Illiterate adults in the area are also offered adult literacy classes in Hindi and English by a compassionate, helpful teacher. They are learning so well that they themselves are proud and amazed. Among their 'texts' are sacred scriptures from various religions, so their sincere spirituality coupled with their native intelligence and desire to learn are helping them to advance very quickly.

Citizens of India as well as visiting foreigners have been inspired to share their used clothing with the poor, so Gobind Sadan volunteers are frequently engaged in sorting and distributing the donated clothes to those in need. Many poor men of the area thus proudly wear T-shirts and sweatshirts emblazoned with the logos of Western universities and other organizations, and many children are nicely turned out in clothes previously worn by Swedish children.

Medical care is often beyond the means of poor Indians, so Gobind Sadan offers free medicines and also takes people to doctors and hospitals and arranges for their care. It is very heartening to see that when someone needs an emergency blood transfusion, those who are willing to give blood include people who are not their relatives, nor are they of the same religion, but they have compassion for others as if they were their own brothers or sisters. Such health services offered by Gobind Sadan have saved many lives over the years. But when people have died, whether from old age or sickness, their survivors receive great support from other members of the community who are not their blood relations. Many members of the community pitch in to help with cremation and memorial arrangements, share in the grieving, and console the survivors.

Malnutrition is a great problem among the poor people of India. To help alleviate this scourge, Gobind Sadan sponsors many feeding programmes, including weekly distribution of nutritious sweet bread (*roti)*, sweet rice, and black grams. *Langar* (free kitchen) is being run constantly to provide three hot meals plus tea daily to the volunteers, working staff, and visitors. A programme is also being initiated to provide a mineral supplement that should help to prevent stunted development, weakness, and frequent illnesses among small children and their nursing mothers.

In addition to support for the materially needy, Gobind Sadan offers support to the spiritually needy. Many people come or send e-mail requests for prayers and spiritual practices to help overcome their depression, anger, fears, family problems, financial difficulties, educational challenges, legal problems, and the like. They are encouraged to share their resources with others in order to improve their own karma, so they often help to sponsor feeding programmes or bring fresh fruits to distribute to the poor. One volunteer has been blessed by Babaji to pray for people every hour, twenty-four hours a day. Another has been given the duty of praying for people of all religions every evening before a compassionate statue of Jesus. Miracle stories and cases of personal transformation are quite common following these prayers and offerings.

Gobind Sadan's compassionate services are inclusive. Every one of all castes, religions, and genders is invited to partake, and everyone is included in serving, as all are considered fellow members of one human family. From the elderly to teenagers and toddlers, the feeble-minded as well as the highly educated are all involved in *seva* (volunteer service) as respected members of the community. Gobind Sadan serves as a refuge for many differently-abled or rejected people who cannot survive in the outside society, and all are given some useful *seva* to do.

Not only the people but also the plants and creatures are treated compassionately in Gobind Sadan. The young men who serve in the dairy give very loving care to the cows and buffalos, and the animals respond by being peaceful and easily manageable and giving copious amounts of delicious milk. The ox that pulls the cart is huge, but he calmly steps into the traces and lowers his head for the harness whenever he is needed. Vegetables and flowers respond very positively to the organic methods and tender care of the gardeners, and trees planted on the rocky hillside have formed their own natural jungle to help preserve the environment.

These practical services have never been trumpeted or even mentioned on Gobind Sadan's website. They are a constant feature of Gobind Sadan life, but services go on quietly, naturally, with no fanfare. Baba Virsa Singh advised his devotees to just keep serving without self-interest, never expecting any praise or reward. 'Just do and keep moving ahead', he said. 'Every person has to work and help others, for this is God's *hukam* (divine command). One who simply sits idle and meditates will not find favour in God's court, and because he is not helping people, he will not find favour in the world either.'[3]

Notes

1. *Guru Granth Sahib*, p. 15.
2. Baba Virsa Singh, 'What is Dharma and True Spirituality?' – His Holiness Baba Virsa Singh's Message to the Parliament of the World's Religions held in Capetown, South Africa, 1999, www.gobindsadan.org
3. Baba Virsa Singh, *Loving God*, 3rd edn., New Delhi: Sterling, 2006, pp. 69-70.

CHAPTER 6

To Be Holy is to Practise Compassion

ROBERT CHODOS

AS I WRITE this, in May 2016, we are just three days past Shabbat Kedoshim – the Sabbath on which the Torah portion Kedoshim (Leviticus 19-20) is read. *Kedoshim* means holy, and the Torah portion begins with the commandment to be holy as YHWH our God is holy. There follow a series of directives as to how we are to do that. Some of these involve ritual acts – the proper way to prepare an animal sacrifice, a prohibition against wearing clothing made of mixed materials – but most involve ethical conduct.

Don't lie, steal or cheat. Judge people fairly, whether they are rich or poor. Don't mock or take advantage of people because of their disabilities. Leave a corner of your field for the poor and the stranger. My personal favourite, as a freelance writer and editor having often had to wait months to get paid for work I have done: don't keep a worker's wages overnight until morning. All the specific acts of compassion that are mandated in this portion are encapsulated in three words in its eighteenth verse: *Ve'ahavtale're'achakamocha* – 'You shall love your neighbour as yourself.' The overall message of the 'Holiness Code', as it is called is that holiness is a practical matter; more specifically, to be holy you need to practise compassion.

An example of the compassionate practice of the commandments in the Holiness Code is found in a later book of the Bible, the book of Ruth. Observing the commandment that 'you shall not reap all the way to the edges of your field, or gather the gleanings of your harvest', Boaz, a wealthy landowner in Bethlehem, allows gleaners to find food in his field. One of the gleaners is Ruth, a destitute young Moabite widow who is herself a model of compassion in her relationship with her mother-in-law Naomi, with whom she has come to Bethlehem. Boaz treats Ruth with kindness; eventually they marry, and it is noteworthy that the House of David, the royal line of Israel – and, according to both Jewish and Christian tradition, the line of the messiah – is descended from this chain of compassion.

Of course, in common with all peoples, Jews have a mixed record when it comes to actually carrying out their highest teachings. From biblical times to our own, instances of Jews being cruel, callous, dishonest, oppressive, even murderous, abound. But while practices of compassion may not be the whole of the Jewish story, they are part of the story, and it is that part that I sketch briefly here.

The commandment to love my neighbour as myself comes with an implied question: who is my neighbour? In other words, whom am I obligated to love as myself? At the synagogue I attend, Temple Shalom in Waterloo, Ontario, that question was addressed on Shabbat Kedoshim by the thirteen-year-old boy who was celebrating his bar mitzvah on that day: 'Some people think it is someone you can relate to or know pretty well, some people think it is someone who lives near you because of the name "neighbour", some people think it is other Jewish people, and some people think it is someone in your community. But I think everyone qualifies as your neighbour.'

He went on to cite another verse in the Torah portion, Leviticus 19: 34, in which we are commanded not to oppress the stranger and, in fact, to love the stranger as ourselves. So in relation to the commandment to love others as oneself, no distinction is made between Israelites and non-Israelites. This remains controversial in the Jewish world, and while the intent of the Torah portion seems clear to me, there are others who interpret it differently. In practice, compassion can be seen at all levels: in personal relationships, in community structures and in concern for the world as a whole.

Compassion in personal relationships is at the core of rabbinic teaching. It has been emphasized in some times and places more than others, and can be seen especially in the nineteenth-century eastern European ethical movement known as *Mussar* (the word means discipline or instruction), which focused on the cultivation of *midot*, or personal qualities. Stories about the rabbinic leaders of the movement celebrated the lengths to which they would go to practise compassion. One of these leaders was Rabbi Nosson Zvi: 'One of the congregants had difficulty reading the prayer book. This man became a mourner, and it was customary for mourners to lead the congregation in prayer. In order to alleviate the man's embarrassment, Rabbi Nosson Zvi led the prayers and began to stammer and stutter.'

Another story concerns Rabbi Yisroel Meir, who alongside his rabbinic work helped his wife run a grocery store to support the family: 'He was as careful not to cheat his non-Jewish as well as his Jewish customers. On market day a non-Jewish customer left a herring in Rabbi Yisroel Meir's store. Rabbi Yisroel Meir made every effort to find out who the man was, but to no avail. The next market day, he distributed free herring to all his non-Jewish customers.'[1]

Stories I heard in childhood from my mother reflected a similar sensibility. When my mother was born in Montreal in 1911, her parents were recent immigrants from Lithuania, where the Mussar movement was founded. She told me that when she was growing up, she and her siblings were not allowed to find anything. Any object lying on the sidewalk wasn't there for the taking; it belonged to someone, and every effort had to be made to find the owner.

My mother's parents were also involved in establishing Montreal's network of Jewish community institutions to take care of those in need. Such an institutional network is a common feature of Jewish communities in many countries. It reflects a strong communal ethic, and also the particular situation of Jewish minorities. Because of discrimination or simply because of difference, Jews were often poorly served by state- or Christian-run institutions. Jewish doctors, for example, were often excluded from practising in Christian or secular hospitals. And Jewish patients would not be able to get meals that conformed with Jewish dietary laws. Hence Jewish communities established their own hospitals, funded from Jewish sources.

In Montreal, the first organized charitable institution, the Young Men's Hebrew Benevolent Society, was established to aid refugees in 1863, when the city's Jewish population was under 500. As the community grew, the network of institutions grew with it. My mother remembers visits from the 'Greene Yidene' ('green' or recently arrived Jewess), Toba Kaplan, who was raising money for the fledgling Hebrew Maternity Hospital, established in 1914. Two decades later, the Maternity Hospital became the nucleus for the Jewish General Hospital, one of Montreal's major medical institutions.

Other community institutions included the Jewish Immigrant Aid Society, a home for the aged and a tuberculosis sanatorium. An immigrant from Poland, Zigmond Feinberg, established the Hebrew Free Loan Society in 1911. While Jews, like Christians, had long since learned to find ways around the biblical prohibition on taking interest, Jewish free loan societies, providing small, interest-free loans primarily to Jews, but to non-Jews as well, are remnants of the ethic underlying that prohibition.

This network of institutions received occasional financial support from Jewish philanthropic sources elsewhere in the world. Thus, a gift from the prominent German-Jewish philanthropist Baron Maurice de Hirsch led the Young Men's Hebrew Benevolent Society to change its name to the Baron de Hirsch Institute in 1890. But such gifts were the exception. Primary support for the institutions came from within the Montreal Jewish community itself.[2]

Building a strong community that takes care of its members is admirable; limiting one's concern to members of that community, to the exclusion of others, is not. For Jews, with their history of living as a precarious and often persecuted minority, the more exclusive approach to compassion is a constant temptation. But foundational teachings at the core of Jewish tradition argue against that temptation. Hillel, an influential teacher of the first century BCE (it was he who reformulated the commandment to love one's neighbour as oneself into the Jewish version of the Golden Rule, 'What is hateful to you, do not do to your neighbour'), expressed the balance between concern for one's own and concern for others in a sequence of three aphorisms: 'If I am not for myself, who is for me? And if I am only for myself, what am I? And if not now, when?'

Among the Jewish organizations seeking to stretch compassion beyond the bounds of the Jewish community is *Ve'ahavta*, which takes its name from the first word of the biblical commandment to love one's neighbour – which is also the first word of the commandment to love the stranger, and of yet another central commandment, this one in Deuteronomy, telling us to love God with all our being. Based in Toronto, Ve'ahavta provides a number of services including an outreach van providing food, clothing and companionship to Toronto's homeless; health promotion for First Nations in north-western Ontario in cooperation with local chiefs; support for health, education and water supplies in Ethiopia; and international disaster relief wherever needed.

In the fall of 2015, my own community in Waterloo was faced with a choice that highlighted the question of how far our compassion extends.

The synagogue service for the holiest day of the Jewish year, Yom Kippur or the Day of Atonement, theoretically lasts all day, but in practice there is a break of a couple of hours in the afternoon. At Temple Shalom it is the custom to hold a discussion on a topic of interest to the congregation during that break. In 2015 Yom Kippur fell on September 23. A hotly debated issue in Canada at the time was how the country should respond to refugees fleeing the civil war in Syria. The country was in the midst of an election campaign, and the governing Conservatives, citing security concerns, favoured a cautious response, admitting only a very limited number of refugees. The opposition Liberals, who eventually won the election, were prepared to open the gates wider and pledged to admit 25,000 Syrian refugees by the end of 2015.[3] Meanwhile, religious organizations and other private groups were making their own arrangements to sponsor refugee families. This was the question discussed at Temple Shalom on Yom Kippur afternoon: should the temple get involved in efforts to bring Syrian refugees to Canada?

The answer was not a foregone conclusion. Syria and its neighbour, the Jewish state of Israel, have never been on friendly terms. People who had grown up in Syria would likely be coming with anti-Israel, and therefore anti-Jewish, attitudes. There were already enough anti-Semites in Canada; did we need to bring in more?

Weighed against that argument was the central Jewish teaching, and long tradition, of welcoming the stranger. Added to that was the tragic history of Canada's response to Jewish refugees before, during and after the Second World War. While no Western country welcomed Jewish refugees with open arms, Canada's record was the worst of all: fewer than 5,000 refugees admitted between 1933 and 1945, the period of Nazi rule in Germany.[4] Just as significant as the commandment to love the stranger is the reason given for that commandment: 'Because you were strangers in the land of Egypt.' We know what it is like to be turned away when we are in need. How can we do that to others in a comparable situation?

Both sets of arguments were heard at Temple Shalom on Yom Kippur afternoon. I am pleased to say that it was the second set that prevailed. Since Temple Shalom is too small a congregation to sponsor a family on its own, it formed a partnership with three Christian churches and an Islamic social service organization. At the time of writing, the necessary funds have been raised, the paperwork has been done, the application to sponsor a family has been submitted and approved, and a family has been chosen. Unless there are unanticipated hurdles, the Mardini family will arrive in Canada within the next few months.

The story that began when Leviticus was written two and a half millennia ago continues.

Notes

1. Stories adapted from Rabbi Chaim Ephraim Zaichik, *Sparks of Mussar: A Treasury of the Words and Deeds of the Mussar Greats* (Jerusalem: Pisgah Foundation, 1985).
2. See Joe King, *From the Ghetto to the Main: The Story of the Jews of Montreal* (Montreal: Montreal Jewish Publication Society, 2000), especially chapters 10 through 12 and 16.
3. It took a few extra months, but the Liberals, once in government, did eventually meet their target of 25,000 refugees.
4. The story of Canada's response to Jewish refugees is told in Irving Abella and Harold Troper, *None Is Too Many: Canada and the Jews of Europe 1933-1948* (Toronto: Lester & Orpen Dennys, 1982).

CHAPTER 7

Dreamwork as a Practice of Compassion

JAMES GOLLNICK

IN THE BROADEST sense, dreamwork refers to all efforts to uncover the meanings of dreams, although particular connotations of the term have emerged over the course of time. The methods used to understand dreams have varied widely throughout human history and have taken place in many different contexts. In this essay, I shall argue that dreamwork, whatever the method or the context in which it is carried out, is potentially a practice of compassion. In order to highlight the compassionate nature of dreamwork, it is first necessary to clarify the meaning of compassion in this context.

The Canadian Oxford Dictionary defines compassion as 'pity inclining one to help or be merciful' as derived from the ecclesiastical Latin word *compassio*, meaning 'to suffer with'. According to *Merriam-Webster's Collegiate Dictionary*, the word 'compassion' denotes a 'sympathetic consciousness of others'. These definitions highlight the connective nature of compassion as a state of consciousness in which we share the feelings, hopes, and anxieties of others. We shall see that the empathetic connection to others is a key link between compassion and dreamwork.

The Dutch priest and psychologist, Henri Nouwen, emphasizes that compassion is at the heart of our prayer life because when we pray for others, our souls expand to embrace them and bring them into the presence of God. Nouwen (2009: 108) notes, 'Compassion is hard because it requires the inner disposition to go with others to the place where they are weak, vulnerable, lonely, and broken...Our ability to enter into solidarity with those who suffer is our greatest gift.' 'Here we shall see that working with dreams can bring us into a profound solidarity with our fellow human beings as well as with the many other inhabitants of our world.'

Before presenting a brief historical sketch of dreamwork and discussing its compassionate nature, I want to provide some context regarding my own experience of, and standpoint on, dreamwork. My first systematic study of dreams took place at the University of Toronto in a graduate seminar on J.W. Dunne, an engineer and aviation pioneer. In his striking work, *An Experiment with Time* (1934), he examined a number of his own extraordinary precognitive dreams and maintained that dreams can reveal aspects of the future. In order to explore further and test his ideas, I learned to recall and record my dreams in considerable detail, a process that took several weeks of concentrated effort. Finally, much to my surprise, I was able to confirm a number of future references in my own dreams, such as seeing a person I didn't know a day or two before I first met them. Especially in the time surrounding the death of my mother and father (1978-81), dreams communicated precognitive events distant in time and space. Fascination with these enigmatic dream phenomena has led to my life-long interest in the astonishing world of dreams.

After completing my doctorate in religious studies (with a focus on the psychology of religion) at the University of Toronto, I began training and research into clinical approaches in psychology. I was particularly interested in two of the psychological perspectives emphasizing the value of dreamwork for understanding the human personality, namely Gestalt Therapy and Analytical Psychology (Jungian analysis). At the Gestalt Institute of Toronto, I completed the three-year training programme in psychotherapy and received certification from the International Gestalt Association. The director of the Gestalt Institute at that time, the late Jorge Rosner, had a deep appreciation of the role of spirituality in psychotherapy and personality development and he fully supported my exploration of dreamwork within a Gestalt framework.

Later, Carl Jung's major contributions to dreamwork drew me to the training programme at the C.G. Jung Institute in Zurich, Switzerland. I eventually decided not to complete the Zurich training programme and instead underwent a Jungian analysis in Toronto with Frazer Boa, Canada's first Jungian analyst. This three-year analysis helped me integrate my study of the psychology of religion with the ever-surprising world of dreams. During my years of training in psychotherapy and while in analysis, I recorded my dreams regularly, a practice I continue to this day. Over the last forty years, I have catalogued over 6,000 of my own dreams and have examined thousands of dreams of others from both clinical and historical sources. This experience, along with more than a decade of practicing psychotherapy and over thirty years of teaching courses on dreams, first at the University of Toronto and then at the University of Waterloo, in Ontario, Canada, is the basis for my observations about the compassionate character of dreamwork.

Dreamwork in Historical Perspective

Since the dawn of human history, people have wondered about the mysterious images, symbols and stories that appear in their dreams. The earliest historical records indicate that the ancients considered dreams to offer a link between human beings and the divine (Bouche-Leclercq (1879); Buechsenschuetz (1967); Eliade (1960). In the 'cradle of civilization' the Sumerians, Babylonians and Assyrians believed that, in dreams, the gods help people to discern the divine will and see into the future; they also viewed demons and spirits of the dead as the source of bad dreams. Literary texts dating back to the third millennium BCE in Mesopotamia, the first civilization to develop writing, provide some of the oldest written evidence about ancient views on dream interpretation. The earliest of these texts dealing with dreams is 'Dumuzi's Dream', which concerns the journey-to-the-Netherworld motif and is likely the earliest recorded dream in history (Hoffman, 2004: 240).

Ancient Egyptians maintained that dreams were messages from various divinities to warn of dangers, heal the sick, predict the future, demand repentance, and answer important questions. The earliest collection of dreams in Egypt dates from the twelfth dynasty (*c.* 2000-1790 BCE) and may be 'the earliest dreambook in existence' (Gardiner, 1935: 9). Dreamwork in these ancient cultures highlights the religious and future orientation of the dreamworld which we find in all the major religions of the world (Gollnick, 2013). In that context, a religious figure or authority would decipher the meaning of dream images and symbols. We see this approach in the Hebrew

Scriptures, where Joseph interprets Pharaoh's dream of seven fat cows followed by seven lean cows who eat up the fat cows as a symbolic prophecy of seven years of famine in Egypt which would consume all that was produced in the prior seven years of plenty.

We also see this religious view of dreamwork in Egyptian dream temples where the dream god Serapis would appear in a dream to answer a crucial question or heal an illness. In early Egyptian history, dream temple communications were given in direct (non-symbolic) language where no dreamwork was required to decipher their meaning, but in a later epoch, symbolic dreams required interpreters, such as 'the Learned Men of the Magic Library', who formed a guild in Memphis (Jayne, 1962: 30). The ancient Greeks, influenced by Egyptian customs, also focused on healing and raised the practice of dream incubation to a highly developed art, with their earliest temples founded *c.* 500 BCE. The dreamwork in this context involved purification rites and abstaining from food and wine for a period of time before sleeping in the dream temple. Inscriptions from these temples indicate a development in the method of dream healing over the centuries. In pre-Roman centuries, Asklepios, the god of medicine, performed healing miracles in the dream itself, while in later centuries, the god prescribed medications that corresponded to then-current medical treatment (Edelsteins: 1945). Religious authorities at these temples would help supplicants to understand dream images and the treatments they symbolized.

The Greek practice of attending to the divine dreams of Asklepios lived side by side with the development of Greek medicine as represented by the Hippocratic tradition, which dates back to the fourth century BCE (Kerenyi, 1959). Hippocrates, known as 'the Father of Western Medicine', used dreams to diagnose physical disorders. He held that dreams often express the dreamer's physical condition in terms of the world of nature, such as weather, cycles of growth, the sun, moon and planets. If a dream contained images of what normally happens in the outer world (the macrocosm), then the dreamer's body was healthy; conversely, a dream showing irregularities in nature or the cosmos signaled a disorder in the corresponding body system (the microcosm). For instance, dream images of flooding might indicate high blood pressure while images of drought could signal anemia. Here we see the close parallel between religious and medical dreamwork in the ancient world. In both cases, an authoritative figure would interpret dreams for the dreamer within a traditional religious or medical framework.

Dreamwork through the centuries followed the lead of these early traditions, carrying on the belief that dreams can express the divine will and aspects of the spirit-world, foresee the future, and monitor the dreamer's physical condition. However, with the advent of modern science, people increasingly came to believe that science would supplant previous centuries of superstition and ignorance. By the seventeenth century, science was reshaping the world by developing more precise measurement, greater mathematical analysis, and experimental methods for exploring the natural world. These developments seemed to call into question any role for dreams as a possible source of future knowledge or divine guidance.

When science did turn its attention to dreams, it focused primarily on how the body and mind influence dream content. For example, Robert Burton (1854: 102) held that the dreamer's physiological and psychological condition generated dream images, leaving no room for anything like god-sent dreams. In a similar vein, Thomas Hobbes (1994: 11) maintained that imperceptible physiological changes are the real cause of dreams; in his view, dream images reflect only the activity of the dreamer's internal organs and warned against the traditional notion that spirits appearing in dreams could foretell the future. The English neurologist David Hartley (1834: 242) considered dreams to be the result of impressions from the preceding day. From this early scientific vantage point, there appears to be little value in dreamwork, and that is limited to those few medical practitioners who can discern how prodromal dream images can reflect the body's condition before physical symptoms appear.

Sigmund Freud's Psychoanalysis represents a major shift away from the medical-science emphasis on the somatic dimension of dreams. Freud's monumental work, *Die Traumdeutung* (1976) (*The Interpretation of Dreams*), introduced the analysis of dreams as a psychotherapeutic tool and showed convincingly that dreams can provide a psychological portrait of the dreamer. Freud (1976: 283-513) added another dimension to the term dreamwork (*Traumarbeit*) when he distinguished between the manifest dream (the dream as remembered) and the latent dream (the dream thoughts that give rise to the manifest dream). For Freud, it is the latent dream which allows us to disentangle the dream's psychological meaning.

Freud defines dreamwork as the process which transforms the latent dream thoughts into the manifest dream content. For him, dream interpretation actually reverses the dreamwork that created the dream, i.e. he uses each element of the manifest dream as a springboard (via free association) to discover the thoughts that gave rise to that element. It is beyond the scope of this essay to discuss the process of dream formation or Freud's method of unraveling the puzzle posed by the manifest dream; I merely want to highlight Freud's idea of using the dreamer's associations to uncover the psychological meaning behind the manifest dream. This is the key: the dreamer's associations, and not a dream book or dream dictionary, lead us to discover the psychological meaning of a dream.

In the early years of psychoanalysis, the analyst was considered the person in the best position to interpret how dream stories and symbols shed light on the patient's psychological conflicts. In this model drawn from the medical sciences, the analyst is seen as the expert doctor and the only one sufficiently trained to understand dreamwork. This situation began to change dramatically in the 1970s when dreamwork entered the public domain in what Richard Wilkerson (2003: 23-5) calls the 'couch to culture break-out.' Humanistic psychology paved the way for this shift of authority in dream interpretation away from the analyst to the dreamer when it demonstrated how people participate in their own psychological health and how psychotherapy involves clients in resolving their own problems.

This development in turn gave birth to the 'grassroots dreamwork movement', a term which surfaced in popular usage in the early 1980s to describe the growing interest in dreams outside the clinical setting. The *Dream Network Journal*, first appearing in 1982, fostered dream appreciation among ordinary dreamers, an interest which often highlighted spiritual, cultural, religious, environmental, cosmic, and even parapsychological dimensions of dreams that were typically overlooked in a strictly therapeutic setting. Anthropologist Deborah Hillman (1990: 13-20) attributes the rise of the dreamwork movement to the work of spiritual organizations such as the Association for Research and Enlightenment, with its interest in Edgar Cayce's remarkable psychic dreams, and to the feminists' emphasis on raising consciousness through dream groups.

Even from this brief overview of the history of dreamwork, we can see that dream interpreters and researchers have identified a wide range of meanings and possible functions of dreams, such as permitting contact with the spirit-world and the divine, foreseeing future events, showing the condition of the dreamer's body, revealing the dreamer's mental dynamics, commenting on the dreamer's relationships and society, and portraying the state of our environment and the world. The common thread that runs through this variety of observed and hypothesized aspects of *dreamwork shows dreaming to be a multi-dimensional feedback system that provides a metaphorical or symbolic portrait of the entire range of human experience.* From this vantage point, dreamwork can enable a deeper perspective on what is happening in every area of the dreamer's existence.

The Compassionate Nature of Dreamwork

In this section, we shall consider particular aspects of dreams that highlight the compassionate character of dreamwork, beginning with the physical and divine dimensions. In ancient Egypt, Greece, and the Roman Empire, the long tradition of dream incubation temples testifies to the physical healing that was often associated with dreamwork. We see the compassionate aspect of this somatic and religious dreamwork in the belief that the divine is involved in the dreamer's physical condition and actively seeks to bring the dreamer's body back into harmony with the order of nature. The view that the body (the microcosm) is linked to the world of nature (the macrocosm) places human existence in a larger context, where the world reflects and gives meaning to a person's physical health and suffering. From this viewpoint, we might say that God and the world reflect, and even have compassion for, the individual human being.

When a god appears in dreams to heal an illness or provide images of a physical disorder or its possible treatment, compassion is involved in every step of the dreamwork. In this worldview, human beings, the divine, and nature are inextricably bound together. Healing takes place in a world where the divine engages human beings and can either heal physical illness directly in dreams or work with nature's imagery to show what ails the dreamer and what measures to take for recovery. The temples' dream interpreters practice compassion in that they enter into supplicants' dreams and relate dream images and symbols to the then-current religious and medical practices. A practice associated with the ancient dream temples is particularly noteworthy in relation to compassion: If a person was too ill to journey to a dream temple, a surrogate could travel to a temple to dream on behalf of the sick person. Here we see a literal enactment of compassion as 'suffering with' another person, in that the proxy actually represents, and dreams for, the suffering person.

In modern times, too, we find many instances where dreams envision serious illnesses before the dreamer is aware of the physical problem, allowing for early intervention to alleviate suffering. Carl Jung (1935: 65), for instance, discussed dreams showing premonitory symptoms of illness in the course of his psychiatric practice. In one case he diagnosed an organic disease (progressive muscular atrophy) on the basis of two dreams of a young patient. In another case, he interpreted a dream of a pond being drained as symbolic of the damming up of cerebrospinal fluid circulation. More recently, Marc Barasch (2000) and Jeremy Taylor (1992) cite a number of cases where dreams alerted people to serious medical conditions of which they were completely unaware. In England, Dr. Robin Royston has collected 250 such instances of prodromal dreams and Russian psychiatrist Vasily Kasatkin has catalogued over 10,000 dreams from 1,200 patients suffering from a wide range of illnesses (van de Castle, 1994: 364). Kasatkin states: 'By correctly interpreting dreams we've been able to discover and treat serious illnesses long before they would be diagnosed by any traditional means. We have been able to save many lives.' So, at the physical level, dreamwork exhibits compassion by actually healing or ameliorating an illness, or by recognizing dream images of a disorder as an early warning system.

At the psychological level of dreamwork, various schools of psychotherapy have confirmed Freud's view that dreams portray the dreamer's instinctual life and emotional conflicts and have expanded that perspective to show that dreams help people deal with a variety of new, confusing, conflicting and difficult situations in their lives (Levin: 1990). In psychotherapy, the therapist enters into the client's dreamworld in order to clarify the dreamer's emotional difficulties and focus on images that can lead to a way out of these problems. Although psychological dreamwork can be painful for both the therapist and the dreamer, it often brings about an enlarged perspective that contributes to the healing process. For example, people suffering from post-traumatic stress as a result of war experiences, accidents, or the death of loved ones may have nightmares that replay the trauma for months or even years in an attempt to integrate these indigestible experiences. Helping dreamers work through such psychological pain in order to adapt to their new circumstances is a fundamental act of compassion.

Considering the dynamics of group dreamwork may further illustrate its compassionate nature. Group dreamwork is currently practiced both in and outside of the clinical setting. Outside the clinical setting, Montague Ullman's (1987) method is now widely used because of its simplicity, efficacy, respect for the dreamer, and concern for the emotional safety of the dreamer. In this method, dreamgroup members listen carefully to the dreamer tell her or his dream. Then they take on the dream as if it were their own and each, in turn, tells what feelings emerge for them in this process, using some phrase such as 'if this were my dream, I would feel...' or 'in my dream, I feel fear when I see a knife on the table'. Here the group experiences and shares (suffers with) the concerns, fears, joys, and sorrows that are imaged in the dream. On a second time around the group, again using the 'in my dream' protocol, members express what the images, symbols or metaphors in the dream mean to them. In this process, the dreamer benefits from how others experience and understand the dream. The success of this process rests on our common human experience of dreaming and the benefit we gain from other people's empathetic sharing of their dream feelings, images and symbols.

The grassroots dreamwork movement of the 1980s and 1990s has extended the compassionate aspect of dreamwork beyond the physical and psychological healing long associated with dreams to include recovering a wider view of reality that calls into question the mechanistic and materialistic world-view of mainstream science that has dominated the last 300 years in Western societies, 'leading inevitably to atheism and a belief in the meaninglessness of physical existence' (Davies, 1999: 263). Nobel laureate Jacques Monod (1972:167) sums up the world-view underlying modern science: 'The ancient covenant is in pieces: man at last knows that he is alone in the unfeeling immensity of the universe, out of which he has emerged only by chance.'

According to physicist David Bohm (1988), this materialistic and fragmentary world-view of mainstream science has contributed to a whole range of psychological, social, political, economic, and ecological crises in the individual and in society. For Bohm (1980), the undivided wholeness that underlies our everyday world means that we must go beyond the kind of mechanistic view of the universe that has been basic to physics for many centuries. This mechanistic perspective considers human beings to be biological machines composed of cells, tissues, and organs and consciousness to be strictly a function of brain physiology. While this materialistic viewpoint has enabled substantial gains in our understanding of the world, it is, at best, a partial truth, because it has not been able to account for many experiences and states of consciousness associated with dreams.

The grassroots dreamwork movement encouraged dream appreciation among the general population and thereby involved them in features of the dreamworld they might have overlooked in an exclusively therapeutic setting. This movement now represents a significant number of people who regularly record their dreams in detail and note, in addition to other things, telepathic and precognitive dream phenomena. Non-clinical dreamwork can help balance the current one-sided materialistic view governing most mainstream science because it provides an 'experiential laboratory' in which we can experience directly and study for ourselves phenomena that go against cultural expectations and current scientific views. Non-clinical dreamwork is particularly important in this effort to overcome the materialistic and mechanistic excesses of much mainstream science because dreams are the most frequently reported source of precognitive experiences.

The mechanistic model dismisses extraordinary dream phenomena such as pre-cognition and telepathy as anomalies or exceptions so rare that they do not challenge the validity of the mechanistic model itself. However, such remarkable dream phenomena as well as other extraordinary experiences reported in a number of related sciences have reached the point where it is increasingly difficult to ignore them. Noted consciousness researcher Stanislov Grof (1985) maintains that the significant body of data now existing in the fields of psychology, psychiatry, medicine, parapsychology, anthropology and thanatology is too massive to ignore or dismiss as anomalies. Dreams involving telepathy and pre-cognition show that human identity is more like a web extended in space and time than like 'isolated egos inside bags of skin' as Alan Watts (1966: 8) characterizes our typical sense of self in Western society.

Although it will likely take considerable time to alter current mainstream conceptions of consciousness and the human being, dreamwork can play a primary role in changing our view of these matters. When people record their dreams in detail and communicate possible precognitive or telepathic dreams to another person or put them on the web, they are establishing an important bank of data that may help to overcome the weight of traditional scientific objections to the possibility of precognition and telepathy. This movement towards an enlarged view of the human being and the world may turn out to be the most important contribution that dreamwork makes towards a more compassionate, less materialistic, and more accurate world-view.

When we contemplate and work with our dreams, they can show us possibilities that we frequently miss from our usual conscious and cultural perspectives on life. Dreams often surprise us with insights into our emotional conflicts, our physical and spiritual condition, and even the state of our relationships, society, and world. Psychotherapy, medicine, and science have built upon and refined the ancient belief that dreams are meaningful communications with the dreamer's world. We are slowly rediscovering through continuing dreamwork just how large the dreamer's world actually is. It turns out that this remarkable inner world is as infinite as the unfolding external universe. Dreams that show us future or distant events, remind us how limited our present scientific world-view is. Dreams that illuminate the transcendent dimensions of our lives remind us that we dwell in a more sacred and much larger universe than the ordinary stuff of everyday life generally permits us to see.

References

Barasch, M. (2000). *Healing Dreams: Exploring the Dreams that can Transform Your Life*. New York: Riverhead Books.

Bohm, D. (1980). *Wholeness and the Implicate Order*. London: ARK Paperbacks.

——— (1988). 'Consciousness and Self-Consciousness: A Working Paper', *Psychological Perspectives* 19/1: 44-9.

Bouche-Leclercq, A. (1879). *Histoire de la divination dansl'antiquite*, vol. I. Paris: E. Leroux.

Buechsenschuetz, B. (1967). *Traum und TraumdeutungimAlterthume*. Wiesbaden: Saendig Verlag.

Burton, R. (1854). *The Anatomy of Melancholy*. London: William Tegg.

Dunne, J. (1934). *An Experiment with Time*. London: Faber & Faber.

Edelstein, E. and L. Edelstein (1945). *Asclepius: A Collection and Interpretation of the Testimonies*, 2 vols. Baltimore: John Hopkins University Press.

Eliade, M. (1960). *Myths, Dreams, and Mysteries*. New York: Harper & Row.

Freud, S. (1976). 'Die Traumarbeit', in *Die Traumdeutung*. Frankfurt am Main: S. Fischer Verlag, pp. 283-513.

Gardiner, A.H. (1935). *Hieratic Papyri in the British Museum*, no. 3, *The Dream Book*. London: The British Museum.

Gollnick, J. (2013). *The Spiritual, Social, and Scientific Meanings of Dreams*. Lewiston, NY: The Edwin Mellen Press.

Grof, S. (1985). *Beyond the Brain: Birth, Death, and Transcendence in Psychotherapy*. Albany, NY: SUNY Press.

Hartley, D. (1834). *Observations on Man*. London: Thomas Tegg & Son.

Hillman, D. (1990). 'The Emergence of the Grassroots Dreamwork Movement', in S. Krippner, ed., *Dreamtime and Dreamwork: Decoding the Language of the Night*. Los Angeles, CA: Jeremy Tarcher, pp. 13-20.

Hobbes, T. (1994). *Leviathan*. Ed. E. Curley. Indianapolis, IN: Hachot Publishing.

Hoffman, C. (2004). 'Dumuzi's Dream: Dream Analysis in Ancient Mesopotamia.' *Dreaming* 14/4: 240-51.

Jayne, W. (1962). *The Healing Gods of Ancient Civilizations*. New Hyde Park, NY: University Books.

Jung, C.G. (1935). 'Tavistock Lectures', in *The Collected Works of C.G. Jung* (vol. 18), ed. H. Read, M. Fordham and G. Adler, trans. R.F.C. Hull. Princeton, NJ: Princeton University Press, pp. 1-182.

Kerenyi, K. (1959). *Asklepios: Archetypal Images of the Physician's Existence*. New York: Pantheon Books.

Levin, R. (1990). 'Psychoanalytic Theories on the Function of Dreaming: A Review of the Empirical Dream Research', in J. Masling (ed.), *Empirical Studies of Psychoanalytic Theories*, vol. 3. New York: Analytic Press.

Monod, J. (1972). *Chance and Necessity*, trans. A. Wainhouse. London: Collins.

Nouwen, H. (2009). *The Essential Henri Nouwen*, ed. R. Jonas. Boston: Shambhala.

Ullman, M. (1987). 'The Experiential Dream Group', in *The Varieties of Dream Experience*, ed. M. Ullman and C. Limmer. New York: Continuum, pp. 1-26.

van de Castle, R. (1994). *Our Dreaming Mind*. New York: Ballantine Books.

Watts, A. (1966). *The Book: On the Taboo Against Knowing Who You Are*. New York: Random House.

Wilkerson, R. (2003). 'Tending to the Soul of the World', *Dream Network: A Journal Exploring Dreams and Mythology* 21/4: 23-5.

PART III

PRACTICES OF COMPASSION IN HINDU AND JAIN WAYS

CHAPTER 8

Interwoven into the Way of Life: Compassion Practised in the Hindu Tradition

SWAMI CHIDANANDA

WHEN THE SPORTS teacher was harsh to a group of eighth grade boys in a co-education school and made us crawl some distance on our knees as a punishment for the loud noise that we had made, it was more emotionally humiliating than physically painful. As another expression of his anger, he also took away the ball that we were playing with. It was the size of a basketball. One of us had brought it from home. We were very resentful and some of us even thought of some kind of retaliation. Then Rajiv Shetty, our math teacher, came to know what was going on. On his own, he intervened. He spoke kind words to us, got the ball back and told the sports teacher not to treat students like that.

This was compassion in action. It did not involve any obvious marks of religion or of tradition. It was simply the kind gesture of our teacher, Rajiv Shetty. Yet it was, all the same, an expression of the religion he belonged to – Hinduism – and of the tradition or Indian ethos which he was raised in.

The Practices

- With much diversity, and significant freedom, Hindus practise compassion in ways that come from their hearts.
- Some Hindus are regularly engaged in acts of charity without making their religion visible in the process.
- Individuals display compassion in various settings and Hinduism supplies the inspiration for such displays of compassion.
- Some Hindu temples have multi-faceted programmes rooted in

compassion for serving the wider society. But not all Hindu temples are necessarily involved in social service.

- A number of organizations carry out great acts of service. Many of them are Hindu religious bodies, but some are not. Yet even in those organizations that are not explicitly religious, their inspiration typically comes from one or another Hindu saint.
- Many of the family values of Hindus have roots in Hinduism and include practices anchored in compassion.
- Hindus have been active in fields of service-oriented education, health, rural service, and animal care.
- Compassion can be towards oneself too. Hindu scriptures have written at length on the importance of compassion for oneself.

Religion, Tradition, Way of Living

Compassion, it seems to me, is not limited to or found only in religion. Of course, all religions speak of compassion, but we could debate whether or not organized religion can really instil true compassion in all its adherents. This is in no way a call for abandoning religion. It rather reminds us that we can look beyond the structures of religion to discover compassion in ourselves and to awaken it in others. Religion and tradition have a tendency to become mechanical. They tend to get caught up in formalities. Often they speak of values like compassion without necessarily having them deeply rooted in their own hearts.

In this world, we encounter many people who are not involved with any religion and yet are very kind and compassionate. We also encounter many who go to places of worship regularly, but lack sensitivity towards people who are suffering.

Similarly, tradition can also get caught in mere repetition of some external act – that might be very artistic and beautiful – yet lacking at the same time in genuine feeling or sentiment.

Religion and tradition, alas, tend to get compartmentalized in our lives rather than informing all aspects of our life.

It is the way of living, which is the result of many factors, rather than religious or traditional training, that seems to reflect compassion and other important human values.

Freedom, Hinduism's Strength

Given the cleverness of the human mind, anything imposed from the outside can have mixed results. For example, what happens when we say to somebody with the voice of authority 'Be compassionate?' Does a person thus advised simply behave in ways that conform to our demand? Or does that person begin to inwardly rebel against the command to conform? Perhaps they do so without even being fully conscious of the inner workings of her or his mind.

So how do we go about teaching values? How do we rise in our own understanding and practice of values? How do we impart them to others?

Learning takes place most successfully when, with a few broad parameters of discipline in place, the student is given the freedom to find out for herself. We are not talking about freedom that takes the form of wanton behaviour. We are rather talking about an environment where a person suffers the least, if not zero, imposition or pressure.

Hinduism, which is a very ancient religion, has accepted, accommodated and assimilated numerous schools of thought. At its philosophical height, it has made room for non-dualism, dualism, qualified dualism and many more variations with regard to a soul's relation with God. At the level of forms of worship, a Hindu enjoys a great amount of freedom. He may worship a male form, a female one or a graphic symbol or just a sound string, too. (This apparent polytheism is translated to One God by the higher philosophy, which the common man may not know.)

In the process, Hindus have always enjoyed much greater freedom with regard to the practice of their religion than, I suppose, is found in other religions. This has also led them to look at their own and others' lives with a relatively higher degree of freedom. I tend to believe that they discover real 'compassion' in their own bosom, when they observe life in such an atmosphere of freedom.

A Blend of 'A Way of Life' and 'A Religion'

For a Hindu, goodness is not confined to his religious practices. Being good is a part of his way of living. What we mean here is that he does numerous acts of kindness at home and in the society, without invoking the name of God. He shows compassion without raising a flag with a symbol of his religion. While his thoughts, words and deeds are much influenced by his religion, he may not show it openly.

A Hindu may be seen, for example, doing a significant amount of charity – to very worthy causes – and yet he may say that 'I do not believe in supporting temples. I simply want to help the needy and the deserving to have a better standard of living.' Though he indirectly criticizes his temples, the very values he attaches to supporting non-religious causes is actually inspired by what Hinduism preaches in temples and other structured facilities!

In this way, comparing Hinduism with another great religion of the world is often like comparing an orange with an apple! We have to go closer to the religion and only then can we appreciate its rich sources for ethics and values.

Compassion under the Banner of Religion

Numerous religious organizations, under the broad banner of Hinduism, are seen in today's world, especially in India, to be engaged in acts of compassion in various ways. An example that can be cited is the Sadhu Vaswani Mission with its headquarters in Pune, Maharashtra, India. Adhering to Hinduism and showing respect for all the other great religions of the world, this Mission has been a shining example of great social service for a century now. 'The way to be happy is to make others happy', says its present head, Dada J.P. Vaswani. Feeding the poor; building houses for the homeless; imparting education to large numbers at an affordable cost, if not free; providing drinking water at places where it is scarce; supplying medical aid to the poor; and many more ways of 'compassion displayed in action' have been going on under the banner of this Mission for decades. This Hindu organization is ever ready to rise to any occasion. Disaster relief when there is an earthquake or tsunami and providing succour to the suffering during any other natural calamity have been part of their programme. 'Never leave out the poor and the needy' has been the advice of these spiritual teachers.[1]

Ramakrishna Mission, officially incorporated in the year 1902, can also be cited as another example of a Hindu organization serving the poor and needy. With branches worldwide, this establishment has a large number of monks as well as householder members who are engaged in regular acts of service and are always ready to swing into action when people, in different parts of India, need help. Swami Vivekananda (1863-1902), the founder of the Ramakrishna Mission, made it clear from the beginning that we are to see God in a human being and we can go to heights of spiritual excellence if we serve man with love and care.[2]

There are numerous organizations like the two cited above which are run by followers of Hinduism. Then there are many more, which do not directly announce their adherence to Hinduism but are indeed inspired by Hindu gurus or scriptures.

Individuals or families belonging to Hinduism often perform great acts of service, marked by much compassion, in many ways. Once more, they may not display symbols of their religion but where do their values come from? More often than not, it is some Hindu saint that is behind these acts. Baba Amte, Vinoba Bhave, and of course Mahatma Gandhi himself, can be given as examples. Recently, Kailash Satyarthi received the Nobel Prize for Peace (2014) and though he did not do all his good work – protecting children against forced labour – in the name of a religious body, the fact remains that he was born a Hindu.

Compassion towards Animals

A high percentage of Hindus, as everybody knows, are practising vegetarians. Not to kill animals for food has been a value that is a part of Hinduism for ages. This was, however, not imposed on all because it was recognized that 'life subsists on life in Nature.'[3] The sages of Hinduism held the view that food affects the mind[4] and meat was considered less conducive to a contemplative living. Great Hindus like Mahatma Gandhi were pure vegetarians by both upbringing and personal choice. Gandhi in fact even tried to avoid cow's milk. For some time he drank goat's milk as part of his experiments with food, trying to find the best choice in terms of the least violence and the maximum healthy influence on the mind.

Hindus do see, however, that food alone does not decide the quality of our thoughts. They believe that other factors are also important. While food can be a decisive factor in ensuring calm, balanced and compassionate thoughts, they also believe the converse is true.

It is well known that Hindus see the cow as worthy of worship. The cow is not God, but the animal stands apart in Hindu eyes as one that is not to be hurt. Certain scriptures have described the cow as 'something where divine forces reside'. While logic and science may not support this, time alone may tell the hidden truth behind the revelation of the sages (*rishis*)! Lastly, if people in India are seen to ill-treat the cow anywhere, it is simply a case of animal cruelty and of 'not following true Hinduism'.

There is, in some spiritual centres of Hinduism, the practice of feeding cows, birds and certain other animals before people eat. In some other ashrams, they first feed poor sadhus (those who have taken to spiritual practices by abandoning regular household life, and who live on alms) and then their guests.

Compassion towards Oneself

Though forgotten by the majority, the Hindu scriptures actually make earnest appeals to everyone to 'safeguard the true well-being of oneself.' This means compassion towards oneself. 'They go to dark worlds after their death, who kill themselves (by ignoring self-knowledge)', says an ancient text.[5] While this 'lack of self-knowledge' connects directly with suicide, it also makes a good case for avoiding all forms of self-condemnation or self-pity. It is an appeal to live with self-respect, putting in fresh effort to rebuild one's life in the face of failure, fall or loss.

Those Hindus who have understood their religion, therefore, do not misuse the idea of 'karma' and curse themselves when things go wrong. They rather say to themselves, 'What I am facing today could indeed be the result of my past actions; I can however create a happy future for myself by "acting wisely" in the present.' Swami Chinmayananda (1916-93) used to say, 'What you face is the result of your past actions; how you face it is your self-effort!'

Similarly in the case of others' suffering, the right understanding of karma in Hinduism is certainly not blaming their suffering on their past karma. If somebody is sick, poor or failing repeatedly, certain factors from his past may indeed be the causes; the right Hindu vision is, however, to help him, to give him a touch of love and care. By doing so, we add 'good karma' to ourselves and we help others to come out of their suffering. The explanation that the present is the result of the past does not prevent us from doing our two cents of service.

Therefore compassion towards oneself and towards others is an 'empowering principle' that helps in living a meaningful life and in working towards the highest spiritual goal of liberation (*moksha*).

Compassion in Family Life

Children taking care of old parents, wife and husband staying together for all their lives, younger members respecting the older ones, etc., are facets of Hindu family values, all of which are based on noble values like 'putting others first', 'sacrificing one's own interests for the sake of the group', etc. They connect with compassion in as much as there is self-denial and broadmindedness.

There are many cases for example, where a daughter-in-law serves the parents of her husband with tremendous dedication and a lot of personal sacrifice. She may regard it as her good fortune rather than looking at it as a burden. But the reverse is not true with most son-in-laws.

Business houses, often led by certain communities (like Marwari, Shetty, Chetty[6]), are often seen in our country to be devout followers of Hindu gurus. They are seen to spend a portion of their profit for service to the poor. Some of them may give money to temples, and it may seem there is no compassion towards suffering humanity. The temples, however, are seen to spend a portion of their earnings to serve the society in *annadāna* (free food to people), building orphanages, schools and hospitals. In the south (India), there are many temples which offer free food to all devotees who come to the temple. The numbers that throng these places of worship can sometimes be tens of thousands daily if not more. Dharmasthala in Karnataka can be cited as one example.

Rural Service

In the past, every village used to be self-sufficient. Due to industrialization, there is now dependence on products made somewhere else. The urban-rural divide has widened. Hindu spiritual organizations have risen to the occasion and have launched various programmes through which they contribute to rural uplift. An example is the Chinmaya Organization for Rural Development (CORD), they are doing extensive rural service in the sectors of medical aid, awareness generation and education.[7]

The 'hugging saint' or 'Amma' – as she is called – Ma Amritanandamayee has also been a symbol of compassion and service, as she goes to nooks and corners of the country (India) and serves the poor. She has built a large number of houses for the poor who have no roof over their heads. She travels all over the world, healing wounds and bringing light, and collects funds to help the poor in India.[8]

Satya Sai organizations are another example that should not be missed. Satya Sai Baba exhorted his millions of followers to carry 'service of the needy' together with their personal spiritual practices.[9]

Individuals Display Justice and Compassion

Former President of India (2002-7), A.P.J. Abdul Kalam (1931-2015)[10] used to narrate a piece of story from his own childhood days. He grew up in Rameshwaram in south India, a town known for a major Hindu temple. At his primary school, he used to sit in the front row next to his good friend who was from a Brahmin family. The friend's father was in fact a well-placed and much respected priest in the town. All was well until a new teacher joined the school. This gentleman was highly conditioned by the prevalent bigotry in the society. He literally ordered Kalam, the Muslim boy, to go to a back row! The boy, much puzzled, obeyed. The best part of this story is that when the Brahmin boy's father came to know what happened at the school, he right away called the new teacher, his own son and Kalam to his house. He reprimanded the new teacher in front of the little boys and told him to allow Kalam to sit in the front row with his own son, a Brahmin boy.

This episode has two points to convey. One is that there are very good, broadminded people in every religion in whom we can perhaps see the true, essential spirit of the religion. The second point is that human goodness is only partly nurtured by religion and partly independent of religion!

True sympathy means, putting yourself in another's place.
To ease another's pain and sorrow is to dispel your own.

SWAMI SHIVANANDA

Notes

1. The Sadhu Vaswami Mission was initiated by Sadhu T.L. Vaswami (1879-1966) in Hyderabad, Sind, now a part of Pakistan. Following Partition it moved to Pune, India, where it is still located. It runs schools including St. Mira's College for Women, hospitals, rural development projects, and many other projects to empower the poor and especially women. It has Chapters around the world.
2. The Ramakrishna Mission was founded by Swami Vivekananda, a shining star of the 1893 Parliament of the World's Religions in Chicago, in 1897, and officially incorporated in 1902. It has a mission of social service especially in education, medicine, and improving village life. Vivekananda also brought Vedanta and Yoga to the West.
3. *jeevojeevenajeevati* is an old saying in Sanskrit meaning 'life forms depend on other life forms for them to live on…'.
4. *āhāra-shuddhau sattva-shuddhih* is found in the '*Chāndogya Upanishad*' (*Sāma Veda*) 7.26.2.
5. See the *tyekechātmahanojanāh* – '*Ishāvāsya Upanishad*' (*Yajur Veda*), mantra 3.
6. These terms are variously described as family names, ethnic groups, or castes.
7. The Chinmaya Organization for Rural Development is a branch of the Chinmaya Mission founded by Swami Chinmayananda Saraswati. It has branches world-wide.
8. Ma Amritanandamayee (1953-) is an India spiritual teacher or guru. She is from Kerala. She teaches that 'true love transcends all barriers. It is universal. It is this love that I consider my religion.' Her *darshan* is by embracing people.
9. Sathya Sai Organizations emerged following the death of Sathya Sai Baba (1926-2011).
10. Dr. Kalam was one of India's leading nuclear scientists. He was also a deeply spiritual person.

CHAPTER 9

The Silence of Compassion: The Practices in Words

SUDHAMAHI REGUNATHAN

With rising waves lashing the shores, the turbulent sea rumbled
The quiet moonlit night aided the spread of its roar
But the huge mansions and trees on its banks stood unmoving
They had not a bit of fear,
the reason for which was the sea itself
for it
never transgresses its limits.[1]

The verse above, was composed by Acharya Mahapragya as he sat watching the sea at a place called Dholawad in Maharashtra. In the words of this poem he captures the deathly silence of fear by its absence. And that which is present is a chorus rising in high octave, it is un-worded, yet it reverberates. Is this called compassion?

Compassion is interchangeably called *daya*, *anukampa*, *karuna*, *dana* or *maitri* and each term has its own specific connotations and some overlapping commonality. Essentially they all indicate an empathy with the other, a close quarter appreciation of the other's pains, being moved by it, alleviating it either by service or by donating something and nurturing a universal love towards all. Compassion is used to represent any of the above ideas or a combination of them.

Compassion is a sentiment common to all faiths for it forms the very basis of faith. Their expression is varied, their perspective is multi-dimensional. In Jainism, its definition moves beyond the ideas enumerated above to include the root cause of them all … fear. The removal of all fear, known as *abhayadānam*, is the highest quality, charity, action … the supreme manifestation of compassion.

What causes fear? A feeling of not being good enough, a feeling of insecurity with respect to a stronger being, a more powerful being, ignorance of the rules that operate in the world, the possibility of losing possessions in terms of material wealth or relationships, the apprehension of being called to own up for a wrong, a revengeful enemy, the crying ache of lust. All these feelings cause or bring in their wake, exploitation. And this gives birth to fear.

Therefore it is, that the Jainas believe that to remove fear in all beings is the highest act of compassion. It is logical to find they have identified five principles which can help remove fear and enhance compassion. The five principles take the form of the five vows or *mahavratas* that a monk or nun takes when he or she is initiated into the fold: *ahimsa*, *aparigraha*, *achautya*, *brahmacharya* and *asatya*.

Ahimsa: non-violence, causing no harm
Aparigraha: non-possessiveness not only about material possessions but even about ideas
Achautya or non-stealing, not coveting the other's possessions
Brahmacharya: overcoming lust
Asatya: to refrain from speaking untruth.

On taking and following these five vows, *karuna* or *daya* or *anukampa* begins to manifest. It is thus associated with *samyaktva* or *samyak drishti* or the right perspective. When a mendicant takes these vows (or a lay follower who follows these vows with some caveats), he is essentially giving *abhayadana*: he will not hurt, will not fight for his ideas or possessions, will not steal, be overcome by lust or tell lies. Of such a person one has no fear.

The *Tattvartha* sutra mentions compassion as one of the *bhavanas* or contemplations that strengthen the five vows. So compassion is born of these five vows and also strengthens these five vows for these vows lend the right perspective and compassion is indicative of the right perspective. Only if you are inclined towards compassion will these vows appeal to you and you will sincerely follow them. Only if you sincerely follow them will you become a compassionate being.

The interesting thing is that each of these principles is followed for the purifying of one's own soul, but the route taken is through social action ... that is why the three culverts in the journey of Jainism are right perspective, right knowledge and right conduct. Good conduct alone translates into spiritual benefits. Drawing in the world and social life thereby, Jainism integrates personal goals with harmonious living.

However, because of the manner in which compassion is defined, the practices of compassion are also different. The reason why dispelling of fear is considered paramount is because every soul is equal, even if it be lodged in an insect, plant or human. So to cause harm to another is to cause harm to one self. It is disrespecting the universality of the soul. In order to understand compassion better, the Jainas delved deep into the study of all living beings in such detail that they have classified them as having one, two, three, four or five senses. Further, they all also have a soul which desires to live:

Savvism jiviyam piyam[2]
To each, his life is dear

Therefore it is that one finds many *goshalas* and bird hospitals set up by Jainas. Jainas have been leaders in setting up medical services for animals. Since the Jaina idea of compassion goes beyond human life to all living beings, they cover their mouth, lest they harm some air bodies, walk barefoot, to minimize the harm they may cause to a small being (like an ant) crawling on their pathway, that is why they are careful using water, in fact this defines many of features of their lifestyle. Though this is contained in their concept of *ahimsa*, it is, in my opinion, more than *ahimsa* for it is an understanding and a true appreciation of other forms of life. It is not limited to refraining from doing harm, it goes further to allow for an environment where the other too can flourish.

It may appear obvious to many, but the subtle difference in understanding compassion in the Jaina world arises because it talks about compassion at the level of the soul. To recognize that one should not cause fear and that everyone should be able to live free indicates an understanding of the equality of one soul with other souls. And souls look after each other's interest.

Parasparo upagraho jivanam
Souls render service to one another[3]

It is not surprising, therefore that Acharya Bhikshu, the founder of the Swetambar Terapanth sect differentiated further between two kinds of compassion: worldly compassion or *laukika daya* and spiritual compassion: *lokottara* or *dharma daya. Laukika daya* is that which pertains to worldly affairs … the rich help the have nots with donations, charity and other philanthropic activities. In India the Jains are among the highest donors and managers of charities and charitable institutions.

The other type of compassion is called Lokottara daya, or other worldly compassion, or compassion beyond this world. According to this thought the compassionate are the ones who steer people to the path of rectitude. As we have seen the monks and nuns who take the five vows are expected to have compassion which leads them to take these vows and are also supposed to develop compassion through the practice of these vows. They see people who are not aware of the spiritual scheme of things making blunders that will cause them to suffer in future lives. They guide them, therefore, back to a life of rectitude by showing them the right path and thereby help reduce the bad karmas that they could have acquired. By acquiring bad karmas they may be born in hell in their future births. Their soul may be captured in organisms that have to remain for several years in that state before they can be born as human beings. In order to help the beings from falling into such states, the compassionate one guides them. Therefore it is that in most stories in the Jaina tradition, the ending is always such that the hero and/or the heroine is initiated into a life of rectitude by becoming a monk or a nun.

The core act involved in this kind of compassion is to spread the word of restraint: do not be led by temptation to commit acts such that you fall low in the type of birth you may get in the next birth and lose all the merits you have so far acquired. Generally monks and nuns are the ones to direct erring followers. Sometimes it can happen the other way round too as told in the following story:

A monk after several years of severe penance was practising restraint while living in a prostitute's house. It did not last. Soon he fell prey to her whims. She asked him for an expensive shawl. He managed to get a king to donate it to him, for a monk has no posessions. The temptress wiped her mud soiled feet on the expensive shawl when the monk gifted it to her while waiting to be favoured by her. As the monk was aghast, the woman replied, 'I threw away just a shawl, you are throwing away all your years of penance and restraint…'.

The monk realized his folly and in repentence of his conduct went back to his fold to make amends and reach higher levels of spiritual progress.[4]

Those who show compassion of this nature are indeed showing the highest form of compassion. The Tirthankara is so called because after attaining enlightenment or *kaivalya,* he comes back to the world to help others see the right path. That is why they become Tirthankaras or ford makers while those who get realization but do not come back to help the lesser mortals are not adored as the Tirthankaras are.

Does delivering a sermon, however wise, benefit a dying man? The question is tricky. At one level it does for it can make him repent. In sincere repentence alone, much damage can be controlled and the bad karmas accruing may actually be dispelled. Every human being has the potential to be a Jina or a conqueror so even at this last stage, if he sees the right path, he has made a better future for himself.

Laukika dharma helps in day to day living. It can lead us to donate medicines, build charitable hospitals and so on. Jaina thought sees life as continual. Each birth and death are like changing rooms where you acquire a new body. Every action, every event in life is a result of previous actions. Our actions also decide the nature and fate of the future. So the long term goal of salvation is the one deemed most important to address. For ultimately we are not just this body, we are the soul. So service in this life is not given separate focus.

Yet another story illustrates both *laukika* and *lokottara dharma*:

There once lived an elephant called Meruprabh. When a forest fire broke out, Meruprabh rose quickly to rescue the animals by tearing down some trees and creating a small space through which fire could not spread. In this small space all animals huddled together waiting for the fire to wane. Meruprabh too stood there. As he picked up one foot to scratch his other leg, a rabbit came and took refuge under that raised foot. Meruprabh, not wanting to hurt the rabbit kept his foot aloft till the fire died out, which took three days. Unfortunately he succumbed to the pain in his leg, thereafter.

He was reborn as Meghakumar, a prince. Meghakumar decided to join the fold and on the first night of his initiation suffered such discomfort that he made up his mind to go and tell the Master, revered Mahavira, himself that he would go back to the palace. Then Mahavira understanding why the young monk had come to him reminded him of his previous birth where he had been so compassionate that it had won him a human birth in which he would attain monkhood.

Mahavira's compassion restored Meghakumara's determination and he once again committed himself to purifying his soul as an ascetic.

As the Seminar includes silence, words and practices compassion, may I end with another poem of Acharya Mahapragya where he says to dispel fear is the ultimate spiritual aim, to understand and be sensitive to the causes of pain is the true measure, and to see the other soul as equal to your own is the true realization:

Don't you hum: to speak in silence alone is speech

Look! The painter's brush has drawn a moon ray in darkness pitch
Frightened was I, seeing the dazzling expression of lightning from the mute
But, to fearlessly mix nectar in poison alone is the true mixture.

Is the translation of the translation of this poem of fate, sufficient?
Are you perceptive enough to be able to read the original script?
To unleash imagination in freedom is alone true evolution.

Sorrow is filled with sensitivity, the void is laughing all the way
Meaning is veiled in words, tear laden clouds are sneering
To weigh in the balance of the inner self is alone the true measure.

Notes

1. Acharya Mahapragya, *Yatra Ek Akinchan Ki* (Jain Vishva Bharati, Ladnun, 2010), p. 97.
2. Acharya Mahapragya, *Acarangbhashyam* (Jain Vishva Bharati, Ladnun, 2012) 2.64.
3. Umasvati, *That Which Is: Tatvartha Sutra*, trans. Nathmal Tatia (London: The Institute of Jainology and Harper Collins) 5.21, 131.
4. Acharya Mahapragya, *Uttaradhyayana Sutra* (Jain Vishva Bharati, Ladnun, 2000), p. 2.

CHAPTER 10

Gandhi and Compassion

M.P. MATHAI

WHAT IS THE place of compassion in Gandhian philosophy? Was Gandhi a man of compassion? These questions call for an enquiry into what compassion is and how Gandhi can be credited with the quality of being compassionate. This is particularly important as there are detractors of Gandhi who accuse him of being too demanding of his coworkers and sometimes even cruel. The well-known British historian Andrew Roberts, for example, alleged that Gandhi's love of humanity was more conceptual than real. In his controversial review of Joseph Lelyveld's book, *Great Soul: Mahatma Gandhi and His Struggle with India* Roberts characterized Gandhi as 'downright cruel to those around him,' and even argued that 'Gandhi was the archetypal twentieth-century progressive intellectual professing his love for mankind as a concept while actually despising people as individuals.'[1] In all fairness to Andrew Roberts it must be conceded that he was not alone in Gandhi baiting; there are others as well who accuse Gandhi of being cruel and insensitive.

I

Though compassion as an ethical principle is common to all major world religions, it is Buddhism which put the greatest emphasis on this principle and elevated it to the status of one of its four cardinal virtues. The Buddhist terms *metta* and *karuna* translated as loving-kindness and compassion stand for empathetic care, the practice of which is essential for attaining the level of *bodhisattva* or *arhant*. Both Mahayana and Theravada schools of Buddhism agree that it is by a diligent use of *metta* and *karuna* that the right way for liberating sentient beings from the suffering of *samsara*, the cycle of birth and death, is found. More specifically, *karuna* is the desire to remove harm and suffering from the lives of sentient beings (*ahita dukkha apanayakamata*) and *metta* is the desire to ensure their welfare and happiness (*hitasukhaupanayakamata*). In Buddhism faith without works is dead and therefore, faith, to be true faith, must be translated into compassionate action. Many anecdotes had been cited from the life of the Buddha to elucidate this like that of Buddha's nursing the monk who was seriously sick with dysentery.

Just as in the life of Shakyamuni Buddha, there are numerous examples of Gandhi's compassion not only towards sentient beings in the Buddhist sense of the term (in Buddhism sentient beings are beings with consciousness; sentient beings are composed of the five aggregates/*skandhas*: matter, sensation, perception, mental formations and consciousness), but also towards non-sentient creatures. There are also many personal witnesses offered by people who had the opportunity to work with Gandhi of the personal care and attention they received from him. When members of the Ashram fell sick he personally attended to their needs and nursed them.

There is the classic case of Parchure Shastri, a Sanskrit scholar and poet from Pune/Poona. He was a prisoner along with Gandhi in the high security Yeravda jail in Pune in 1922. After leaving prison, he somehow contracted leprosy but the treatments he received had no effect. He thought that his days were numbered and wanted to have a final *darshan* (view) of Gandhi. He, therefore, came to Gandhi's Sevagram Ashram and waited at a distance just to see him when he came out for his regular walks. Gandhi was so moved to see Parchure Shastri lying on the roadside that he had him moved to the Ashram for shelter. Gandhi started nursing him personally by dressing his wounds and massaging his feeble limbs. The inmates of the Ashram hesitated to follow Gandhi's example for several days as leprosy was considered an incurable disease those days and the inmates of the Ashram were mortally afraid even to approach Shastri. But eventually Gandhi's example inspired several co-workers who took up Shastri's nursing in earnest. After some weeks Shastri's condition improved considerably. Then Gandhi began to utilize Shastri's services for teaching Sanskrit to the children of the community. He was also requested to solemnize some marriages in the Ashram.

Winston Churchill's caustic comment on Gandhi as 'that half-naked fakir' insinuating his scanty dress was a political stunt has become classic from the day it was made. Gandhi's sartorial experiments have been interpreted by scholars from different perspectives and almost all of them have arrived at a common conclusion that Gandhi's style of dress was political. But for Gandhi it was more than political. The compelling reason why he decided to change his way of dressing and adopted the loincloth of an ordinary Indian villager was the deep compassion he felt for the poor and deprived villagers of rural India. The decision he took in Madurai, south India, on 22 September 1921, to identify himself with the common man by slipping into the loincloth dress code stayed with him till the very end of his life as a indelible mark of his deep compassion.

It is legendary that he refused to change his dress to comply with the strict dress code for meeting the King Emperor George V when he led the Indian delegation to the Second Round Table Conference (September-December 1931). As he came out of the meeting with the Emperor a reporter asked him if he did not feel ashamed in his meagre dress. Gandhi answered: 'Why should I feel ashamed? The Emperor was wearing enough clothes for the both of us.' Humour apart, for Gandhi his sartorial integrity was the result of his compassion for the exploited masses of India and, therefore, changing that dress code was unthinkable for him.

The number of people who thronged to meet him seeking his advice was astoundingly large, yet no genuine seeker had to go away disappointed. The care he took to write replies in his own hand to the incredibly large number of letters he received daily is another point in hand. Mahadev Desai, Gandhi's personal secretary till 1942, in his famous dairy *Day to Day with Gandhi* has recorded several anecdotes elucidating Gandhi's compassion.[2]

II

Although it was a personal insult suffered by him at the hands of colonial powers in South Africa that propelled Gandhi into social action he never took any humiliation or discrimination personally or tried for a personal redress to any grievance. On the contrary, he saw them as structural problems, a civilizational malaise, and viewed them from a communitarian perspective. This was possible because he could and did identify himself completely with the community. This, of course, was the result of his capacity for empathy and compassion. He wanted to save the community from the oppressive and discriminating structures of a colonial, racist regime and ensure their human dignity. He realized that he could help achieve that only if he became a true servant of the people. He tried his best to free himself completely from everything that separated him in any measure from his fellow human beings. It was total identification and empathy that he wanted to achieve. So he practised austerities and observances, almost similar to the penances undertaken by Indian sages of yore, which would personally empower him to be a true servant of his fellow human beings. He also developed methods to liberate his people from exploitation and oppression.

It has been generally recognized that Gandhi's greatest contribution to humankind has been *satyagraha* – truth force, the unique method of applying non-violence for the removal of injustice and for bringing about social transformation leading to the creation of a just social order. A closer and critical examination of Gandhi's concept of non-violence and his method of *satyagraha* will reveal that compassion both as *metta* and *karuna* is woven into their texture.

Ahimsa or non-violence is, primarily, a negative term and it literally means abstaining from using physical violence, that is, non-injury and non-killing. But for Gandhi non-violence was far more positive than negative. Viewed positively, non-violence meant love and goodwill towards all life. According to Gandhi not to hurt anything was, of course, part of *ahimsa* but it was its least expression. He wrote: 'the principle of *ahimsa* is hurt by every evil thought, by undue haste, by lying, by hatred, by wishing ill to anybody. . .'.[3]

Note the following passages by Gandhi on non-violence:

> In its positive form Ahimsa means the largest love, the greatest charity. If I am a follower of Ahimsa I love my enemy. I must apply the same rules to the wrong doer, who is my enemy or a stranger to me, as I would to my wrong-doing father or son. . . .[4] The first step in non-violence is that we cultivate in our daily lives, as between ourselves, truthfulness, humility and loving kindness.[5]

Such statements abound in his writings on non-violence and they clearly show that Gandhi's understanding and definition of *ahimsa* come very close to the Buddhist position on compassion.

Gandhi delved deep into all aspects of non-violence and wrote extensively on this topic. But primarily he valued non-violence as an ethical principle. Therefore, he insisted that a follower of *ahimsa* should first internalize the spirit of non-violence. This was the first step and a necessary pre-condition for the practice of non-violence. Gandhi insisted that one should seek to be non-violent in thought, word and deed. One should make *ahimsa* the organizing principle of life. For Gandhi non-violence was not a cloistered personal virtue to be practised by accomplished individuals for the sake of their spiritual benefit but a principle that was relevant in all activities of life.

Gandhi did not dispute the fact that a person who practised non-violence with care will become spiritually accomplished; but for him even more important was the collective use of non-violence in mitigating the sufferings of people, particularly those who were victims of injustice, 'the last, the lowest and the least'. Gandhi would certainly agree with the Buddhist position that *karuna* means the desire to remove the suffering of sentient beings; but he went further and argued that it was the duty of human beings, whom he considered 'moral agents', to try to remove suffering through conscious intervention and through non-violent methods. That was why he developed *satyagraha* or non-violent direct action for resisting social evils and for demolishing unjust socio-political structures and for the creation of a just social order. That was essential for liberating human beings from the suffering of exploitation and for ensuring their ultimate liberation or *moksha*.

Gandhi insisted that the means you use for the creation of a new social order must be completely non-violent. He did not make any distinction between the means and the end for he believed that attainment of the goal depended completely on the nature of the means you employ. Therefore he gave the dictum: 'As the means, so the end.' The method of *satyagraha* for Gandhi was not aimed at defeating any person or persons but at changing the system and transforming the individuals who run the system. In *satyagraha* you have no enemies to fight; you have only adversaries or opponents to convert. So Gandhi insisted that you must distinguish between the evil and the evil-doer. *Satyagraha* is an attempt to remove or destroy the evil but not the evil-doer. A *satyagrahi* must always consider the opponent as your brother or sister and try to convert and reform the person and save her/him from the coil of evil in which he/she is caught. One can discern that *satyagraha* is *karuna* in action. Although it is true that Buddhism did not develop a collective method based on *karuna* like *satyagraha* for liberating sentient beings from suffering and exploitation, it had developed the *sangha* (community) which would act as the vanguard of change, engaging in liberative praxis by using a distinctive method of its own.

For Gandhi compassion was not a soft option; it was sacrificial just as non-violence, in the sense of love, was suffering love for him. A follower of *ahimsa* will never inflict any suffering on her/his opponents but will take all suffering upon oneself and lay down her/his life, if need be, for vindicating one's truth or position. This, undoubtedly, is compassion/*karuna* in its ultimate form. Gandhi also argued that if non-violence as suffering love is to be effective it must be undertaken not only without regrets but joyfully just like the early Christian martyrs. He also argued that *ahimsa* as *soul force* will never fail and wherever *ahimsa* appeared to fail it was not truly the failure of *ahimsa* but the failure of the agents who used it defectively.

In Gandhian action, particularly in his 'constructive programme', one will be able to identify the elements of Buddhist *metta* in the sense of ensuring the welfare and happiness of sentient beings. The 'constructive programme' was conceived and carried out by Gandhi as a method to reconstruct society on the basis of non-violence. He explained that his 'constructive programme' was an attempt to construct *swaraj* – self-rule from below, which meant the creation of a *sarvodaya (well-being for all – development of the community as a whole)* social order in miniature, hoping that it will serve as a model for the future.

III

Gandhi famously said that he had nothing new to teach the world. His basic principles of truth and non-violence, according to him, were as old as mountains. This is obviously an understatement and it only acknowledges that most of the ideas he used were borrowed from other sources. And his main sources were the scriptures of the major religions of the world and the thought corpus of the thinkers of alternative schools like John Ruskin, Leo Tolstoy, Edward Carpenter et al. But Gandhi was in possession of a special alchemy by which he transmuted and reoriented the borrowed ideas, thus making them his own and then incorporating them into his practice and theory of life. Thus most of the ideas of Gandhi could be traced to a source but they are uniquely his own as he transformed them and gave them his own original definition and interpretation. This underlying pattern is maintained in the way he borrowed ideas from Buddhism as well. He was influenced by the Buddhist concepts of *karuna* and *metta* but he did not accept them as such but developed and reoriented them by using his special alchemy.

Notes

1. See Joseph Lelyveld, *Great Soul: Mahatma Gandhi and His Struggle with India* (New York: Alfred R. Knopf, 2011) and the controversial review by the British historian Andrew Roberts in the *Wall Street Journal* in 2011.
2. See Mahadev Desai, *Day to Day with Gandhi* (Varanasi: Sarva Seva Sangh Prakashan, 1972).
3. See M.K. Gandhi, *Yeravda Mandir (Ashram Observances)* (Ahmadabad: J.T. Desai, 1932), p. 7.
4. See M.K. Gandhi, *Speeches and Writings of Gandhi* (Madras: Naesan & Company, 1922), p. 346.
5. See D.G. Tendulkar, ed., *Mahatma*, vol. 4 (New Delhi: Govt. of India, 1953), p. 236.

PART IV

PRACTICES OF COMPASSION IN BUDDHISM

CHAPTER 11

The Four Immeasureables

ANNE C. KLEIN

BUDDHISM TEACHES THAT there is no such thing as the self as we think we know it: a separate, bounded self, strictly cordoned off from what is 'other'. When we are freed from the reactive patterns sprung from the boundaries we live by – good and bad; love and hate – we are not the self we were before. And when the boundaries themselves dissolve, self as we understand it disappears.

Buddhist tradition offers two central paths to dis-establish our overwrought, constricting sense of self: enlightened love (*bodhicitta*) and enlightening wisdom (*jnana*). The four boundless qualities, enumerated in the early canon's *Mettanisamsa Sutta* (SN 46.54) as the 'four Brahma dwellings', further both of them. These four boundless qualities, which literally have 'no measure' (*apramana*), are equanimity (*upekkha*), love (*metta*), compassion (*karuna*) and joy (*mudita*). By dissolving the boundaries that constrain us, these four qualities expand our capacity for experience.

By practicing the four boundless states, we avoid the fate of T.S. Eliot's poor Alfred Prufrock, who lamented, 'I have measured out my life with coffee spoons.' The ease of equanimity, the full-heartedness of love, the tenderness of compassion, the radiance of joy – these are things we don't want in meagre doses. Let us consider them one by one, with an emphasis on equanimity, as it provides the foundation for the other three.

The fourth-century Indian Buddhist philosopher Asanga speaks of two types of equanimity: a meditator's own equanimity toward all beings and his or her wish that those beings develop equanimity. The former is limitless because equanimity can develop without end. The latter is limitless because beings are limitless. Longchen Rabjam (Longchenpa) (1308-64), the master Nyingma philosopher and

LONGCHENPA DRIME OZER, TIBET, 1800-99, NYINGMA LINEAGE, GROUND MINERAL PIGMENT ON COTTON. COURTESY RUBIN MUSEUM OF ART.

practitioner of Dzogchen who wrote in fourteenth-century Tibet, taught both. A practitioner's equanimity toward others, he writes, comes from recognizing that everyone seeks happiness.

Tsongkhapa, the revered founder of the Tibetan Gelug order, writing in the late fourteenth and early fifteenth centuries, defined equanimity as freedom from powerful reactions, positive or negative, to another person or an event – the ability to be even-minded toward everyone, no matter how they behave. Longchenpa and the eighteenth-century Nyingma treasure revealer Jigme Lingpa identify equanimity as the portal to two of the five Buddha wisdoms, the special knowing that characterizes fully developed Buddhahood. An antidote to pride, equanimity opens us to the first Buddha wisdom, the wisdom of sameness: this primordial knowing recognizes that everything is suffused by the same true nature – empty, stainless, and unchanging. Equanimity also relaxes the hard hold we have on things. As grasping eases, ignorance itself is undone. Now the practice of equanimity becomes a portal to the second Buddha wisdom, wisdom of the expansive reality known as the stainless real or basic space (*dharmadhatu*), the true home of everything, which Longchenpa equates with Buddha nature.

In the Theravada tradition, the four Brahma dwellings are practices of concentration that culminate in equanimity, which is found only at the fourth level of concentration (*jhana*), when the mind has moved past the conceptualizing of the lower concentrations. In Mahayana, the four qualities are part of *bodhicitta* training and begin with equanimity. Just as one must flatten hilly ground to create a stable base for building, so, Tsongkhapa writes, is it vital to even out the mind's attachment to some persons and disdain for others. Then love and compassion can develop without bias, standing tall and sturdy. Longchenpa and Jigme Lingpa also instruct the beginner to start with equanimity. (The more seasoned practitioner is encouraged to order the four states in accordance with his or her experience.)

With equanimity as their base, the next three boundless states deepen our connection with others. Boundless love, in contrast to clinging and attachment, is the wish for everyone everywhere to have happiness and its causes. It banishes hatred. Love sees everything without distortion, and eventually transforms into the third Buddha wisdom, mirror-like wisdom, which sees everything clearly, just the way it is.

Boundless compassion, which is distinct from being overwhelmed by emotion, is the wish that everyone everywhere be free of pain and its causes. It banishes desire. Tsongkhapa teaches that compassion becomes wisdom when it recognizes the empty nature of those who are suffering. The understanding of cause and effect, according to Jigme Lingpa, gives rise to the all-discerning wisdom that effortlessly knows the details of everything. 'Compassion is nothing but the glow and display of emptiness',

says Kangyur Rinpoche in his commentary on Jigme Lingpa's *Treasury of Precious Qualities.*

Boundless joy, not to be mistaken for frenzied exultation, is delight in others' happiness. It banishes jealousy and stabilizes our capacity for engagement. As such, it is a portal to the only remaining Buddha wisdom, the all-accomplishing wisdom that transforms intention into action.

Each boundless quality supports the balance of equanimity. Longchenpa and Jigme Lingpa point out that meditation on love prevents the mind from getting stuck on any of the four states. If love-meditation deviates and furthers attachment, compassion frees us from this suffering. If meditation on compassion is deficient, leading us to feel mired in despair at others' suffering, we turn attention to joy. If practicing joy incites an agitated yen for more joy, we focus on the great equanimity free of all attachment.

Recognition of our own harmful patterns and our wish to be free from them makes the prospect of cultivating any of these states at once alluring and daunting – daunting because our patterns, harmful though they may be, are at present thoroughly conflated with our sense of who we are. Cultivating each boundless state involves integrating body, mind, emotions, and energies to protect against unhealthy and distorted unbounded states – for example, allowing ourselves to be treated inappropriately by confusing defenselessness for the boundless states that are the goal of these practices. Effective practice proceeds slowly and with care. Gradually, our patterns lose their constricting power, and we live more expansively than before.

With practice – lots of practice! – of the four boundless states, our effort resolves into ease, the self-other divide resolves into wholeness, and ideas resolve into direct experience. The deep ease that practice makes possible furthers our capacity for clarity. What relaxes, ultimately, is the deeply entrenched sense of 'being me', the error that gives rise to all other errors. Freedom from the reactivity created by pride, ignorance, hatred, desire, and jealousy endows an ease of intimacy with our own feelings as well as those of others, and we can live our own stories even while engaging with theirs. No longer dividing the world into good and bad, love and hate, we not only have more freedom and ease in daily life; we also gain access to the wisdom of our real nature.

CHAPTER 12

A Bouquet of Quotations on Compassion and Loving-kindness

VEN. OLANDE ANANDA THERA

MY CONTRIBUTION IS a series of quotations concerning compassion and loving-kindness drawn from a number of Buddhist sources. I have drawn mainly on contemporary sources, especially those of H.H. the Dalai Lama.

I began with a quotation from Bhikshuni Thubten Chodon, better known in North America as Pema Chodron.

Often we see other sentient beings as hassles: 'This mosquito is disturbing me. Those politicians are corrupt. Why can't my colleagues do their work correctly?' and so on. But when we see sentient beings as being more precious than a wish-fulfilling jewel, our perspective completely changes. For example, when we look at a fly buzzing around, we train ourselves to think, 'My enlightenment depends on that fly.' This isn't fanciful thinking because, in fact, our enlightenment does depend on that fly. If that fly isn't included in our *bodhicitta*, then we don't have a *bodhicitta*, and we won't receive the wonderful results of generating *bodhicitta* – the tremendous purification and creation of positive potential.

Imagine training your mind so that when you look at every single living being, you think, 'My enlightenment depends on that being. The drunk who just got on the bus – my enlightenment depends on him. The soldier in Iraq – my enlightenment depends on him. My brothers and sisters, the teller at the bank, the janitor at my workplace, the president of the United States, the suicide bombers in the Middle East, the slug in my garden, my eighth-grade boyfriend, the babysitter when I was a kid – my enlightenment depends on each of them.' All sentient beings are actually that precious to us.'[1] [ed. note: *bodhicitta* is the wish to attain enlightenment for the benefit of all sentient beings.]

Paul Farmer, a noted interpreter of Buddhism, made the following remark: 'The idea that some lives matter less is the root of all that's wrong with the world.'[2]

The Venerable Lobsang Gyatso makes the following observations in his book on *Bodhicitta: Cultivating the Compassionate Mind of Enlightenment:*

> We ordinary individuals share the characteristic of having our attempts to gain happiness thwarted by our own destructive self-centeredness. It is unsuitable to keep holding onto the self-centered attitude while ignoring others.
>
> If two friends find themselves floundering in a muddy swamp they should not ridicule each other, but combine their energies to get out. Both ourselves and others are in the same position of wanting happiness and not wanting suffering, but we are entangled in a web of ignorance that prevents us from achieving those goals. Far from regarding it as an 'every man for himself' situation, we should meditate upon the equality of self and others and the need to be helpful to other beings.[3]

And Thich Nhat Hanh observes that 'To love our enemy is impossible. [But] the moment we understand our enemy, we feel compassion towards him/her, and he/she is no longer our enemy.'[4]

Dilgo Khyentse Rinpoche writes that

> The practice of compassion begins at home. We have our parents, our children, and our brothers and sisters, who perhaps irritate us the most, and we begin our practice of loving-kindness and compassion with them. Then gradually we extend our compassion out into our greater community, our country, neighbouring countries, the world, and finally to all sentient beings equally without exception.
>
> Extending compassion in this way makes it evident that it is not very easy to instantly have compassion for 'all sentient beings'. Theoretically it may be comfortable to have compassion for 'all sentient beings', but through our practice we realize that 'all sentient beings' is a collection of individuals. When we actually try to generate compassion for each and every individual, it becomes much more challenging. But if we cannot work with one individual, then how can we work with all sentient beings? Therefore it is important for us to reflect more practically, to work with compassion for individuals and then extend that compassion further.[5]

His Holiness the Dalai Lama writes in *How to Practice: The Way to a Meaningful Life* that

The more we care for the happiness of others, the greater is our own sense of well-being. Real compassion comes from seeing the suffering of others. You feel a sense of responsibility, and you want to do something for them.

Sometimes your dear friend, though still the same person, feels more like an enemy. Instead of love, you feel hostility. But with genuine love and compassion, another person's appearance or behavior has no effect on your attitude.

Through universal altruism, you develop a feeling of responsibility for others and the wish to help them actively overcome their problems.

Nirvana may be the final object of attainment, but at the moment it is difficult to reach. Thus the practical and realistic aim is compassion, a warm heart, serving other people, helping others, respecting others, being less selfish. By practicing these, you can gain benefit and happiness that remains longer. If you investigate the purpose of life and, with the motivation that results from this inquiry, develop a good heart-compassion and love. Using your whole life this way, each day will become useful and meaningful.

With regard to compassion and altruism there is no limit, and thus we should not be content with the degree that we have. We are just the opposite; in the spiritual field we are content with slight amounts of practice and progress, but materially we always want more and more. It should be the other way around. Everyone needs to practice this, whether lay or monastic.[6]

His Holiness continues to develop this theme in his *Healing Anger: the Power of Patience from a Buddhist Perspective* when he writes:

Every human being has the same potential for compassion; the only question is whether we really take any care of that potential, and develop and implement it in our daily life. My hope is that more and more people will realize the value of compassion, and so follow the path of altruism. As for myself, ever since I became a Buddhist monk, that has been my real destiny – for usually I think of myself as just one simple Buddhist monk, no more and no less.

This is my own practice, and I frequently speak about it to others. Imagine that in front of you on one side is your old, selfish I and that on the other side is a group of poor, needy people. And you yourself are in the middle as a neutral person, a third party. Then, judge which is more important – whether you should join this one selfish, self-centered, stupid person or these poor, needy, helpless people. If you have a human heart, naturally you will be drawn to the side of the needy beings.

One of the reasons there is a need to adopt a strong countermeasure against someone who harms you is that, if you let it pass, there is a danger of that person becoming habituated to extremely negative actions, which in the long run will cause that person's own downfall and is very destructive for the individual himself or herself. Therefore a strong countermeasure, taken out of compassion or a sense of concern for the other, is necessary. When you are motivated by that realization, then there is a sense of concern as part of your motive for taking that strong measure.

... One of the reasons why there is some ground to feel compassionate toward a perpetrator of crime or an aggressor is that the aggressor, because he or she is perpetrating a crime, is at the causal stage, accumulating the causes and conditions that later lead to undesirable consequences. So, from that point of view, there is enough ground to feel compassionate toward the aggressor.[7]

In 'Compassion, the Supreme Emotion', His Holiness the Dalai Lama writes that 'If you want others to be happy, practice compassion. If you want to be happy, practice compassion.'

Sometimes we think that to develop an open heart, to be truly loving and compassionate, means that we need to be passive, to allow others to abuse us, to smile and let anyone do what they want with us. Yet this is not what is meant by compassion. Quite the contrary. Compassion is not at all weak. It is the strength that arises out of seeing the true nature of suffering in the world. Compassion allows us to bear witness to that suffering, whether it is in ourselves or others, without fear; it allows us to name injustice without hesitation, and to act strongly, with all the skill at our disposal. To develop this mind state of compassion ... is to learn to live, as the Buddha put it, with sympathy for all living beings, without exception.[8]

In *The Compassionate Life*, His Holiness addresses compassion without attachment.

Love and compassion are necessities, not luxuries. Without them, humanity cannot survive.

Compassion without attachment is possible. Therefore, we need to clarify the distinctions between compassion and attachment. True compassion is not just an emotional response but a firm commitment founded on reason. Because of this firm foundation, a truly compassionate attitude toward others does not change even if they behave negatively. Genuine compassion is based not on our own projections and expectations, but rather on the needs of the other: irrespective of whether another person is a close friend or an enemy, as long as that person wishes for peace and happiness and wishes to overcome suffering, then on that basis we develop genuine concern for their problem. This is genuine compassion.

For a Buddhist practitioner, the goal is to develop this genuine compassion, this genuine wish for the well-being of another, in fact for every living being throughout the universe. [9]

In *An Open Heart, Practicing Compassion in Everyday Life*, His Holiness the Dalai Lama takes another approach to compassion. He writes,

If we have been reborn time after time, it is evident that we have needed many mothers to give birth to us ... the first cause bringing about *bodhicitta* is the recognition that all beings have been our mother.

The love and kindness shown us by our mother in this life would be difficult to repay. She endured many sleepless nights to care for us when we were helpless infants. She fed us and would have willingly sacrificed everything, including her own life, to spare ours. As we contemplate her example of devoted love, we should consider that each and every being throughout existence has treated us this way. Each dog, cat, fish, fly, and human being has at some point in the beginningless past been our mother and shown us overwhelming love and kindness. Such a thought should bring about our appreciation.

... if all other sentient beings who have been kind to us since beginningless time are suffering, how can we devote ourselves to pursuing merely our own happiness? To seek our own happiness in spite of the suffering others are experiencing is tragically unfortunate. Therefore, it is clear that we must try to free all sentient beings from suffering.[10]

In *Generous Wisdom*, His Holiness takes up the subject of loving-kindness and writes:

The Buddha Maitreya's name is derived from the Sanskrit 'maitri'. The very name 'maitri' means 'loving-kindness' ... now, in today's world, we really need maitri, Maitreya, loving-kindness.

... Shakyamuni Buddha, even when he was a trainee on the path, was solely concerned in both thought and action with others' welfare. Whenever he found an opportunity to work for others, no matter what difficulties he faced, he was never discouraged. He never hated obstacles and hardships encountered on the way. Instead, the difficult situations facilitated his being more courageous and determined to accomplish others' welfare. Just because he was so determined to work for others in the past, even as a trainee on the path, it is needless to say how much more it is so with him now as a completely enlightened person.

... We say this prayer at the time of taking vows:

I shall relieve those who are distressed;
I shall establish beings in the bliss of enlightenment.

Therefore, after saying such a prayer and also pledging to fulfill it, we should not neglect our roommates and neighbors who are sick and old, etc. We must do our best to help others literally in whatever way we can, even with our words, as if Buddha had created such opportunities for us to help others; we must create virtues. In regard to situations in which we cannot help others literally, we can mentally dedicate our body, wealth and virtue to them. Otherwise, we are just helpless.

While you give, do not expect something in return. Do not give to fulfill selfish motives. Do not be discouraged in giving. Generate the altruistic mind of enlightenment as best you can, and then give out of sole concern for others. Having been reborn as human beings and having come into contact with Dharma, we know something about what to do and what not to do.'[11]

His Holiness the Dalai Lama also writes of compassion and the need for action:

Real compassion extends to each and every sentient being, not just to friends or family or those in terrible situations. To develop the practice of compassion to its fullest extent, one must practice patience. Shantideva tells us that if the practice of patience really moves your mind and brings about a change, you will begin to see your enemies as the best of friends, even as spiritual guides. Enemies provide us some of the best opportunities to practice patience, tolerance, and compassion.[12]

It is not enough to be compassionate. You must act. There are two aspects to action. One is to overcome the distortions and afflictions of your own mind, that is, in terms of calming and eventually dispelling anger. This is action out of compassion. The other is more social, more public. When something needs to be done in the world to rectify wrongs, if one is really concerned with benefiting others, one needs to be engaged, involved.

When we speak of the welfare of ourselves, we are speaking of only one individual, whereas the welfare of others encompass the welfare of an infinite number of beings. From that point of view, we can understand that others' welfare is much more important than our own.[13]

Sakyong Mipham in *Ruling Your World: Ancient Strategies for Modern Life* offers the following advice:

When the feeling of compassion arises, we meditate on our response for a moment, and compassion begins to flow. Now that we've generated compassion, we can extend it to our family and friends, little by little. This is how we make it bigger. If we bring intelligence [or wisdom] into our compassion, we can extend it even to our enemy. People are always being pushed around by their own anger and pride. When we're in an adversarial relationship with someone, if we can see that his suffering arises from the negative emotion that is torturing him - like a victim and his bully – we can feel compassion.

Compassion even has the power to overcome demons – invisible beings who are trapped in negative emotions and wrong views. Caught between lives, they harm others out of ignorance. There are stories of Tibetan Buddhist lamas trying to banish demons with exorcisms and spells, to no avail. But when the lamas extended their compassion to them, the demons found peace and were liberated from their painful state.

There are two kinds of compassion: compassion mixed with clinging, and compassion mixed with prajna – best knowledge. The compassion we feel toward friends and family is usually mixed with clinging. We want the best for them, but our wish is colored by jealousy, attachment, or fear. Clinging makes it hard to be straightforward in our compassion. We're still thinking of ourselves. We want someone's suffering to go away because it is inconvenient for us, it scares us, or it causes us personal pain. Through contemplative meditation, we filter out the dirt of negative emotions and hit the mother lode – unadulterated, openhearted compassion.[14]

Madmilla Moacanin writes that: 'Wisdom by itself is like an empty gold vessel, it needs to be filled with compassion. Wisdom and compassion are the two sides of the same coin, one representing personal and the other transpersonal consciousness and both equally indispensable for the attainment of enlightenment.[15]'

In *The Wisdom of Imperfection*, Rob Preece argues that:

Compassion does not arise from ideals of perfection but from a recognition of and concern for our own fallibility. At the heart of our potential for health and wholeness is the need for a fundamental quality of acceptance, an unconditional compassionate presence. Without this capacity either for ourselves or for others, even our spirituality can become harsh and uncompromising.

As we deepen our sense of ease with ourselves, the fundamental wounding to our self-identity will soften. This softening leads to a greater inner space that can more naturally respond to others. While we are caught in our wounded self-preoccupations, we have no space for others. An inner atmosphere of compassion and acceptance slowly softens the rigidity of our wounding. As we become less self-preoccupied we begin to find a capacity to respond to others, and we may discover that we are able to be present, compassionate, and caring without judging. Our compassion grows as we allow others to be who they are with their faults and struggles, their unique qualities and gifts.

Sharon Salzberg in *Loving-kindness: The Revolutionary of Art of Happiness* clarifies the meaning of an 'open heart' when she writes

> Sometimes we think that to develop an open heart, to be truly loving and compassionate, means that we need to be passive, to allow others to abuse us, to smile and let anyone do what they will with us. Yet this is not what is meant by compassion. Quite the contrary. Compassion is not at all weak. It is the strength that arises out of seeing the true nature of suffering in the world. Compassion allows us to bear witness to that suffering, whether it is in ourselves or others, without fear; it allows us to name injustice without hesitation, and to act strongly, with all the skill at our disposal. To develop this mind state of compassion ... is to learn to live, as the Buddha put it, with sympathy for all living beings, without exception.[16]

Shantideva, the eighth century Buddhist at Nalanda University, wrote:

> For as long as space exists
> and sentient beings endure
> may I too remain
> to dispel the misery of the world.
> Whatever joy there is in this world
> all comes from desiring others to be happy
> and whatever suffering there is in this world
> all comes from desiring myself to be happy.

Sogyal Rinpoche at his website 'Glimpse of the Day' posted these words: 'Compassion is a far greater and nobler thing than pity. Pity has its roots in fear and carries a sense of arrogance and condescension, sometimes even a smug feeling of 'I'm glad it's not me.'[17]

Stephen Levine, the well-known spiritual writer, wrote that:

> When your fear touches someone's pain it becomes pity; when your love touches someone's pain, it becomes compassion. To train in compassion is

to know that all beings are the same and suffer in similar ways, to honor all those who suffer, and to know that you are neither separate from nor superior to anyone.

To realize what I call the wisdom of compassion is to see with complete clarity its benefits, as well as the damage that its opposite has done to us. We need to make a very clear distinction between what is in our ego's self-interest and what is in our ultimate interest; it is from mistaking one for the other that all our suffering comes.

Self-grasping creates self-cherishing, which in turn creates an ingrained aversion to harm and suffering. However, harm and suffering have no objective existence; what gives them their existence and their power is only our aversion to them. When you understand this, you understand then that it is our aversion that attracts to us every negativity and obstacle that can possibly happen to us, and fills our lives with nervous anxiety, expectation, and fear.

Wear down that aversion by wearing down the self-grasping mind and its attachment to a nonexistent self, and you will wear down any hold on you that any obstacle and negativity can have. For how can you attack someone or something that is just not there?

Evoking the power of compassion in us is not always easy. I find myself that the simplest ways are the best and the most direct. Every day, life gives us innumerable chances to open our hearts, if we can only take them. An old woman passes you with a sad and lonely face and two heavy plastic bags full of shopping she can hardly carry. Switch on a television, and there on the news is a mother in Beirut kneeling above the body of her murdered son, or an old grandmother in Moscow pointing to the thin soup that is her only food. ...

Any one of these sights could open the eyes of your heart to the fact of vast suffering in the world. Let it. Don't waste the love and grief it arouses. In the moment you feel compassion welling up in you, don't brush it aside, don't shrug it off and try quickly to return to 'normal', don't be afraid of your feeling or be embarrassed by it, and don't allow yourself to be distracted from it. Be vulnerable: Use that quick, bright uprush of compassion – focus on it, go deep into your heart and meditate on it, develop it, enhance and deepen it. By doing this you will realize how blind you have been to suffering.

All beings, everywhere, suffer; let your heart go out to them all in spontaneous and immeasurable compassion.

Compassion is not true compassion unless it is active. Avalokiteshvara, the Buddha of Compassion, is often represented in Tibetan iconography as having a thousand eyes that see the pain in all corners of the universe, and a thousand arms to reach out to all corners of the universe to extend his help.

One technique for arousing compassion for a person who is suffering is to imagine one of your dearest friends, or someone you really love, in that person's place.

Imagine your brother or daughter or parent or best friend in the same kind of painful situation. Quite naturally your heart will open, and compassion will awaken in you: What more would you want than to free your loved one from his or her torment? Now take this compassion released in your heart and transfer it to the person who needs your help: You will find that your help is inspired more naturally and that you can direct it more easily.

You can have no greater ally in the war against your greatest enemy, your own self-grasping and self-cherishing, than the practice of compassion. It is compassion, dedicating ourselves to others, taking on their suffering instead of cherishing ourselves, that, hand in hand with the wisdom of egolessness, destroys most effectively and most completely that ancient attachment to a false self that has been the cause of our endless wandering in samsara. That is why in our tradition we see compassion as the source and essence of enlightenment and the heart of enlightened activity.

Imagine that you are having difficulties with a loved one, such as your mother or father, husband or wife, lover or friend. How helpful and revealing it can be to consider the other person not in his or her 'role' of mother or father or husband, but simply as another 'you', another human being, with the same feelings as you, the same desire for happiness, the same fear of suffering. Thinking of the other one as a real person, exactly the same as you, will open your heart to him or her and give you more insight into how to help.

As you continue to meditate on compassion, when you see someone suffer, your first response becomes not mere pity but deep compassion. You feel for that person respect and even gratitude, because you now know that whoever prompts you to develop compassion by his or her suffering is in fact giving you one of the greatest gifts of all, as you are being helped to develop that very quality you need most in your progress toward enlightenment.

That is why we say in Tibet that the beggar who is asking you for money, or the sick, old woman wringing your heart, may be the buddhas in disguise, manifesting on your path to help you grow in compassion and so move toward buddhahood.

Your compassion can have perhaps three essential benefits for a dying person: First, because it is opening your heart, you will find it easier to show the dying person the unconditional love he or she needs so much.

On a deeper, spiritual level, I have seen again and again how, if you can embody compassion and act out of the heart of compassion, you will create an atmosphere in which the other person can be inspired to imagine the spiritual dimension or even take up spiritual practice.

On the deepest level of all, if you constantly practice compassion for the dying person, and in turn inspire him or her to do the same, you might heal the person not only spiritually but perhaps even physically. And you will discover for yourself, with wonder, what all the spiritual masters know: that the power of compassion has no bounds.

Compassion is the best protection; it is also, as the great masters of the past have always known, the source of all healing. Suppose you have a disease such as cancer or AIDS. By taking on the sickness of those suffering like you, in addition to your own pain, with a mind full of compassion, you will – beyond any doubt – purify the past negative karma that is the cause, now and in the future, of the continuation of your suffering.

In Tibet there have been many extraordinary cases of people who, when they heard they were dying of a terminal illness, gave away everything they had and went to the cemetery to die. There they practiced taking on the suffering of others; and what is amazing is that instead of dying, they returned home, fully healed.

As you continue to meditate on compassion, when you see someone suffer, your first response becomes not mere pity but deep compassion. You feel for that person respect and even gratitude, because you now know that whoever prompts you to develop compassion by his or her suffering is in fact giving you one of the greatest gifts of all, as you are being helped to develop that very quality you need most in your progress toward enlightenment.

That is why we say in Tibet that the beggar who is asking you for money, or the sick, old woman wringing your heart, may be the buddhas in disguise, manifesting on your path to help you grow in compassion and so move toward buddhahood.

What is compassion? It is not simply a sense of sympathy or caring for the person suffering, not simply a warmth of heart toward the person before you, or a sharp clarity of recognition of their needs and pain, it is also a sustained and practical determination to do whatever is possible and necessary to help alleviate their suffering.[18]

In *The Door of Satisfaction* Lama Zopa Rinpoche writes that 'The purpose of human life, why we survive, why we live, is to pacify others' sufferings and disease, and to give happiness to them. Even if we cannot do everything now, just to stop one problem of another person is worthwhile.'

All the peace and happiness of the whole globe
the peace and happiness of societies
the peace and happiness of family
the peace and happiness in the individual person's life
and the peace and happiness of even the animals and so forth
all depends on having loving kindness toward each other.
When you cherish others, all your wishes are fulfilled
Living your life for others, cherishing them with loving kindness and compassion
is the door to happiness, the door to enlightenment.[19]

His Holiness the Dalai Lama has written extensively on compassion and the following quotes are from *The Art of Happiness*.

Love and compassion are necessities, not luxuries. Without them, humanity cannot survive.

If you want others to be happy, practice compassion. If you want to be happy, practice compassion.

Only the development of compassion and understanding for others can bring us the tranquility and happiness we all seek.

I believe compassion to be one of the few things we can practice that will bring immediate and long-term happiness to our lives. I'm not talking about the short-term gratification of pleasures like sex, drugs or gambling (though I'm not knocking them), but something that will bring true and lasting happiness. The kind that sticks.

A truly compassionate attitude toward others does not change even if they behave negatively or hurt you. Compassion is the radicalism of our time.

Love and Compassion are the true religions to me. But to develop this, we do not need to believe in any religion.

We can reject everything else: religion, ideology, all received wisdom. But we cannot escape the necessity of love and compassion. ...This, then, is my true religion, my simple faith. In this sense, there is no need for temple or church, for mosque or synagogue, no need for complicated philosophy, doctrine or dogma. Our own heart, our own mind, is the temple.

The doctrine is compassion. Love for others and respect for their rights and dignity, no matter who or what they are: ultimately these are all we need.

So long as we practice these in our daily lives, then no matter if we are learned or unlearned, whether we believe in Buddha or God, or follow some other religion or none at all, as long as we have compassion for others and conduct ourselves with restraint out of a sense of responsibility, there is no doubt we will be happy.

The purpose of all the major religious traditions is not to construct big temples on the outside, but to create temples of goodness and compassion inside, in our hearts.

When we are motivated by compassion and wisdom, the results of our actions benefit everyone, not just our individual selves or some immediate convenience. When we are able to recognize and forgive ignorant actions of the past, we gain strength to constructively solve the problems of the present.

Compassion is not religious business, it is human business, it is not luxury, it is essential for our own peace and mental stability, it is essential for human survival.

You must not hate those who do wrong or harmful things; but with compassion, you must do what you can to stop them – for they are harming themselves, as well as those who suffer from their actions.

Every single being, even those who are hostile to us, is just as afraid of suffering as we are, and seeks happiness in the same way we do. Every person has the same right as we do to be happy and not to suffer. So let's take care of others wholeheartedly, of both our friends and our enemies. This is the basis for true compassion.

I have found that the greatest degree of inner tranquility comes from the development of love and compassion. The more we care for the happiness of others, the greater is our own sense of well-being. Cultivating a close, warmhearted feeling for others automatically puts the mind at ease. It is the ultimate source of success in life.

I believe all suffering is caused by ignorance. People inflict pain on others in the selfish pursuit of their happiness or satisfaction. Yet true happiness comes from a sense of inner peace and contentment, which in turn must be achieved through the cultivation of altruism, of love and compassion and elimination of ignorance, selfishness and greed.

Sometimes when I meet old friends, it reminds me how quickly time passes. And it makes me wonder if we've utilized our time properly or not. Proper utilization of time is so important. While we have this body, and especially this amazing human brain, I think every minute is something precious. Our day-to-day existence is very much alive with hope, although there is no guarantee of our future. There is no guarantee that tomorrow at this time we will be here. But we are working for that purely on the basis of hope. So, we need to make the best use of our time. I believe that the proper utilization of time is this: if you can, serve other people, other sentient beings. If not, at least refrain from harming them. I think that is the whole basis of my philosophy.

So, let us reflect what is truly of value in life, what gives meaning to our lives, and set our priorities on the basis of that. The purpose of our life needs to be positive. We weren't born with the purpose of causing trouble, harming others. For our life to be of value, I think we must develop basic good human qualities – warmth, kindness, compassion. Then our life becomes meaningful and more peaceful – happier.

Whether you believe in God or not does not matter so much, whether you believe in Buddha or not does not matter so much; as a Buddhist, whether you believe in reincarnation or not does not matter so much. You must lead a good life. And a good life does not mean just good food, good clothes, good shelter. These are not sufficient. A good motivation is what is needed: compassion, without dogmatism, without complicated philosophy; just understanding that others are human brothers and sisters and respecting their rights and human dignity.

The topic of compassion is not at all religious business; it is important to know it is human business, it is a question of human survival.'[20]

Thich Nhat Hanh observes that

The essence of love and compassion is understanding, the ability to recognize the physical, material, and psychological suffering of others, to put ourselves 'inside the skin' of the other. We 'go inside' their body, feelings, and mental formations, and witness for ourselves their suffering. Shallow observation as an outsider is not enough to see their suffering. We must become one with the subject of our observation. When we are in contact with another's suffering, a feeling of compassion is born in us. Compassion means, literally, 'to suffer with'.[21]

I want to conclude this bouquet with these words from the *Dhammapada*: 'One is not called noble who harms living beings. By not harming living beings one is called noble.'[22]

Notes

1. See Pema Chodron, *Cultivating a Compassionate Heart: The Yoga Method of Chenrezig* (Denver, CO: Shambala Publications, 2006).
2. See Paul Farmer, 'The Existential Buddhist' at www.existentialbuddhist.com.
3. See the Venerable Lobsang Gyatso in *Bodhicitta: Cultivating the Compassionate Mind of Enlightenment* (Ithaca, NY: Snow Lion, 1997).

4. See Thich Nhat Hanh, *The Heat of the Buddha's Teaching: Transforming Sufferings into Peace, Joy, and Liberation* (New York: Harmony Books, 1998).
5. See Dilgo Khyentse Rinpoche, *Trainings in Compassion: Manuals on the Meditation of Avalokiteshvara* (Boston: Shambala Publications, 2007).
6. See HH the Dalai Lama, *How to Practice: The Way to a Meaningful Life* (New York: Pocket Books, 2002).
7. See HH the Dalai Lama, *Healing Anger: The Power of Patience from a Buddhist Perspective* (Ithaca, NY: Snow Lion, 1997).
8. See HH the Dalai Lama, 'Compassion, the Supreme Emotion' at www.viewonBuddhism.org.
9. See HH the Dalai Lama, *The Compassionate Life* (Somerville, MA: Wisdom Publications, 2003).
10. See HH the Dalai Lama, *An Open Heart: Practicing Compassion in Everyday Life* (Boston: Back Bay Books, 2002).
11. See HH the Dalai Lama, *Generous Wisdom: Commentaries by H.H. the Dalai Lama XIV on the Jatakamala* (Ann Arbor MI: Library of Tibetan Works & Archives, 1992).
12. See *How to Practice: The Way to a Meaningful Life*, op. cit.
13. See His Holiness the Dalai Lama, *The World of Tibetan Buddhism: An Overview of its Philosophy and Practice* (Somerville, MA: Wisdom Books, 1995).
14. See Sakyong Mipham, *Ruling Your World: Ancient Strategies for Modern Life* (New York: Morgan Road Books, 2005).
15. See Madmilla Moacanin, *Jung's Psychology & Tibetan Buddhism* (Boston: Wisdom Publications, 2002), p. 47.
16. See Sharon Salzberg, *Loving-Kindness, The Revolutionary Art of Happiness* (Boston: Shambala, 1995).
17. See 'Glimpse of the Day' at www.usa.rigpa.org.
18. See Stephen Levine, *Becoming Kuan Yin: The Evolution of Compassion* (San Francisco: Red Wheel/Weiser Books, 2013).
19. See Lama Zopa Rinpoche, *The Door to Satisfaction* (Boston: Wisdom Books, 2001).
20. See His Holiness the Dalai Lama, *The Art of Happiness* (New York: Riverhead Books, 2009); and as an Audio CD from Simon & Schuster, New York, 1998.
21. See Thich Nhat Hanh, *The Heart of the Buddha's Teaching: Transforming Suffering into Peace, Joy, and Liberation* (New York: Harmony Books, 1998).
22. For more quotes on Compassion and Buddhism go to the following: http://www.realbuddhaquotes.com/tag/compassion/https://www.goodreads.com/author/quotes/2167493.Gautama_Buddhahttp://quotesnsmiles.com/quotes/calming-buddha-quotes/https:/and www.youtube.com/watch?v=lyUxYflkhzo.

CHAPTER 13

Compassion from the Buddhist Perspective

WANGCHUK NEGI

Introduction

GENUINE HAPPINESS DOES not come from external forms or through material objects. It is obtained from within oneself by being a light to oneself and knowing oneself. Can a comparison be drawn between the saints, great beings, Buddhas, Bodhisattvas and the political leaders and rich people of today's world? I believe that a person will be happy in his/her life when he/she possesses the qualities of loving-kindness and compassion towards others. Yet, the irony is that today we try to imitate that belief and culture which believes in the 'survival of the fittest' principle. While in reality the most humble and greatest thing to do is to live as simply as you can. Is it possible for everyone to become the richest person? No, it's not, because there can only be one richest person. Therefore, there will certainly be competition and jealousy. When competition and jealousy are there, there will be no peace. On the other hand, in terms of great compassionate beings, there can be many saints and Bodhisattvas. We should seek to overcome selfishness and cultivate a sense of sacrifice within all of us. Thus, it seems to me that inward, spiritual peace is real and lasting while material riches are temporary and passing.

Today, many people fight for power, run away from duty, and are biased in one way or another. Such situations are indeed a matter of sadness. Many of us talk about compassion, but we do that for social, political and religious reasons. We say that we should be compassionate, and we often give big lectures on compassion but harbour another agenda inside us. Listeners are viewed as mere spectators. And we just seek to have them listening and watching us. The result is like coming out of a movie theatre after watching a movie but not having any genuine sympathy or empathy towards the characters of the movie. We know that it is just a movie. Sadly, there is a somewhat similar attitude towards teachings on compassion that we give and receive these days. These days when many talk about compassion or spirituality, it is often in the form of a lecture or a performance. It is like professionals working on their profession. When this happens there is absence of deep feeling towards the topic. Consequently, there are few, if any, positive results of the talk on the listeners or on society. However, I will not follow that course. Here, in this contemplative seminar, I am expecting something different. I am happy to be here today to share some of my experience and thought with you.

What is Compassion in Buddhism?

The Buddha was born a prince, but abandoned all his royal comforts. He struggled for a long time to achieve enlightenment. He became a world-renowned teacher. He propounded a philosophy that is immensely beneficial and applicable to society. I begin by highlighting some of the things that the Buddha taught regarding compassion.

Compassion is to see others' suffering through one's eyes and through one's experience. Just as we wish to alleviate our suffering, it is to feel the same for others and to try to alleviate their suffering. The goal of Buddhist practitioners is to attain Buddhahood for the benefit of others. As the *Maitreyanatha Sutra* has said, 'Buddhobhave jagat hitaya',[1] meaning that it is for the benefit of the world that we aspire to become a Buddha. In this way, the goal and means are both for the benefit of others. Therefore, when perfection is achieved in benefiting others then we have achieved the perfection of compassion. As long as there is intense suffering, poverty and starvation in society we should not be happy in our happiness. As long as the protection of small living beings is not assured and as long as they are not happy, our work is not finished, our happiness unjustified. Because they are also a part of the world and they too have a right to well-being. The world is unhappy when we only care about ourselves and fail to care about those who are suffering. If we care about them and are concerned of them, then there will be happiness in the world and such a motivation is indeed, for me, compassion.

We not only need to understand reality, we also need the blessing, wisdom and method of Buddhism. Wisdom and method are akin to eyes and feet that take us to our destination. Hence, not only understanding but applying it in practice is very important. And that must also be done genuinely, without any bias or favouritism towards ones' own community or religion, nor for one's self-benefit. If done in this manner, then we will have accomplished what is said in the *Avalokitesvara Avadana*:[2]

Having one thing in the palm of one's hand is the same as having everything. What is that one thing? It is the great compassion.

In the *Dharmasangraha Sutra* we read that the Buddha says that: Wherever the wheel of a Universal king exists, there exists his entire troop. Similarly, wherever the great compassion of a Bodhisattva exists, there exist all the dharmas/qualities of a Buddha.[3]

Similarly, in the *Tathagataguhya Sutra* too, it is said that: The primordial wisdom of the Buddha has arisen from the root of compassion.[4]

The great Buddha taught compassion as one of the methods for the complete liberation from cyclic existence. Among many skilful means, compassion is indeed the foundation or the essence of Buddhism because the entire Buddhist practice is based on it. What is the goal of Buddhism? It is the welfare of others. When we ask what it is to become a Buddha? It is simply the embodiment of compassion. Just as a seed, sprout and fruit of barley are the same in being barley while differing in their stages, similarly, the innate nature of our mind is compassionate while it may be in different stages of development. Therefore, to practice the Buddhist path is mainly to develop compassionate qualities.

In Buddhism, a person is made up of 'five aggregates': physical form, feeling, perception, mental formation, and consciousness[5]or the 'name and form' or matter and mind. And just as the body requires proteins, minerals, vitamins, etc., to maintain life, so to the mind for peace and well-being requires or needs loving-kindness, compassion, altruism, and wisdom. It is said in the *Bodhicaryavatara* that, 'a person affected by a physical disease will not be able to do any physical work, in the same way, a person affected by ignorance and other afflictions will not be able to function properly'.[6] Between matter and mind, mind is the more dominant factor. As we are all aware, all the sciences of the world such as arts, philosophy, physics, biology, and so on were originally created by the intelligence and the mind of people. Hence, just as the human mind has unlimited power in creating all these sophisticated sciences, similarly, the human mind has unlimited mental power in developing mercy, empathy, and compassion. Such emotional qualities are indeed the qualities of mind. In order to produce electricity, one has to have the knowledge of all the different electrical elements. Similarly, in order to develop the qualities of the mind, knowledge of the mind is necessary. Knowledge and development of these qualities of the mind can be done through Shamatha and Vipasyana meditations. I strongly believe that our ancient masters – Buddhas and the Bodhisattvas – were not wrong in instructing us to understand our mind.

As the Buddha says in the Dhammapada: 'Tame your mind completely'.

Similarly, Acharya Shantideva has also said, 'Those who have not understood the feeling of secret mind, the core of spirituality, they will never be able to obtain genuine happiness'.[7]

There are various kinds and forms of mind training/taming and here I will be talking about how compassion can be developed. The Sanskrit term for compassion is *karuna*; it is constructed by two syllables: 'karun' root + 'tap' affixation. Compassion is a strong emotion that arises in relation to sentient beings suffering in the world. Suffering is due to ignorance and compassion is the desire to protect and save them from suffering.

It is said in the Sadhanamala: Kakaruna? ya triduhkhaduhkhitanam sattvanam samsarasagaraduddharanakamana.[8] This can be translated as 'What is karuna? It is the wish that wishes to liberate sentient beings from the three sufferings.'

And according to the Trimsikabharya of Sthiramati (*c.* 510-70) *Avihimsa* or non-violence is the mental factor in the nature of compassion.

Avihimsa vihimsapratipakrah. Vadhabandhanadibhih sattvanam avihethanam avihimsa, sattveru karuna. Kam runaddhiti karuna. Kamiti sukhasyakhya, sukham runaddhitiyarthah. Karuniko hi paraduhkhadukhi bhavatiti – Trimsika sthiramatibharya.[9]

Compassion is a mental factor – chaitsik dharma – and its object is the suffering of beings. This mental factor prevents a person from harming others and thus avihetan/*ahimsa* or non-violence is the action of compassion. This mental factor is called compassion because it cannot tolerate the suffering of others. This is the true compassion. A compassionate person is always concerned for the suffering of others. A compassionate person never cares for mere personal happiness. Furthermore, the definition of compassion we find in the Madhyamakavatara by the great Chandrakirti is this: 'Completely protecting those who suffer is the great compassion.'[10]

In order to generate compassion, we need to know what the object of compassion is. An artist, for example, will need to have a clear vision of the image he wants to draw on the canvas before actually drawing it. Similarly, in order to develop a genuine compassion, we need to understand why beings are suffering and unhappy and what the causes are. Lacking this knowledge will be similar to treating a patient without diagnosis of the disease and such a treatment will not be effective. To me, it seems that the cause of suffering is the feeling of the emptiness of material things and ignorance. Consequently, we experience physical and mental problems, which are explained in Buddhist literature as the suffering of suffering, the suffering of change, and all pervasive suffering. Among the three sufferings, we can say that the first is mainly physical and the other two are psychological. Hence, merely saying that all beings want happiness and do not want suffering and that we have to take others' sufferings as ours will neither help generate a genuine compassion within us, nor will we be able to alleviate the suffering of others.

If the thought of preventing others' suffering is compassion then we must acknowledge that it does not occur naturally; one has to work on it to develop it. Just as we need various types of yogas and exercises to keep our body fit and healthy, similarly, good thoughts and analysis is necessary in order to develop good qualities of the mind. It is important to know that the seed of compassion lies within us and it has to blossom as all beings have the essence of Buddhahood. For instance, just as butter permeates milk, similarly, the essence of the Buddha nature pervades all sentient beings. As is written in the *Uttaratantra Shastra*,

> Because the perfect form of the Buddha radiates,
> Because there are no distinctions within suchness and,
> Because all are in a family [share the same nature],
> All sentient beings are always of the essence of enlightenment.[11]

For example, in the absence of other necessary conditions or resources such as water, air, and heat the seed will not germinate. The seed of compassion is within all of us; there is not a single person who does not possess the seeds of mercy, love and compassion. No beings can survive in the absence of compassion and love. The very existence of the present life of all sentient beings began with their birth and at that time they were born through the love of their mother. This proves that love and compassion are innate in the nature of beings. On the other side, we can say that there is not a single person who is without anger. This is certainly true. While particular causes such as jealousy, hatred, etc., are required to arouse anger, compassion can be developed towards all beings – both good and bad. In fact, a practitioner of compassion develops even more compassion towards his/her enemies, because the practitioner knows that the angry person under the influence of anger is on the verge of destroying oneself. Therefore, a compassionate practitioner becomes worried and wonders how he/she may save that person from being destroyed.

A compassionate person can defeat an angry person but an angry person cannot win over a compassionate person. Compassion is innate by nature. Thus, while the victory of ignorance over wisdom is not possible, the victory of wisdom over ignorance is possible. This is the reason why wisdom and compassion are a person's innate qualities but their development is necessary. For this reason, we need to know which of these two emotions make us feel good. Is it compassion or is it afflictive emotions such as anger?

Consider this: was the Buddha unhappy after giving up his kingly throne? Was he unhappy staying among begging monks? What if he had remained a king? Would he have been able to benefit innumerable sentient beings and would there be the vast collection of his teachings that is today available in the great libraries of the world? Does real happiness lie in material gain or spiritual practice? In order to earn money, people manufacture very sophisticated weapons and sell them and create problems between different communities and countries by bullying each other. Would you find peace in being involved in such negative activities or would you find peace in trying to understand others' suffering and working to overcome their suffering? Which one is more suitable to engage in? It seems clear to me that if we feel good through compassion then we should sincerely contemplate how these feel good states can be developed. If the mind feels good from its depths and thinks accordingly, then one will never follow violence and will progress naturally. One will be very concerned for others and will be honest, sincere and sensitive.

In the course of development of one's compassion, one will encounter more averse situations than favourable ones. Yes, before being able to develop compassion towards enemies, it is necessary to develop selfless compassion towards one's family and friends. It is just as sportsmen initially play among their team-mates and gradually, after much progress, play at the district level, then nationally and finally internationally. For instance, the tougher your opponent is in a playground, the better your performance will be. The basic need is that you will need to have a strong will-power towards that game and that depends on the depth of your interest in the game. If you are very interested you will work very hard and no physical pain will be a hindrance. Or consider those who aim to reach the top of Mount Everest. There are young and older people who excitedly take on this venture. They experience enjoyment in doing what they are interested in. Similarly, if you see the importance of compassion and aspire for it then you will find your own methods to develop it. Later, I will discuss some techniques employed by Buddhists seeking to develop compassion.

The mind possesses remarkable power. Acharya Shantideva remarks in the *Bodhicharyavatara*, that 'there is nothing that is not easy when familiarized.'[12]A compassionate Bodhisattva gives his life to save a tigress and its cub. King Shibi cut his hand to save a pigeon. Reflecting upon these examples, we see that the masters are masters of the heart. When we talk about compassion, if we say it from the heart and if the listeners also listen from the heart and both sides genuinely wish to become compassionate, then I think the result will be compassionate heart. But in the absence of such intentions from either side, it will not be possible.

These days we talk a lot about mercy, compassion, and the virtues of all religions. But we do little work on these topics. Too often, we are just giving a lecture, or putting on a clinic for one's personal benefit. The Buddha used to emphasize the importance of making oneself pure and sacred in order to help others become pure and sacred. He believed that the betterment of others is indeed the betterment of oneself. Confidence in his intelligence/wisdom was the Buddha's legacy.

When I look at the Buddha, I see that he did not do anything for himself but did everything for others. He left home, relied on begging, almost gave up his body, spent six years practicing rigorously and after enlightenment though he appeared as a prince externally, he was a realized being internally. Nevertheless, he continued to go from door to door begging for alms and working for the benefit of all sentient beings by giving teachings and so on. Even when he was about to pass away, though he had many monasteries built by many kings, he chose to pass away in a remote place. Despite Ananada saying that it would be better to go to a bigger city so that he could be accessible to more people, the Awakened One, the Buddha died underneath a tree in the remote village of Kushinagar. The Buddha passed away after having the last meal offered by a devotee named Cunda. Knowing that when he passes away after having the meal offered by Cunda, people might say to Cunda that the Buddha died after taking the meal offered by him. Therefore the Buddha said to Ananda to convey to Cunda his thanks for the meal offered by him, it was very precious. He said it was indeed just as he attained enlightenment after having the rice porridge offered by Sujata, he is now entering into *Mahaparinirvana* (realm of eternal bliss) after having the meal offered by him. These two incidents of meal offering are similar in their preciousness and thus Cunda should rejoice. Such simplicity and such a compassionate attitude of the Buddha make us respect him.

Compassion can be developed through three types of thoughts and wisdom by understanding the suffering of suffering, suffering of change and all pervasive suffering just as Dipamkarasrijana has said in the *Bodhipathapradipa*, One who always wishes to remove all the suffering of others through their own suffering is the superior person.[13]

1. By contemplating the experience of tiny problems and sensations of one's own physical and mental suffering, we learn to see other beings' suffering with a sense of empathy. And we then begin to find compassionate ways to eliminate their suffering. In order to accomplish this task, one has to give one's valuable time to this valuable task by going to orphanages, hospitals, villages, and slums to do whatever you can to alleviate their suffering. If one is not able to go personally, one should provide monetary assistance to those people who are engaged in such tasks as well as provide them guidance. In brief, one should have a place for needy beings in our heart and be compassionate to them because they are a part of our society, village, city and nation.

   Compassion should be extended gradually from one's family, neighbour, village, city, district, state, nation and internationally towards all sentient beings.

   We often talk about compassion but fail to seriously examine our own attitudes and actions. When we do we sometimes find that we don't possess genuine compassion even towards our family and friends. In fact, I wonder if we are as compassionate as we should be towards those who work day and night with us and for us. Compassion should not be just lip service but be applied in practice, initially towards our family by loving and caring for their happiness and suffering and being of assistance to them. Then we should be compassionate towards our workplace authorities and staff and to those we are related to in work and respect all of them and be loving towards the children in the schools, patients in hospitals, orphans in orphanages, towards those living in spiritual centres. The brothers and sisters living in care of centres are those who are in real need of compassion.
2. The housemaid, the milk man, the cook, the watchman – they all help us in our daily chores from the break of the day till the end of the day. We should have a sense of indebtedness and gratefulness towards them. This is indeed a first step in developing the feeling of compassion. We should be indebted to house builders, road

makers and all those hard working labourers for their hard work as we enjoy a comfortable lifestyle due to their hard work. We should wonder what would happen if they stopped working for even one day? Imagine how our life would be and what a loss it would be in our daily business. Reflecting in this way should lead us to have respect for their work and empathy for their suffering. This sort of thought is indeed one of the means and methods of developing compassion.

3. Everyone is born into a country. And everyone has a right to access to its resources. We should be especially concerned for the poor, the orphan, the physically disabled and labourers. Because we are using a share of their resources on top of using our own as they are not able to fully use their resources due to their lack of knowledge and capability. Hence, I think our compassion should be especially extended to them.
4. The other significant thought is this: whatever work we do, we should do it for others. Teachers, businessmen, writers, doctors, technicians, scientists, farmers, and officers all work for others. If a teacher realizes what a fortunate person he/she is that they have got the opportunity to serve so many children and a sense of service is developed within that person, then such a teacher will perform his duty very well and enjoy doing it. This is great. Similarly, if officers also think in the same way in terms of their duty by thinking what a great joy it is that I get to serve so many people, it will give them immense joy. All the workers, whatever they are doing, if they generate a similar thought, what a wonderful society it will be to live in. Instead of scientists creating destructive weapons,they will generate positive creativity in the society. If people simply change their thought patterns the world could become like heaven/ paradise or what Buddhists call a 'Buddha field'.[14]
5. Human beings are social beings, they depend on society, and a person cannot survive alone. Others have produced the clothes that cover our body through their hard work and sweat. Similarly, the food we eat and the house we live in – all these were produced by others. People should feel indebted to others. This feeling of indebtedness is indeed a potential cause of compassion.

Look at the way we live our life and all those who assist us.

There are people sweeping, mopping, doing the dishes, cleaning our homes, preparing our food, delivering the milk, and taking care of all our needs and facilities. Often we don't even feel slightly indebted towards those who take care of all these tasks. On the contrary, we often treat them as inferior. Is it ok to do so? We pay them little and often exploit and fool them. Can compassion develop within a person who behaves in such ways? Can they experience genuine peace and happiness? If we want happiness and peace then it is necessary to change our attitudes and our behaviour. If one is able to develop a feeling of gratitude and indebtedness towards others, all of us will be changed. This will bring love and respect towards each other. This feeling is indeed one of the methods of developing compassion within us.

6. Apart from that, the first suffering – suffering of suffering – is generally to suffer physical and mental stresses in the world and we have to see ones' own as well as the suffering of others' as equal and all are similarly wanting happiness and not wanting unhappiness. Verses 90 to 110 of the 8th chapter of the *Bodhicharyavatara* have a detail discussion on these matters.
7. We should also see all sentient beings as our mothers. As Buddhists, we believe in rebirth. According to our teachings on rebirth, every single being that we encounter has been our mother or a well-wisher in one of our innumerable lives. Thus, we should feel indebted to all sentient beings. That feeling of indebtedness will help us develop compassion. Believing in rebirth helps generate compassion towards all.

Even though we may enjoy a high status and all sorts of happiness in this life, we should not become arrogant or self-centred. Such attitudes will have consequences in our future lives.

If we only had this life-time then we could accept the view of 'survival of the fittest' and behave in self-centred ways. But people behaving in this way would lead the new generation in an inappropriate direction. Do we really want self-centred people to be the role models or heroes of today's youth? I think not. We have to understand that happiness comes from within. If this feeling is understood, many families will be saved from being destroyed and the future for children will be stable. The effect of a broken family falls mostly on the children. If one is not able to give love to one's own family, then what right does one have to talk about compassion?

8. Another thing is that we can see how compassion is developed through the four immeasurables (*caturbrahmavihara*) demonstrated in the following story found in Buddhist treatises. In the story, there is a mother who has three sons and she views all as equal. Similarly, we know that all beings are the same in wanting happiness and not wanting unhappiness. We have to have equanimity, and to see all as equal is *loving-kindness*. If one of the sons of that mother is slightly physically disabled then the mother will be bit more attentive towards that child. Similarly, we should be more sensitive in alleviating the problems of the needy people and to do so is an act of compassion. Then rejoice. Just as a mother would never be jealous when her children progress and obtain a high status through their effort or merit, we should rejoice in their achievement. If we fail to rejoice in the achievements of others, then our compassion for all beings is not complete.

   Next there is equanimity (*upeksha*). Suppose that an infant child of that mother unknowingly breaks an important thing? The mother simply forgives the child because she knows that the child is innocent. Similarly, when a person, under the influence of attachment, anger and ignorance, harms us, we should pity their ignorance and forgive them. Whether someone helps or harms us, we should view them with equanimity.

   These thoughts help us to develop a good attitude toward others, to become compassionate.

   In ancient India – and even today – mothers in Indian villages are very caring of their children. Thus, these are the four types of immeasurable (*caturbhrahmavihara*) attitudes that will prove helpful in the development of compassion. The moment a person becomes selfless like the genuine mother reflected in the above story, all impurities are overcome.

9. We should all be accountable for the defects/shortcomings of the society we live in and accordingly make every effort to remedy those defects. Leaving those defects alone will not help; they won't go away by themselves. I am aware that people have been trying to solve this problem but it hasn't been as effective as it might have

been. I think this is simply because we have been using the means to remedy the problem in a wrong way. We have been simply doing lip service and writing bundles and bundles of books on how to develop great attitudes like compassion and so on. We are ourselves not following what we have written in our papers and books. When we ourselves have not changed our attitudes, how can we expect others who listen to or read our writings to change? Therefore, I think we – political leaders, spiritual masters and concerned authorities – should seriously think of taking a holistic approach that is practical, applicable and thus effective.

If we trust ourselves, it is not a difficult task to change ourselves. We have to overcome all negative thoughts, even those hiding deep inside. Then, if one is constantly alert, mindful, introspective, compassionate, and honest, there will be change.

10. Whatever duties and responsibilities one has obtained – whether obtained because of one's abilities or karma – one has to fulfil it sincerely. Teachers have to teach their students sincerely. Companies and businessmen cannot develop their business or company if sellers and buyers betray one another. Sellers and buyers are inseparable parts like our hands and feet are part of one body. Business only works if both parts work together and we proceed honestly.

    We have to apply this approach to all fields, as everything is interdependent. A family depends on their family members, they in turn depend on their society and the society depends on the nation, the nation depends on the world and the world depends on the diverse eco-system. Every one of us and everything are linked with each other, none of us can survive alone on our own in this world. Understanding this interdependent\causation and interdependent nature is the foundation of the development of a genuine compassion according to Buddhism.

11. Generally, when we draw a conclusion or make a decision about an individual, we do it conditioned by our own likes and dislikes, while that individual or the event depends on various causes and conditions. In fact, we should actually have a holistic approach that is of benefit to the maximum whenever we are to draw a conclusion or make a decision regarding a person or an event.

Failing to approach it holistically, we come to conclusions and decisions that are of advantage for one and disadvantageous to others and to society.

12. In everything we do, we have to try to view them through different perspectives, otherwise we may create misunderstanding. In this regard, I can say something from my own experience. A male student of my class came into the classroom and banged his book on the table creating a loud noise. I got very angry feeling that he was insulting me. However, in reality he came into the classroom right after he had an argument with his girlfriend. I took his action as an insult to me when his action was actually a reaction to his own frustration. It was my misunderstanding to take it as an insult to me. Before, I realized that it was my own misunderstanding, I was very angry. But after that student came and explained to me his situation, I felt very sorry for him. We often become unhappy due to our own misunderstandings. It is very important to take a holistic approach. Generally, all our actions and decisions are based on our own judgements and perspectives. We fail to see things from the others perspective. Therefore, a practitioner of compassion should be very patient and contemplative. When a practitioner is patient and contemplative then genuine compassion can be further developed.

In summary, people should not be hypocritical but be honest, sincere, and do what they say. These are some points which help us generate compassion based on the first type of suffering, the suffering of suffering.

For the second type of compassion, the object of compassion is dharma and the connotation of dharma in this context is the momentary nature of things. Due to our failure to understand the impermanent nature of all things, people face various sorts of psychological problems. For instance, one holds in mind an incident that happened many years before as if it happened today. And then constantly holds a grudge against the person even though that event was a past thing that does not have any existence in the present moment. In fact, life is momentary and therefore, there is no reason to either be too excited or too sad. A thing that was not there yesterday but it is here today may not be there tomorrow. Someone who understands this will be able to handle various kinds of problems because understanding the impermanent nature of all things will develop compassion towards those who suffer due to a lack of understanding impermanence.

An awareness of the impermanence of all things is a type of compassion which is used generally today by psychologists. One should try to see the others' problem as one's own and help them through genuine compassion rather than only doing it as a means of earning money. We need to seriously ask ourselves whether we want to become happy through money or through a wish to serve needy persons. When helping others gives us extreme joy and happiness, why not choose the latter and why don't we make that happiness our happiness and celebrate.

The third type of compassion is objectless compassion; its purpose is to counteract the lack of understanding the impermanent, non-intrinsic nature of things. And, consequently, thinking of the 'self' as permanent, unitary and intrinsically existent, and acting accordingly. Due to these sorts of profound misunderstandings, one has to face various kinds of physical and mental problems. If this life is like an illusion, that is, interdependently originated, inherently non-existing in itself, formless, empty, 'lack of elaborations'[15]and impermanent – then what is there to be stuck about? When one is able to establish in oneself what happiness and unhappiness is, then one will have achieved a transcendent state. Through this experience of oneself, we come to realize that others with the lack of this knowledge unnecessarily and unknowingly experience problems. To be compassionate towards those suffering thus is indeed the object-less compassion.

In a nutshell, I think that generating compassion towards those suffering from *suffering of suffering is there in all religions*. However, the compassion that is generated by those who have realized impermanence, towards those who have not seen the impermanent nature of all phenomena and hold everything as fixed and permanent and the compassion generated, after realizing the non-inherent existence of all phenomena, towards those who have not done so is, I think, only in Buddhism.

This view is found in the *Bodhicharyavatara* of Shantideva: 'Fear is born when you hold things exist in reality, while they don't exist in reality and are in the form of emptiness; emptiness is pain relieving, so why should there be any fear from it. Thus, understanding emptiness is the genuine cause of genuine compassion.'[16]

These two types of compassion: compassion generated through understanding impermanence and compassion generated through understanding emptiness are qualities of Buddhism.

I have, in brief, attempted to shed some light on how to develop compassion according to the Buddhist tradition. A mere pity towards someone is not a genuine compassion, a genuine compassion is that which arises towards sentient beings suffering from the various sufferings of *samsara* (cyclic nature of life) like suffering of poverty, old age, illness, depression, loneliness, death, grasping things as permanent and inherently existing, etc., and having a strong feeling to protect them from such sufferings. Compassion is indeed one of the most substantive qualities of a Bodhisattva, just as it is said thus in the *Madhyamakavatara:*

'Because for this bountiful harvest of the conquerors, compassion itself is like the seed, like water for growth, and like ripening, remaining for long enjoyment; at the beginning I praise compassion.'[17]

Bhavantu Sarva Mangalam

Notes

1. See the Ornament of Realization (Abhisamayalanka), an early *Mahayana Sutra*, much loved by Tibetan Buddhism, 1/16.
2. *Avadana* is a type of Buddhist literature that seeks to correlate the virtuous deeds of past lives to subsequent events in lives. Avalokiteshvara is the Bodhisattva of Compassion in the Tibetan Buddhist tradition. See the *Tohuku Catalogue*, no. 238, p. 84.
3. See the *Dharmasangraha Sutra* in the *Tohuku Catalogue*, no. 238, p. 84.
4. See the *Tathabataguhya Sutra* in the *Tohuku Catalogue*, no. 494, p. 153.
5. The five aggregates are *rupa*/physical form, *vedana*/feeling/sensation, *sanna*/perception, *sankhara*/mental formation, and *vinnana*/consciousness.
6. See the *Bodhicaryatatara* by Shantideva (685-753) for the classic account of the Mahayana Way, p. 14.
7. See Shantideva, ibid., 5.17.
8. Ibid.

9. See Sthiramati, the *Trimsikabharya*, p. 223.
10. See Chandrakirti, *Madhyamakavatara*, a commentary on the work of Nagarjuna (150-250 CE), p. 212.
11. See the *Uttaratantra*, a treatise on the Buddha nature, p. 1/28.
12. See Shantideva, op. cit., 6/14.
13. See Atisa's (982-1054 CE) *Bodhipathaprodipa* and its teaching of three levels of spiritual aspiration, p. 5.
14. 'Buddha Field' is a celestial realm or the abode of a Buddha or Bodhisattva in Mahayana Buddhism.
15. Ed. note: The phrase 'lack of elaborations' occurs in Buddhist literature in relation to the teachings of anatta or 'no self' in the sense of a fixed permanent self and in relation to shunyata or the 'emptiness' of all things/existence.
16. See Shantideva, op. cit., 9/52.
17. See Chandrakirti, op. cit., 1/2.

CHAPTER 14

The Need for Compassion and the Attainment of Buddhahood

TASHI PALJOR

You embraced compassion,
to rid us of all wrong perceptions,
you showed us right Dharma,
We pay homage to the Gautama Buddha.

THE GREAT COMPASSIONATE Lord Buddha repeatedly stressed the importance of compassion in the texts of the *Tripitika* or Pali Canon.[1] Compassion is to have the feeling that all beings may be free of suffering. Likewise, to have a feeling for their welfare is called loving-kindness. The wish or aspiration to lead all beings into Buddhahood is termed *Bodhicitta*. It is out of compassion that Lord Buddha remains in contact with all beings.

According to Mahayana teaching, all the beings of the 'three worlds' are considered as one's mother.[2] Our births have no beginning and we can never know how many times we have taken birth from the womb of a mother. So we are in this world because of the compassion of mothers. So we should try to develop a compassionate mind by thoroughly understanding this teaching. It is for this reason that Lord Buddha is also called 'the great compassionate one'.

Compassion is necessary to have a peaceful human life. Compassion plays a crucial role in creating cordial and congenial relationships with relatives, friends, and other people. All should be treated with an attitude of loving kindness.

Acharya Chandrakirti (*c.* 600-50 CE) paid homage to compassion instead of to the Buddha in the *Mulamadhyamika Shastra* (Principles of the Middle Way). It is from compassion that *Bodhicitta* arises. *Bodhicitta* is a spontaneous wish to attain enlightenment motivated by great compassion for all sentient beings. It results in an enlightenment that culminates in Buddhahood. Since the attainment of Buddhahood is not possible without compassion, Acharya Chandrakirti has paid homage to it. The *Tathagata* – the term Siddhartha Gautama used in referring to himself[3] – explained compassion in detail in the *Gandavyuh Sutra*, the sutra of the entry into the realm of reality.

Compassion is one among the six causes of *Bodhicitta*. Without compassion it is not possible to develop *Bodhicitta*. Through the practice of *Bodhicitta*, the six perfections,[4] and an understanding of emptiness, followers of the Mahayana Way can achieve the goal of Buddhahood. It is an internal achievement of the Mahayanist. Without compassion the welfare of beings is not possible. So compassion is very necessary for Mahayana practitioners.

I have been asked by Doboom Tulku to write of my experience in the practice of compassion and its importance in my life. I started to understand the concept of compassion from that time when I had the opportunity to learn the texts of Mahayana Buddhism. I was fortunate to be taught its religious practice and philosophy by learned scholars of Mahayana Buddhism. I also learned more about Vajrayana, a Buddhist school especially important in Tibetan Buddhism that emphasizes esoteric and tantric practices as a means to Enlightenment. This helped me to realize the necessity of internalizing loving-kindness, compassion, *Bodhicitta*, and Emptiness (*Shunyata*). It helped me grasp the process of arising and ceasing in their practices. Serious learning and a depth in understanding of a given aspect of the topic of compassion is paramount to any growth and internalization of the Mahayana Way.

The Importance of Great Compassion

Every being has traces of compassion to a small degree. Compassion is evident also in the animal world especially among those that treat their offspring lovingly. Among many animals, the mothers make arrangements for food. Mahayanists teach and embody the thought of the welfare of all sentient beings. They always contemplate the welfare of others.

Since following the teachings on compassion of Mahayana

Buddhism, and especially Tibetan Buddhism, I have quit eating eggs and meat for the last thirteen years. Some used to say that according to the *Tikotiparishud Sutra* consumption of meat was allowed and is considered not a sin. I read the *Lankavatara Sutra* concerning Buddha Nature and the *Nirvana Sutra* on the possibility of all achieving Buddhahood. Here Lord Buddha has clearly said that one will have to take birth as a violent animal in another life because of meat eating. The Mahayana canon and texts say that meat consumption kills compassion.

In Mahayana teachings, all the beings of the three worlds are regarded as our former mothers.[5]

The birth of beings is without beginning. We don't know how many times we have taken birth and how many times we will be born in the future. According to Buddhist religion and philosophy, there is no beginning for sentient beings. By attaining the status of *Arhathood* (Enlightenment) in Theravada Buddhism one is freed from birth due to delusional action and attachment to this world. Rather, after the attainment of *Arhathood* one can take birth in any desired place at will.

All beings because of the law of *karma* and passion have to take birth. Since time immemorial there is no one who has physically lived forever. After death the mind continues to remain. Because of one's *karma* one has to take another life. A being has to live in a transitory phase (*antrabhav*) for 49 days after its death. After this one is bound to go to a higher realm or a lower realm. This is the reason why after gaining the life of a human being one should study the dharma. Without the contemplation of dharma, it is not possible to attain a higher rebirth or *sugati* meaning 'a happy destination, bliss, happiness and/or heavenly realms' or liberation. For this reason it is necessary to think day and night for the benefit of all beings. Without the knowledge of Buddhism we fail to value the importance of human life.

In the canonical texts of Buddhism, Lord Buddha elaborated in detail the importance of life. We can cross the ocean of sufferings only through the medium of a boat. If we do not listen, contemplate and practice Buddhist teaching in this life then it's very rare to gain a life with freedom and endowments.

Acharya Tsongkhapa (1357-1419 CE) said that a human life is greater than a wish fulfilling *chintamani* or jewel. A *chintamani* can only help one get worldly comfort. It cannot buy liberation and omniscience. That's why Acharya Tsongkhapa has taught the importance of the value of a rare birth as a human with the eighteen rare qualities. In the *Bodhicharyavatara* text on the *Way of Awakening* or the *Way of the Bodhisattva*, Acharya Shantideva wrote in the eighth century CE about the rarity of a birth of a human blessed with *kyan* and *samapati*. He stressed working to achieve a fortunate rebirth (*purusharth*) in this very life.

Liberation and Enlightenment

Release from rebirth (*nishreyas*) is also called a purpose to strive for (*purusharth*). To achieve such a goal, intelligent beings should remain committed to the study of Buddhist texts. Such study will lead to the eradication of unwholesome acts, the accumulation of virtues, paying homage to our teachers, and revering holy beings. These acts accumulate merit such that after death those adept at spiritual practices can happily reach their goal. Lord Buddha has said that one can become one's own protector, there is no other. That is why Buddhism does not accept the role of a creator God. Human beings have performed virtuous deeds in previous lives which is why they are born as a human being in this life. By performing virtuous deeds in this life it is certain that in the next life one can get birth in a heaven and *nirvana*.

Empowerment of Arya Avalokiteshwara

His Holiness the Dalai Lama initiates believers into Arya Avalokiteshwara empowerment. Avalokiteshwara (Chenrizig) is the Bodhisattva of Compassion in the Tibetan Buddhist tradition. After the initiation it is necessary for the initiates to maintain their vows and promises (*samaya*). The teacher of HH the Dalai Lama, Yongzin Ling Rinpoche, once bestowed Avalokiteshvara initiation at Sera Jey Monastery in Karnataka. He said that recitation of the *Om Mani Padme Hum* mantra one hundred times a day saves us from going into lower realms of existence after death. From that date onward I have recited the mantra one hundred time everyday for the benefit of sentient beings. Through the recitation of this mantra, sufferings of beings in all six realms can be reduced. Along with the recitation of this mantra, goodwill towards all beings is inculcated. Arya Avalokiteshwara is a manifestation of all the Buddha's compassion, past, present and future. Through recitation of this mantra, compassion arises in the heart of the believer. Having a compassionate heart leads to beneficial work and empathy for all beings. So, teachings of compassion and loving kindness are taught for the welfare of all beings.

HH the Dalai Lama gives the teachings of love and compassion to people so that the minds and hearts of believers may experience happiness and peace. This later becomes the cause for the attainment of the highest stage: that of Buddhahood.

This is the ultimate goal of the Mahayana. Such a big achievement is not possible without the help of compassion. Compassion has three characteristics. It is self-dependent, dharma-dependent and inter-dependent.

Many deities of the Vajrayana appear in wrathful forms. People wonder why deities of Buddhism are in this form. Lord Buddha has shown many forms of fearsome aspects out of compassion to bring his followers into the right path.

His Holiness even at the age of eighty years gives Buddhist teachings to the people. In society a compassionate person is always liked and frequently visited while an angry person is avoided even by their own relatives. So it is necessary to make one's mind compassionate.

The Tradition of Dedication (Sharing One's Merits)

I share with all the beings of the three worlds whatever wholesome deeds I have earned during the day for the welfare of all. Sharing one's virtue is a unique feature of Buddhism. The sharing of one's merits multiplies ones virtues so that anger cannot destroy our virtues. Not sharing one's merits leads to the destruction of virtues due to the occurrence of the slightest anger at any given point of time. So one should immediately pray to share our earned virtues with all beings.

The meaning of *parinamana* is to grow or to give. So to share the virtue for the welfare of sentient beings is called *parinamana*.

Notes

1. The *Tripitika* or Pali Canon is central to Theravada Buddhism.
2. The 'three worlds' of Buddhism are destinations for karmic rebirth: the world of desire (*kamaloka*), the world of form (*rupaloka*) and the world of formlessness (*arupaloka*).
3. The term *Tathagata* is found in Pali and in Sanskrit. It is an honorific term with a literal meaning of 'one who has thus gone' or 'one who has thus arrived.' It is found in Buddhist Sutras and used by Siddhartha Gautama, the Awakened One, the Buddha to refer to himself. In Mahayana Buddhism it has come to mean 'the essential buddha nature hidden in everyone.'
4. The 'six perfections or *paramitas*' in Mahayana Buddhism are (1) *dana*/ generosity, (2)*sila*/morality/ virtue, (3)*ksanti*/patience/tolerance, (4) *virya*/ diligence/effort/energy, (5) *dhyana*/one pointed concentration, and (6) *prajna*/ wisdom. These are all higher or transcendent states of consciousness that overcome ego-consciousness.

PART V

PRACTICES OF COMPASSION IN ISLAM

CHAPTER 15

Namaz: A Practice of Compassion

MOHAMMED FAYYAZUDDIN

THE THEME FOR the present conference is 'Practices of Compassion'. Undoubtedly, compassion is one of the noblest human virtues and of great importance for both individuals and societies. The British author Karen Armstrong has written, 'If we want to create a viable, peaceful world, we have got to integrate compassion into the 21st century life.' Likewise, His Holiness the Dalai Lama has observed, 'If you want others to be happy, practice compassion. If you want to be happy, practice compassion'. The religion of Islam also aims to inculcate the quality of compassion in its followers. The Prophet of Islam is reported to have said: 'God is compassionate and loves compassion. He gives for compassion what He does not give for harshness.' (Sahih Muslim)

Why has such enormous stress been laid on compassion? It is because a compassionate attitude has the ability to induce feelings of kindness and forgiveness in people, which can help deal with situations that very often lead to clash and confrontation. Thus, if we want peace at the individual level and in society, we need to promote and foster a culture of compassion.

One of the practices of compassion in Islam is prayer which is called *salat* in Arabic or *namaz* in Urdu. All religions have certain rituals, ceremonies and acts of worship. Islam likewise has its specific rites, but lays special emphasis on the spirit with which these are carried out. Form, in one sense, is only an external manifestation of the spirit. That is, the spirit is the dominant aspect and is the vital and indispensable element of every sincere religious act, while form is subordinate to the spirit of worship. *Namaz* consists of various acts. In this paper, I would like to explain how the different components of *namaz* help develop in the worshipper the desired qualities of compassion, peacefulness and well-wishing for others.

Prayer or *namaz* as a general duty is frequently enjoined in the Koran. Prayer is the second of the five fundamental principles or pillars of practical devotion in Islam. It is a devotional exercise which every Muslim is required to render to God five times a day. In one of its verses, the Koran says: 'Attend to your prayers in the early morning, at the close of the day and at the approach of the night, prayers are good deeds which drive away sin' (11: 114). At another place, the Koran describes *namaz* thus: 'Timely prayer is a duty upon believers to be conducted at appointed times' (4: 103).

Ablutions

Namaz begins with ablution, that is, with the washing of the face, hands and feet. This bodily cleansing is a symbolic reminder that the believer should lead his life in this world in a state of purification of feelings and of the soul. At the moment of washing himself clean, the worshipper utters these words in prayer: 'O God, purify my inner self along with my outer body.' In this way, the earnest prayer makes his soul clean too, like his body.

Congregation

Prayer in Islam may be carried out at any place, but ideally, is performed in an organized manner, in congregation, within the mosque. There the worshippers arrange themselves in orderly rows behind a single prayer leader, the Imam. The acceptance by the group of just one individual to lead the congregation avoids any dissension which might arise from there being more than one. The number of the worshippers may be ten or ten thousand, but all have to stand in rows behind the Imam. This teaches the lesson of unity. Nevertheless, *namaz*, in essence, is an individual action. Everyone recites his own prayer and is rewarded on account of one's inner rectitude and sincerity.

Allah Akbar

Namaz begins with the invocation *Allah Akbar*, which means 'God is Great'. Throughout the *namaz* the phrase *Allah Akbar* is repeated several times. Implicit in these words is the idea that the person uttering them is not great. Their frequent repetition is a lesson in modesty, designed to rid the worshipper of arrogance and egoism, and turn him into a humble servant of God.

The Compassionate God

After the invocation of *Allah Akbar*, the worshipper recites certain verses from the Koran. Before beginning to recite any verse, one says *Bismilliahirrahmanirrahim*, that is, 'In the name of God, the Most Merciful, the Most Compassionate.' This is also the very first verse of the Koran. It is repeated 114 times in the Koran, clearly showing that the God of Islam is the God of Mercy and Compassion, and the book of Islam, too, is the book of mercy. The followers of Islam must also possess the qualities of mercy and compassion, otherwise they could not be true believers.

Compassion is a principle that helps in fostering a culture of peace between people in society. If you go through the Koran and Hadith, you will find many verses in the Koran and Hadith which lay great stress on compassion. For instance, the Prophet of Islam said: 'O people, be compassionate to others so that you may be granted compassion by God' (Sahih Bukhari). Thus, Islam makes compassion a matter of self-interest for every person. That is, one's own future depends on one's compassionate behaviour to one's fellow beings. In this way, Islam motivates us to be compassionate in our dealings with each other. If one wants to receive God's grace, one shall have to show compassion to others.

A believer has to repeat *namaz* five times a day. As a result, he is repeatedly reminded during the day that he has to live among people with good behaviour characterized by kindness, compassion, and sympathy. Islam attaches great importance to these values because in the present world, problems and differences inevitably arise between different groups, for no human situation is ever absolutely ideal. In these situations, only those individuals can help maintain the peace and calm in society who can remain tolerant of others in spite of differences and in spite of facing unpleasant experiences. Tolerance is a worthy, humane virtue, which has been described in different terms in Islam: for instance, gentle behaviour, showing concern for others, being soft-hearted, being compassionate.

Whenever any negative situation arises one way of dealing with it is a head-on clash, that is, an attempt to solve the problem by direct confrontation. Such attempts only aggravate the problem. In no way will they improve matters. Experience shows that on such occasions instead of behaving violently and fighting, we should opt for the course of tolerance and forbearance; instead of combating violence with violence, we should adopt the policy of avoidance; remaining united in spite of differences.

Prostrations during *Namaz*

The acts of kneeling down and self-prostration are also repeated several times in the course of the *namaz*, in symbolic submission before God. In this way, the worshipper is conditioned by *namaz* to surrender himself to his Maker in all humility.

The real proof of this submission to God will only become manifest, however, in subsequent dealings with other human beings in which it is clear that self-glorification has been replaced by glorification of the Almighty, and that feelings of superiority have given way to profound humility.

When a servant of God bows before his Lord, and does so, not just as a matter of form, but in the spirit of true humility, the effect of his action does not remain confined to the place where it is done, but extends to his everyday existence, pervading it completely. His thinking and actions bear the permanent stamp of his devotions, for it is impossible for a man to fear God and to bow before Him without being influenced thereby in his dealings with others. A true worshipper cannot be humble and meek before God and yet be arrogant and inconsiderate with regard to his fellow human beings. He will certainly avoid asserting his own superiority, and instead will adopt a humble demeanour on a parallel with his self-prostration before his Maker.

The submission which he expresses in prayer to God becomes a reality in terms of his observance of others' rights. At prayer in the mosque, he is the epitome of servitude to God and outside the mosque, he is the perfect citizen – humble in demeanour, morally upright, and kind, considerate and forgiving in all his transactions.

When true God-worship and religiosity is born within a person, he reaches above all those evils, which emanate from selfishness. Instead of living within the confines of the self, he begins to live in the world of reality. The truly pious person begins to look upon people with love and compassion. He does not expect anything from anyone which is why even when others differ from him or do not behave well towards him, he continues, nevertheless, to make concessions to them, and continues to be tolerant and kind towards them.

Ending the *Namaz* with Peace

The *namaz* ends with each worshipper turning his face sideways and uttering these words: *Assalamualaykumwarahmatullah*. It means: 'May God's peace and blessings be upon you.' Every day, all around the globe, Muslims perform this rite. It is as if they were saying to their fellow human beings all over the world: 'O people, we have no feelings for you but those of peace. Your lives, property and honour – all are safe.' It is this spirit with which worshippers are infused before they return to society. *Namaz* thus develops feelings of peace and well-wishing in the worshipper for others. All the acts of *namaz* are not mere rituals but are a part of *namaz* in their sprit. Collectively, these forms of etiquette can be termed *namaz* culture. Therefore, if a person's prayer does not fend away indecency and evil then his prayer is not really prayer at all.

What is prayer? It is to remember the fact that man is living before a God who – though man cannot see Him – can see man. Whoever leaves the mosque with this fact firmly embedded in his mind cannot live forgetful of God. In prayer, one testifies to the fact that God is the greatest of all beings. If one is truthful in one's testimony, then one will not claim greatness for oneself when one has finished praying. Whatever one recites in prayer is a covenant before God that one will keep his commandments; then how is it possible that one should leave the mosque and treat people with arrogance, contempt and cruelty? The actions of prayer are a manifestation of the fact that one's heart is full of fear and love for God. How can one claim to be full of fear and love for God in the mosque, and then live as if one knows neither fear nor love for Him when one goes outside?

This is why if one prays in the true spirit of prayer, then one's prayer will surely make one a good member of society. But if one's prayer is devoid of spirit, then it will be no more than a routine action which has no connection with one's real life. It will be prayer in form, but not in reality: for it will not reform a person's character or change him for the better.

Supplications to God

At the end of *namaz*, the worshipper makes special supplication to God in silence with his hands raised. This supplication is called *dua*. According to the Koran, God disapproves of man praying for evil. (17: 11) The Prophet once said to his Companions, 'God grants to gentleness what He does not grant to harshness' (Sahih Muslim). Praying for good is in accordance with nobility. True belief in God inculcates in a person a temperament of sympathy and of kindness. One so inclined will always pray for good, he will never pray for evil.

The Prophet Muhammad said that God is best pleased when a person prays to Him for peace (Ai-Tirmizi). The Prophet frequently used to say this prayer: 'O God, You are peace, and peace is from You. O God, help us to live with peace and reside in the home of peace, O Lord of Majesty and Glory' (Sahih Muslim)! This invocation sums up the spirit of prayer.

Conclusion

The important thing about prayer is that it nurtures the correct attitude in the devotee, as though the spirit of his prayers were keeping a watchful eye on everything he says and does. When going about his worldly affairs, it is as if the whole world were a mosque; his actions, therefore, at all times and in all places cannot be other than in consonance with what his worship requires of him.

The different acts of *namaz* are aimed at bringing about a spiritual awakening, such as will induce the worshipper to renounce his life of ignorance and heedlessness in favour of a life inspired by moral and human values.

CHAPTER 16

Compassion According to Sufi Masters

SEYED MOSTAFA AZMAYESH

IN SUFISM YOU will find a long history of applied compassion according to the descriptions of some of the great masters of Sufism like Fariddudin Attâr,[1] Mawlana Jami,[2] Nezâmi Ganjavi,[3] and especially Sa'adi Shirazi.[4] That history of applied compassion is found in their stories and poetry.

A Sufi master's deep understanding of love is to experience unity with God and His creation and creatures. When seekers start to follow their path towards unity, their heart is touched by a feeling of deep longing, which they might not be able to explain. They feel an attraction to their Master and connect consciously to the stream of light to which their Master is connected by reaching out to his hand in order to be initiated. By connecting to their own heart during daily life the seekers rest in connection to the heart of their spiritual Master and the stream of love.

Bit by bit their soul grows like a little bird in an egg until it becomes mature enough to spread its wings and leave the hard shell of the egg. Under the guidance of their Master the little birds will accomplish exercises that contribute to their growing. The 'food' of the soul-bird is pure vibration, emanating from the connection to the Master and by exercising specific rhythms of the substantial path. These rhythms can be played on instruments like the *Daff* (a large Persian frame drum), *Dâyereh* (a medium sized frame drum with jingles, a type of tambourine) or a *Tombak* (a single headed goblet shaped drum), or be recited, murmured, or silently performed concentrating on the heart beat of one's own heart. The rhythms are contained in numerous Sufi poems and can be presented live by an experienced Qawal.They are also innate in the names of God. And as it is known, there are many names of God like Haq (reality), Hu (the One) or Ar-rahim (the Compassionate One).

The first part of the Koran, whose verses were composed in Mecca, in fact are hymns and meditative prayers, which should be recited in the correct rhythm in order to carry out the right effect on the heart. In fact, the original and authentic meaning of the word *Islam* according to the Sufi tradition and according to the meaning of the word is: the path from *soghm* to *selm* namely, from illness (*soghm*) of the heart to the health (*selm*) of the heart. Once Sufis have put some effort in their development to reach this kind of health of the heart, they will attain a kind of certainty about their spiritual reality or entity. They thus start to realize, that they are a mere dweller and guest of these earthly bodies. The Sufis know about their mission and need not believe something which they do not experience by themselves.

Thus, by different means – keeping the heart connection to the Master; feeding one's own heart by applying rhythms that propagate vibrations, personal *dhikrs*[5] and collective *samâ*[6] ceremonies; doing a balance of one's own thoughts, emotions and deeds during the day (the technique of *mohassebeh*) – the Sufis clean the 'dust' that covers their heart until their heart is pure, shiny, and calm.

But there is more. And this has to do with compassion.

In one of his most famous poems Sa'adi proposed a condition for being human. According to him compassion is a highly esteemed quality and a necessity for qualification as a human being.

And how do the Sufis develop compassion? Where does the compassion come from? According to them, compassion arises from the heart and it is a consequence or rather an accessory phenomenon of applied action.

We have a story of Sa'adi about empathy that visualizes what this means.

Bàni âdam azâye yekdigarand
Ke dar âfarinesh ze yek goharand
Cho ozvi be dard âvarad roozegâr
Degar ozvohâ ra namânad gharâr
To kaz mehnate digarân bi ghami
Nashâyad ke nâmat nahand âdami.

Human beings are members of a whole,
In creation of one essence and soul.
If one member is afflicted with pain,
Other members uneasy will remain.
If you've no sympathy for human pain,
The name of human you cannot retain!

On one of Sa'adi's extended travels through the Near East in the thirteenth century, he reached Damascus during a drought and famine. The inhabitants of the city were close to starving. Wherever he walked in the streets of Damascus he saw people looking miserable and close to starvation. Finally, he met an old friend who had come into riches in that city and was a very wealthy man. He looked into his face and saw how pale and yellow his skin was and questioned him. 'My friend what has happened to you? You look just as miserable as those poor people around you! Your face is haggard and your skin is yellow. How do you feel?' The friend replied: 'With all these ill people around me I became as ill as them. Their illness affects me, I feel their sorrow and pain. Now I am filled with their grief.'

Sa'adi reflected on this encounter and came to the conclusion that it is not enough to feel the pain of others in a passive or receptive manner. Rather, it is necessary to act and do something about the situation that causes pain to others. So obviously, the rich man could have gone one step further and instead of only feeling the pain, he could have spent the money to organize food for the poor and miserable people who were on the verge of starvation.

Here, Sa'adi describes the principle of *javânmardy*. This principle means: it is not enough to feel a situation, it needs to be understood. And further, it is not enough to understand a situation, there needs to follow an action adequate to the situation according to each person's abilities and possibilities. This is a holistic perspective on compassion according to the Sufi masters.

Another story tells about Shibli[7] who is said to have brought a sack with flour to a Sufi Khanegâh[8] and when he opened the sack an ant was running helplessly from left to right. Shibli became sad about the situation of the ant as he was sure to have deprived her of her home and companions. During that night, he could not sleep at all and decided to not sleep and to not pray, and instead decided to deliver the ant back to its home. And thus he did.

In this story there is a lesson about compassion. The fate of the little animal affected the man and he placed the pain of a being higher than his vow to pray or his body's need to sleep and entered into action to end the pain.

Many stories can be found in books and writings of Sufi Masters. Those stories visualize lessons and principles in a simple form. In this case we learn that for Sufis it is not important to be advanced or powerful or to have many adherents. The important thing is to apply the teachings in daily life – even if that means being respectful towards an ant.

This fact contributed to the historical reality that some mighty rulers chose Sufis as their advisors. Masters like Hafez[9] and Sa'adi did not praise and hail their Sultans, but kept on challenging them with unexpected thoughts in order to make them learn to find a balance, to learn the art of a measured reign and not to be cruel and harsh and severe with people.

According to all these great Sufi Masters, compassion is an applied art of spiritual awareness in daily life.

Notes

1. Known as a poet and Sufi theoretician (scholar) and hagiograph from Nishapour, a major city of medieval Khorasan, north-eastern Iran. Attâr lived during the twelfth and thirteenth centuries. His formal name was Abū Ḥamīd bin Abū Bakr Ibrāhīm. He lived to be more than one hundred years. He is most known for his work *The Conference of the Birds*.
2. Affiliated to the school of ibn Arabi, greatest theologian-poet of the fifteenth century, Jami is known for his achievements as a scholar, mystic, writer, composer of numerous lyrics and idylls, historian, and the greatest Sufi poet of his time. His formal name was Mawlanā Nūr al-Dīn 'Abd al-Rahmān or Abd-Al-Rahmān Nur-Al-Din Muhammad Dashti.
3. Persian romantic epic poet of the twelfth century, born in Ganja in the great Seldjuq Empire, nowadays Azerbaijan. Nezâmis formal name was Jamal ad-Dīn Abū Muḥammad Ilyās ibn-Yūsuf ibn-Zakkī, called Ilyās.
4. A thirteenth century Sufi Master and poet well known for the quality of his writings and for the depth of his social and moral thought. Sa'adi had travelled widely and encountered a wide variety of people. He gained many deep

experiences. His formal name was Abū-Muhammad Muslih al-Dīn bin Abdallāh Shīrāzī.

5. *Dhikr* or *zikr* or *zekr*: reciting a name of God like *Allah Hu* (the unique all-embracing quality of God).
6. Musical ceremony supervised by a Master in order to strengthen the common consciousness.
7. A mystic of Persian origin who served at the court before he embarked on the path of love as it is reported in a rather exalted way. Abu Bakr Shibli lived during ninth and tenth centuries. His Master was Junayd Baghdadi.
8. A place of gathering for Sufis.
9. This genius loved to target religious hypocrisy, Khwaja Shams-ud-Din Muhammad Hafez-e Shirazi. Obviously, he knew the Qur'an by heart, hence his pen name Hafez. His love of poetry has inspired many thinkers and poets after him. Hafez lived in the fourteenth century.

CHAPTER 17

Compassion in Islam: Kindness in Action

IDRISA PANDIT

WRITING ABOUT AN Islamic perspective on compassion in Islam at the present time is a challenge. On the one hand, we have examples of extreme transgression on earth committed by a few hijackers of Islam. On the other, we have super-power war machinery in full action. We have Islamophobes, and even some historians, engaged in erasing and distorting the history of human civilization to claim hegemony over civilizational contributions. Added to it all is the language of conflict and clash based in religions and race, promoted by political pundits and academics.

We live in a broken world driven by *hubris*, ego and greed, a world that is deeply entrenched in fear of the other. It is a world where calls for compassion and care are easily drowned. It is a world that can only heal through true compassion and openness of human hearts to compassionate ways of being and living. Regardless of all the problems of the world often being attributed to religions, and given the present political, social, and environmental global crisis, it is an ideal time to redirect our thinking, to exploring compassion rooted in our faith traditions.

Most Muslims are at a loss to explain the mayhem that is created by some in the name of Islam. The true spirit of Islam is lost on those who use the name of their faith to create *fasad fil ard* (transgression on earth), a grave sin in Islam. Here I will outline compassion as rooted in the Koran, the Islamic scripture, the living example of Prophet Muhammad (Peace be Upon Him) – he was also given the divine title of Mercy to the World – and illustrate compassion through action using the example of a small effort to build a Muslim social service agency whose motto is, 'The best of people are those who serve others'.

The definition and meaning of compassion 'rahma' in Islam is different from the English dictionary definition of the word compassion which limits it to pity and feeling sorry for others. Compassion in Islam encompasses the love and mercy of God. While we often hear that the God of Islam is not the God of love, the word *rahma* (mercy and compassion) and *rahim* (the compassionate), are much broader than the word *hubb* (love). Divine love, as Rumi says in the *Divan Shams Tabriz*, is hard to capture in words, in our speaking and listening, in our books and erudition. It is a mystery hard to unravel.

When asked about God's compassion and love, Prophet Muhammad illustrated with an example of a mother's protection of and sacrifices for her child. In a *hadith* (tradition) cited by Sahih Bukhari, the Prophet saw a woman in captivity who was searching until she found a little infant whom she took in and started to nurse compassionately. The Prophet turned to his companions and asked 'Would that mother deliberately throw her infant in the fire?' The companions replied 'No!' He then replied, 'You should know that God is more compassionate towards you than that mother is towards her infant.'

If a mother's compassion is unbounded, one fails to comprehend the limitless love, mercy, and compassion of the Creator who overlooks our shortcomings, covers our faults, and provides for us regardless of how unworthy we may be..

The root word of *rahma* in Arabic is *rahm*, the womb source of motherly love which surpasses any selfishness, and teaches us sacrifice and altruism. Compassion is part of our primordial being. The question is how best we can as a human race actively cultivate it so we can begin to turn the world into a place where we can live in harmony with each other, sharing, not robbing resources; being part of one community that was created equal in a state of existence, where we all acknowledge the bounty, grace, and compassion of the Creator, regardless of what name one may give to this Almighty force. Compassion ties us to the womb and defines our creation, one that should ideally govern all our actions.Such compassion is meaningless without the love of the other. It is about seeing the other in one's own image, seeing the humanity in the other, and upholding the dignity of the other, no matter how different they maybe in their looks, or ways of living; not wishing harm on another person that one would not wish for oneself, hoping for the same for the other, that one hopes for oneself. Doing *ihsan*, good and beautiful actions towards others, just as we would have them do unto us.

I. The Koran on Compassion

Among all God's attributes, the one that the Koran stresses most is mercy and compassion, the two attributes that every Muslim must emulate and master as a believer. All 114 chapters of the Koran, except one, begin in the name of God the most merciful and the most compassionate. Every action of a Muslim from beginning to end is to be guided by the same phrase, a constant reminder of the primacy of mercy and compassion in every action and thought, an awakening and guide to governing one's life with compassion. As one examines the real meaning of compassion in the Koran, it is an active state of being, a constant enjoining of doing what is good and beautiful, and repelling evil and ugliness. The Koran enjoins a holistic concept of mercy and compassion: being compassionate and merciful to oneself, one's family, neighbours and friends, and all of God's creation – human beings believing and unbelieving, upright and immoral, and beyond the human race to animals, birds, plants and trees – the whole environment.

Harmonious living in which compassion rules is a Muslim guide so as to receive compassion and mercy from God. In Islam, pluralism, not exclusivism, is the norm. Again, it is compassion towards fellow beings and being good and virtuous that ultimately matters for all believers.

'There is no compulsion in religion' (K: 2: 256); 'Truly, those who believe, and the Jews, and the Christians and Sabeans – whosoever believes in God and the Day of Judgement and act virtuously will receive their reward from their Lord; no fear of grief will befall them'. (K: 2: 62) and 'Whoever saves the life of one human being, it shall be as if he had saved the whole of humankind' (K: 5: 32)

The purpose of diversity in creation is described by the Koran as God's intended plan to allow humanity to get to know one another and the only competition among people is around doing good.

'O mankind, We have indeed created you as male and female, and made you as nations and tribes that you may come to know one another' (K: 49: 13); 'And every community has its direction of which He lets them turn towards it. Vie, therefore, with one another in doing good works. Wherever you may be, God will gather you all unto Him'. (K: 2: 148)

The best way to inculcate this level of compassion is first through reflection and contemplation or what the Koran calls *taffakur*: being one with the creation, nature, understanding the mystery of creation, and marveling at the balance and order in the universe, the signs or *ayat* of God.

Every verse in the Koran is also referred to as an *ayah*, a sign, something to contemplate and ponder upon and to try to live up to in the best possible spirit. The Koran exhorts Muslims to engage in compassionate living by being actively and positively engaged in the welfare and well-being of their fellow human beings. In the Koran there is a constant refrain of the best rewards for those who do good and uphold truth and justice.

What does doing good look like from a Koranic perspective? There are various categories of compassion in action outlined in the Koran. It begins with compassion for one's parents, considered as one of the most beautiful actions (*ihsan*), being compassionate to one's spouse and children, taking care of relatives, the poor, the neighbours, the wayfarer and the needy, and the orphans. 'Serve Allah, and join not any partners with Him; and do good – to parents, kinsfolk, orphans, those in need, neighbours who are near, neighbours who are strangers, the companion by your side, the wayfarer…' (K: 4: 36).

In Islam, being compassionate and sharing one's wealth with those in need is not seen as charity, something that would make the recipient obligated to the giver. Instead, *zakat*, the ordained sharing of one's wealth, is regarded as a form of self-purification, a benefit derived as a result of one's compassionate action towards the one in need. That act of sharing is for one's own prosperity.

'And do good, that you may prosper' (K: 22: 77).

This giving does not always have to be material as not everyone is in a positon to share material wealth. As a tradition of the Prophet states, a smile on the face of a human being and saying a good word is considered an act of charity. Since compassionate behaviour enjoins doing good and forbidding evil, standing up to injustice even if it is against one's own self is therefore a duty of every Muslim. 'You who believe! Be upholders of justice, bearing witness for Allah alone, even against yourselves or your parents and relatives' (K: 4: 135).

Any action that leads to harmonious living and betterment of society is an act of charity.

The Prophet Muhammad in one tradition says,

> Smiling at your brother is a Sadaqah (charity), enjoining the good is a Sadaqah, forbidding the wrong is a Sadaqah, guiding someone to the right path is a Sadaqah, and removing harmful things, thorns, bones from road is regarded as a Sadaqah. (Reported by Al-Tirmidhi and Ibn Hibban in his Sahih (nos. 474, 529)

The Koran also lays out how believers should respond when wronged, returning insults and cruelty with compassionate and patient behaviour. At a time when we find severe reaction from some Muslims to provocateurs engaged in insulting Islam or the Prophet, the Koranic commandment of a peaceful response is overlooked. While the pain, humiliation and insult through provocation in the name of religion is understandable, it is in trying times such as these the Prophetic example of rising above the provocateurs and responding with best character is necessary. As the Koran commands, the best way to respond to ignorant people is to bid them peace. 'And the servants of the Most Merciful are those who walk upon the earth easily, and when the ignorant address them [harshly], they say [words of] peace' (K: 25: 63).

II. The Prophet Muhammad as Example

Muslims look at the Prophet Muhammad as the best example for practicing their faith, especially his ways of active compassion. This practice was not always a path filled with ease, as the Prophet endured a lot of pain during his lifetime. At every step of the way he was challenged, his life threatened, as he sought to establish equity and justice in the society of his time. In a deeply traditional and clan-bound society, he challenged discrimination based on race, colour, creed, gender, family/tribal association, economic and social status. His concern for everyone, and his desire to end exploitation and oppression, made him a target of his own tribe. Yet he never relented, challenging the capitalistic and exploitative pagan traditions of the Meccans. He preached that 'no one of you can be a believer unless you desire for your neighbour what you desire for yourself', a practice that his enemies saw as a threat to their social fabric steeped in the exploitation of the other.

There are numerous Koranic verses that enjoin mercy, compassion, kindness, forbearance, patience, courtesy, friendship and seeking peace. Everyone is expected to strive for the good road, the steep ascent that is the way of compassion:

> But he hath made not haste on the path that is steep. And what will explain to thee the path that is steep? (It is) freeing the bondman; or the giving of food in a day of privation, to the orphan with claim of relationship, or to the indigent (down) in the dust. Then will he be of those who believe, and enjoin patience, (constancy, and self-restrain), and enjoin deeds of kindness and compassion. Such are the Companions of the Right hand. (K: 90: 11-18)

Forgiveness and Mercy as practiced by the Prophet towards his arch enemies upon his return to Mecca set an example for Muslims. Instead of seeking revenge, he chose to forgive those who oppressed and humiliated him and his community, eventually taking over Mecca without any bloodshed and declaring a general amnesty. Numerous *hadith* (traditions) of the Prophet repeat that a person who is unkind and hard hearted towards others is also devoid of God's Mercy. Hence, mercy and compassion in Islam is directly linked with one's faith and salvation. As a human being, as a father, grandfather, and husband, Prophet Muhammad was an embodiment of compassion and he led by example. He played and joked with children, spoke with kindness to all, visited the sick, cared for the welfare of all his neighbours, Muslim and those who disbelieved in him. He taught his followers that there is reward in showing compassion towards every living creature, not just humans. The Koran says of the Prophet, 'We did not send you but as a special mercy to the worlds' (K: 21: 71). Mercy is active compassion.

III. Cultivating Compassion through Action: Muslim Social Services of Kitchener Waterloo

A human can have nothing but what he/she strives for. (K: 53: 39)

Compassion cannot happen without our human effort to strive and struggle to change the human condition. Historically Muslims have dedicated their efforts at setting up institutions that help and serve the poor and the needy. In the small Canadian city of Kitchener Waterloo, Muslims Social Services (MSS), is committed to helping anyone: Muslim and non-Muslim in need. It is an agency that educates, creates awareness and also engages the community in active compassion through dialogue and understanding.

In 2007, a year and half after I arrived in Canada from the USA, and after immersing myself in community work, it was obvious that many Muslims, particularly Muslim women, were dedicating themselves to the betterment of other people's lives. Yet this was not an organized effort. In January 2007, a small not-for-profit volunteer driven organization, Muslim Social Services, was born. After seven years of operation without any financial investment, the organization became a full-fledged charity with a well-developed infrastructure and some part time staff, while the majority of the community work is still mainly carried out by community volunteers of all faiths and backgrounds.

The key aspects of MSS work include:

Equitable Dialogue through Action: At a time when 'dialogue' is a fashionable word and interfaith dialogue is often paraded as an expression of good will, very little time is spent on listening and understanding, acceptance and belonging without imposition. The goal of MSS has been to promote respectful and equitable dialogue, often through collaborative action-oriented projects. Those projects include cooking and serving a meal in the local soup kitchens, packing relief kits for victims of disasters and war in far off lands, intentionally seeking opportunities to understand how parenting or financial matters are viewed in different faith traditions and coming together as members of the Abrahamic faith traditions to sponsor and support refugees in our community.

Our emphasis is on moving away from the language of loving thy enemy to loving thy neighbour. Language is a powerful tool and framing another human being or a community as an enemy breeds exclusivism and superiority. Compassion shown towards an 'enemy' reeks of superiority: a superior being, faith, or culture, reaching out to the sinner, the less worthy, and the lost. Such characterization burdens the action with a barrier that is hard to break: a suspicion of the other. It makes the 'enemy' beholden to the 'charitable master' resulting in a power imbalance. Active compassion as an agent of change in interfaith work is one of the key goals of bridge-building through awareness and understanding of the other, real listening, and dialoguing about faith and issues of common concern. But even more importantly, it involves working alongside each other as people believing in the common cause of helping those in need.

Compassion builds through human interaction, encountering the stranger, whether that stranger is a new refugee from a far off land, or our next door neighbour, whom we fear. Humanizing the other through encounters and dialogue, true and equitable conversation, and allowing oneself to be vulnerable through trust building, while sharing one's experiences and faith perspectives without judgement is the way ahead. Dialogue through action and gatherings of friendship have been a great source of building understanding in our community.

Building Compassion through Social Assistance: A vibrant food programme that offers help to families struggling to make ends meet, cooking and feeding people in soup kitchens, shelters and prisons, are of course all basic services MSS offers in line with the religious commandment to take care of the poor, the needy, orphans, the wayfarer and the neighbour.

Creating Safe Families: It is impossible to be compassionate and kind when our souls and families are broken with violence. The Safer Families Program at MSS aims at ending the scourge of domestic violence and providing education on Islamic perspectives on domestic violence to members of the community as well as service providers. Through a culturally and faith sensitive approach, victims of family violence receive counselling and care in an atmosphere where there are no barriers to understanding the cultural and faith perspectives.

Compassionate Integration: In an effort to provide various opportunities to newcomers to belong in their new environment, MSS programmes whether computer literacy workshops, welcome to Canada youth and adult programmes, youth and women empowerment workshops, artistic expression through drama, fine arts or poetry, language lessons, parenting groups or educational workshops, are all aimed at building a welcoming new home for new members of our community. MSS also offers programmes for service providers to prepare them to understand the need of newcomers coming from diverse backgrounds.

Creating Opportunities for Building Compassion through Action: Volunteering as givers, teachers, change makers, educators, spiritual care providers; supporting incarcerated youth and adults, comforting those in prisons and shelters, caring for the families of the bereaved, helping parents struggling to care for their children, reaching out to the sick and the bereaved,finding ways to support end of life decisions and much more are the types of volunteering opportunities provided through MSS.

For Muslims, just as with people of other faiths, the road map to being compassionate and caring is already there, what remains is an active participation and embracing of the guiding principles in their true spirit, free of adulteration and distortions. At a time when Muslims around the world are treated with suspicion for the acts of a few deviants, and the faith itself is attacked, there is a necessity to embrace compassion in one's self care as well as in responding to hate and prejudice with compassion. Compassion is the only cleanser sure to soften our hardened hearts that will make us healthy and caring individuals and societies.

CHAPTER 18

Zakat: A Practice of Compassion

MAULANA WAHIDUDDIN KHAN

THE KORAN, THE book of Islam, is a book of peace. The very first verse of the Koran reads: 'In the name of God, the Most Merciful, the most Compassionate' (1: 2). This verse, which is repeated in the Koran one hundred and fourteen times, clearly shows that the God of Islam is the God of Mercy and Compassion, and the book of Islam is also the book of mercy. Likewise, the people of Islam must also possess the qualities of mercy and compassion, otherwise they could not be true believers.

Mercy and compassion have been accorded a prominent place in the scripture of Islam and also the various teachings and practices of Islam aim to cultivate these qualities in those who follow Islam. Instilling compassion for our fellow-beings is at the heart of Islamic rituals such as *namaz* (prayer) and *zakat* (alms-giving), Islamic festivals of Eid al-Fitr and Eid al-Azha and the Islamic mission of *dawah*, that is, conveying the message of God to all humanity. In the present paper, I would like to expound on the concept of charity as a practice of compassion in Islam.

The Basis for Charity

Charity, preached by every religion of the world, is a way of bringing justice to society. And since justice is the essence of religion, Islam has therefore made charity or *zakat* obligatory and binding upon all those who embrace the faith; it has been made into an institution in order to give it permanence and regularity.

All human beings, according to Islam, have been created by one and the same God, and for this reason they belong to one great brotherhood. All being descendants of the same progenitor, Adam and Eve, they should naturally be each other's well-wishers. They must willingly come to one another's assistance, like members of the same large family. Islam has, therefore, laid the greatest of emphasis on the support of destitute and disabled members of society. It is a sacred duty of the wealthy to give part of their possessions to fulfil the needs of the deprived sections of the community.

A society can flourish only when its members do not spend all their wealth on the satisfaction of their own desires but reserve a portion of it for parents, relatives, neighbours, the poor and the incapacitated. According to a well-known saying, 'Charity begins at home.' A true believer is thus always prepared, after meeting the needs of his family, to assist other people in need of his help.

Compassion for the Needy

There are two forms of charity in Islam – obligatory and voluntary, called *zakat* and *sadaqat* respectively. *Zakat* comes from the verb *zaka*, which signifies 'to thrive', 'to be wholesome' or 'to be pure'. Giving up a portion of the wealth one possesses in excess of what is needed for sustenance is to 'purify' or legalize it so that the remainder may lawfully be used by the almsgiver.

Deducting *zakat* from one's earnings is a material acknowledgment of the fact that the actual giver is God. Since the giver is God, the recipient is duty bound to spend it in His cause. The principle of *zakat* is to take from those who have wealth and give it away to those who do not. This rotation of wealth is a way to balance social inequality.

Islam has established this institution to make concern for the poor a permanent and compulsory duty. This means an annual contribution of 2.5 per cent of one's income to public welfare. The rate on other types of wealth such as agricultural produce and jewellery is more. It is incumbent on minors and adults, males and females, living or dead.

Islamic law empowers the Islamic State or Community to collect such contributions and keep a separate account of them. The funds thus accumulated must be spent on the eight categories specified in the Koran namely, the poor and the destitute, the wayfarer, the bankrupt, the needy, converts, captives, the collectors of *zakat*, and in the cause of God (2: 177). The last category allows such funds to be used for the general welfare of the community – for education of the people, for public works, and for any other need of the Muslim community.

Zakat in spirit is an act of worship while in its external form it is the carrying out of social service. It is thus not just the payment of a tax as it is generally understood, but is rather an act of religious significance. Its importance is underscored by the fact that the Koran treats it at par with *salat* (prayer). The Koran frequently enjoins the believers 'to perform the worship and pay the *zakat*'. It goes to the extent of saying that one cannot attain righteousness unless one spends out of one's wealth for the love of God: 'By no means shall you attain righteousness, unless you give of that which you love' (3: 92).

So the test of charity lies not in giving away something we have discarded but the things that we value greatly, something that we love. It is unselfishness that God demands. It may be in any form – one's personal efforts, talents, skill, learning, property or possessions.

In verse 273 of the second chapter, the Koran states, 'Charity is for those in need.' This is general principle which enjoins us to help people in need, be they good or bad, on the right path or not, Muslims or non-Muslims. We are not supposed to judge in these matters. The chief ends in charity, as reiterated here, should be God's pleasure and our own spiritual good.

The concept of charity in Islam is thus linked with justice. It is not limited to the redressal of grievances. It implies apart from the removal of handicaps, the recognition of the right that every human being has to attain the fullness of life.

Beyond Obligatory Almsgiving

The demand of Islam that all its followers should spend their wealth freely on the common good of society cannot be fully met by the payment of the obligatory levy of *zakat*. According to a tradition, the Prophet observed: 'In one's wealth there is a due (to God and His people) besides *zakat*.' Ali, the fourth Caliph, explained this saying thus: 'God has ordained that the rich are to pay out of their wealth to that extent which is sufficient for the needs of the poor; so that if they do not find food and clothing, or any other need remains to be fulfilled, it would be because the rich are not doing their duty, and for this God will take them to task on the Day of Judgment.'

According to Abdullah ibn Umar, the great religious scholar of the first phase of Islam, 'If the *zakat* levy is insufficient to meet the needs of the poor; then it is the duty of the rich of every town to put the poor on their feet.'

Abu Dharal-Ghifari, a companion of the Prophet, reported that the Prophet, while sitting in the shade of the Kabah wall, said, 'They are the losers.' Abu Dhar enquired, 'Who are they, O Messenger of God?' The Prophet replied: 'Those who pile up heaps of wealth and do not spend' (Sahih Bukhari).

There are many verses in the Koran and many traditions of the Prophet making it quite clear that there is a due over and above *zakat* and that the wealthy are not relieved of their duties solely on payment of *zakat*. The Koran uses the word *haq*, or the right of the poor. So, what the wealthy person is asked to give is not charity but that which should be given to the poor as a matter of right.

All the expenditure of people in need in an Islamic society is covered by *sadaqat* (meaning literally 'righteousness' from the root *sadaqa*, that is, 'to speak the truth', 'to be true'). This is a very wide term used in the Koran. In Islamic literature, this is referred to as *sadaqat al-tatawwu*, or spontaneous almsgiving.

According to Ibn Arabi, almsgiving is called *sadaqat* to indicate the sincerity (*sidq*) of the giver's religious belief (*Akham al-Koran,* 2/946-7). He goes on to say that *sadaqat* is a voluntary act of worship, a choice made of one's own free will. If the act is other than voluntary, it has no religious merit:'For man makes it obligatory for himself, just as God makes mercy obligatory for Himself towards those who repent.'

The only difference between *sadaqat* and *zakat* is that while both kinds of almsgiving are necessarily voluntary (that being the reason for the word *sadaqat* covering both forms of contribution) the former is the result of an inspiration on the part of the donor as befits certain sets of circumstances, whereas *zakat* is given on the basis of a fixed percentage (*nisab*)of the donor's wealth so that the amount given will not vary according to the needs of a particular donee, but according to the earnings of the donor. In the case of *zakat* there is also a system of collection set up under Islamic law and there are persons appointed as collectors of these dues. The money thus collected is meant for the general benefit of the community. In the case of *sadaqat*, the bequest is made directly and spontaneously from one individual to another and the amount given is at the discretion of the giver.

The Spirit of Charity

If a very high standard has been set for charity, it is because *zakat* and *sadaqat* are performed by believers not just as moral obligations to society, but as sincere endeavours to gain God's pleasure. In his commentary on the Koran, Abdullah Yusuf Ali sums up the spirit of charity thus: It must be given in the way of God, it must expect no reward in this world, it must not be followed by reference or reminders to the acts of charity and still less should any annoyance or injury be caused to the recipient, for example, by boasting that the giver relieved the person in the hour of need.

The Koran says that when true believers help others in charity, their hearts tremble with fear (8: 2). When we give something to somebody we are the givers and the other is the taker, so we should develop pride, but why does the Koran say that the believers tremble in fear? The reason is that when a believer gives away in charity to a needy person, he sees his own self in that person. He realizes that this person is needy today, while I may become needy and deprived when we stand before God on Judgment Day. This realization instills fear in his heart and his giving in charity turns into a prayer: 'O God, one day I too will appear before You as a person in need. Do not keep me deprived on that day.' When seeing a helpless person, we should remember that we too are helpless before God.

Thus the spirit of kindness and well-wishing is the essence of charity. The giver is not to expect any reward from the beneficiary as an abundant reward – whether material, moral, or spiritual. And it is God who will deem what is best to confer on His servant.

Since charity is purely for the sake of God, it has value only if something good and valuable is given. It should be lawfully earned or acquired by the giver. It should include such things as are of use and value to others. Charity is, in the words of the Prophet, to place a thing in the palm of God. It is therefore obvious that placing worthless things in the hand of God dishonours Him.

There are some people who think that acts of charity would ruin them. Abdullah Yusuf Ali comments on such doubts: 'No kind or generous act ever ruined one.' We have never heard of anyone who, due to his generosity to good causes, has been impoverished. It is because God has promised to shower such a person with greater bounties (2: 268). On the other hand, false generosity, that is, extravagant expenditure for show or self-indulgence does lead people to ruin.

Extending Help in Education

The spirit of helping others to earn God's pleasure is best reflected in Muslim society in the field of education. Inspired by traditions of the Prophet that the greatest charity for a Muslim being to learn something and then teaching it to others (Musnad Ahmad), Muslims in large numbers have devoted themselves to other's education generation after generation.

Knowledge is the most wonderful thing in the whole universe. That is why there is nothing greater than knowledge being imparted by one human being to another. Muslims on a large scale have engaged themselves in receiving education and imparting it to others, individually as well as by establishing *maktabs* and *madrasas*, that is, primary schools and colleges. These educational institutions established in the house of teachers or in separate buildings, generally made no charges for instruction. During the medieval period, these *madrasas* flourished in tens of thousands throughout the Muslim world. The wealthy people helped in running these *madrasas*, not only through *zakat*, but also by making endowments (*wakf*) of their properties. The income from these properties met the needs of these schools. The orphans and poor people were given stipends over and above free boarding and lodging. *Sadaqa* in the form of *wakf* is known as *sadaqa-e-jariya*, i.e. continued almsgiving. Helping someone to establish himself in business, giving someone a proper education; helping someone to recover from some disease by monetary assistance to looking after the orphans and the destitute; giving scholarships to students, all such charitable works, come under *sadaqa-e-jariya* – that is why so many centres of social welfare have continued to function in the Muslim community.

Conclusion

Sadaqat is a very wide term and is used in the Koran to cover all kinds of charity. Its scope is so vast that even the poor who can have nothing tangible to give can offer *sadaqa* in the shape of a smile or a glass of water to a thirsty person, or they may even just utter a kindly word. Good conduct is frequently termed *sadaqa* in the traditions of the Prophet. Planting something from which a person, bird or animal later eats also counts as *sadaqa*. In this extended sense, acts of loving kindness, even greeting another with a cheerful face, is regarded as *sadaqa*. In short, every good deed is *sadaqa*.

PART VI

PRACTICES OF COMPASSION IN CHRISTIANITY

CHAPTER 19

Practices of Compassion among Anabaptists

VIC FROESE

MY FATHER ONCE told me the story of receiving 20 dollars from a Mennonite donor from Canada who wanted to help him and his family. Knowing my dad was a proud man, I expected him to say that he returned the money. But at the time the donation came, he was living in a small shack in the Paraguayan Chaco, a lowland plain of tough prairie grasses and thickets affectionately known as the 'green hell'. It was 1950, when Mennonites were still experimenting to determine which crops could stand up to the blistering summer sun, and getting far more misses than hits. His 'family' consisted of his mother and two sisters, his father having been arrested and summarily executed in Soviet Ukraine in 1937. Dad was only eighteen years old and had already been the 'man of the house' for thirteen years. And he knew that twenty Canadian dollars could buy much needed food supplies and farm tools, and make life a little less miserable. So he kept the money and promised God that if he ever found his way out of 'this hellhole', he would be as generous as that Canadian Mennonite. A decade later, he was in Canada. He kept his promise, and continues to keep it now that he is in his eighties and living in a seniors' home.

Had he not himself experienced the difference it can make, my father would probably have been charitable anyway. It's what Mennonites do. They are nothing if not a generous, helpful people. These characteristics can be traced back to the Anabaptists (literally, re-baptizers) of the Reformation period, the spiritual ancestors of Mennonites, Amish, Hutterites, Brethren in Christ, and others. Anabaptists made love of God and neighbour the centre-piece of their spirituality and ethics, going so far as to include enemies as neighbours, as Jesus himself had. The teachings of Jesus – 'Turn the other cheek', 'Love your enemies, and pray for those who persecute you' – made every human being, friend or foe, a fit recipient of Christian compassion.

Nowhere is the indiscriminate nature of Anabaptist compassion better illustrated than in the story of Dirk Willems (d. 1569). Willems was a young Dutch Anabaptist arrested one winter by Dutch Catholic authorities for his stubborn membership in the 'heretical' sect. He managed to escape prison, but was chased by a guard. As Willems dashed across a frozen pond, he heard a cry for help. He looked back to see the guard in a hole in the ice, flailing his arms to keep his head above the frigid water. Though he knew the consequences that might follow, Willems quickly ran and rescued the man, at which point he was recaptured and dragged back to prison. Mercilessly tortured there, Willems was later executed by burning at the stake. Anabaptists believed that in this remarkable demonstration of a loving kindness stronger even than the self-preservation instinct, Willems was following the example of Jesus the Christ, whose own extravagant love for the world took him to the cross.

Fortunately, obedience to the Messiah did not always require the ultimate sacrifice. Jesus had also said, 'By this all men will know that you are my disciples, if you have love for one another' (John 13: 35). Loving each other and attending to the needy amongst them was no less a messianic commandment than loving those set on killing them. Much of the history of Anabaptists and their offspring can be seen as working out how to love 'brothers and sisters in the Lord' and, at the same time, malicious neighbours. Menno Simons, a leader of Dutch Anabaptists from whom Mennonites take their name, encapsulated the Anabaptist understanding of Christian love in his famous ode to 'true evangelical faith':

> True evangelical faith cannot lie dormant.
> It clothes the naked,
> it feeds the hungry,
> it comforts the sorrowful,
> it shelters the destitute,
> it serves those that harm it,
> it binds up that which is wounded,
> it has become all things to all people.

Despite holding Jesus as their common measuring stick for Christian compassion, the practices developed by different Anabaptist communities are varied. For the Hutterites, loving each other was expressed in a community of goods, the main purpose of which was to ensure that the poor were no needier than anyone else in the community. In the sixteenth century, 'the poor' typically consisted of widows and orphans, many of whom were the collateral victims of Protestant or Catholic civil authorities who had arrested and executed their husbands or parents. Other Anabaptists, however, rejected the teaching of the community of goods, in part because owning material goods is a prerequisite for the sacrifice of charity, which they agreed was a non-negotiable obligation for true Christians. Not the obligation, but the means of fulfilling it were disputed. Every Anabaptist community developed some system of helping the needy, whether through deacons, a 'poor chest' (*Armenkasse* in German), special collections of money or food, the sharing of tools and equipment, or some combination of these and others. Individual members would naturally be expected to offer what help they could, when they could – baked goods, meals, clothing, feed for animals, or even assisting with the harvesting of crops. No doubt some impetus to care for the less fortunate came from the awareness that they never knew when they themselves might become needy. But obedience to the Bible, to Jesus in particular, was the principal incentive for the devout.

In modern times, especially where Mennonites made their homes in urban settings where a faith community might be scattered in various neighbourhoods across a city, maintaining such compassionate practices has become more challenging than in the intimate communal settings of rural Switzerland, Holland, Prussia, Ukraine, or even in North America, where daily face-to-face interaction kept people in close touch with each other. In the United States, some of those practices were institutionalized in order to address the multiplying needs of Mennonites in the modern industrial age. Mennonite Mutual Aid (MMA), incorporated in 1945 and sponsored by the Mennonite General Conference, was designed to enable American Mennonites of that denomination to continue the time-honoured practice of sharing with financially strapped brothers and sisters, mainly by lending them money. Conscientious objectors returning home from years of Civilian Public Service after the Second World War were the first recipients of MMA assistance. Since its inception, the services offered by MMA have proliferated, and now include banking, insurance, investments, asset management, financial planning, and stewardship education. Now known as Everence, the cooperative no longer focusses narrowly on the indigent, but it hasn't abandoned them either. 'Improved livelihoods of underserved groups through community development investments' remains part of its reason for being.

It was also in modern times that Anabaptists began to broaden the net of their practices to include those outside their tribe. No institution better exemplifies that enlargement of vision than Mennonite Central Committee (MCC), an organization that for the last ninety-five years has worked to provide relief and development aid in more than fifty countries around the world.

MCC was born in the United States in 1920, a response by American Mennonites of various stripes to a severe famine that hit Mennonite colonies in Ukraine in the early years of the Soviet era. Effects of the famine were made worse by the civil war that raged between Imperial and Bolshevik armies, by marauding bands of anarchists targeting Mennonite villages, and by typhoid epidemics that reduced the Mennonite population by a tenth. When news came to Mennonites in the United States that large numbers of Russian Mennonites could soon die of starvation, a small committee met in Elkhart, Indiana, to identify ways of getting food and farming equipment to the most desperate. In eighteen months the new MCC managed to feed 75,000 starving Ukrainian people, 60,000 of them Mennonites. The Committee had overcome huge logistical and bureaucratic obstacles to accomplish the feat, which those involved properly attributed to the miraculous intervention of God.

The famine relief work in Russia was completed in 1926, by which time talk of disbanding MCC had already begun. But MCC, originally an ad hoc committee, refused to die. Over the next fifty years, MCC became a virtual conglomerate of inter-Mennonite cooperative ventures in dozens of countries around the world: post-World War II refugee settlement; experimental farming in Paraguay and Greece; teacher training in Newfoundland and numerous African countries;

medical programmes in Vietnam, Congo, Haiti, Bolivia, and elsewhere; Christmas bundles for children around the world; meat, fruit, and vegetable canning operations to feed the hungry; child sponsorship; self-help programmes; administering the Civilian Public Service during the Second World War; mental health facilities and rest homes; disaster recovery services; and overseeing the international Paxprogram (1951 to 1976).

Since the 1970s, several of these initiatives have grown significantly. Mennonite Disaster Service (MDS), now independent of MCC, is sixty-six years old and has sent thousands of workers across the United States and Canada (and occasionally elsewhere), helping communities recover from devastating floods, droughts, tornadoes, wild fires, earthquakes, and hurricanes. When the Second World War was over, MCC was encouraged by some of those who had worked in psychiatric facilities during their time in the Civilian Public Service to establish hospitals for those suffering with mental disturbances. It finally did so in the 1950s and 1960s, in Maryland, California (2), Kansas, and Indiana.

Though MCC's involvement in refugee re-settlement began in 1929 with Mennonites fleeing the Soviet Union, this kind of work has been a major part of MCC's portfolio for many years. Forty years ago, MCC along with many Anabaptist churches assisted in settling many of the 60,000 Vietnamese, Cambodian, and Laotian refugees (a.k.a., 'boat people') who made their way to Canada, a success story by any measure. Today, thanks to MCC, many of the Syrian refugees now in Europe and Somali refugees in East Africa are finding church sponsors in North America who will do the hard work of helping refugee families learn English, find homes and jobs, pay rent, register children in schools, manage money, obtain health care, and so on. (My own church in Steinbach, Manitoba, has adopted a Somali Muslim family and committed itself to supporting it for the foreseeable future.)

Another example of compassion directed to people outside the Anabaptist camp, though not often described as such, is missions and evangelism. Relative to relief and service work, sharing the Christian gospel elicits far less enthusiasm from many Mennonites. The forces that have dampened zeal for spreading the good news of Jesus the

Messiah are many, the two most potent ones being fears that past mistakes will be repeated (colonialism) and that others will think them narrow-minded and arrogant in regarding their 'belief system' as uniquely and exclusively 'correct' (fundamentalism). Moreover, the conviction is widespread that the gospel is best 'preached' through deeds of love rather than words.

Still, the sense is strong among others that works of compassion alone can only communicate so much. Words are necessary to provide a fuller account of the faith that drives Mennonite Christians to do such works. Inviting others to faith is also to invite them into the community of faith, and this mirrors God's compassionate invitation to all people to draw near to him and so experience fullness of life. Mission agencies like MB Mission and others now recognize that winning souls, promoting social and economic justice, and building churches are tightly interrelated activities. Mission workers, aware that some missions in the past have gone badly wrong, are determined not to repeat those mistakes. They remain certain, however, that helping the lost and unbelieving find the God revealed in Jesus as love is as much an act of compassion as feeding the hungry, giving water to the thirsty, or visiting those in prison.

Notwithstanding the significant compassionate work done by MMA, MCC, MDS, and mission organizations; personal and communal acts of compassion will never cease to be necessary on this side of eternity. The variety of injuries and evils that may visit persons and communities is great, much of it coming from those who are wounded themselves. On 2 October 2006, Charles Carl Roberts IV walked into an Amish school house in West Nickel Mines, Pennsylvania, and shot eight young girls. They ranged in age from six to thirteen. Five of them died. Roberts himself died of a self-inflicted gunshot wound. Not long after learning the identity of the shooter, an Amish neighbour visited Roberts's distraught wife and their children to console them. Other members of the community also went to comfort Roberts's parents and parents-in-law. Realizing that the loss of a husband and father would mean financial hardship, the Amish community established a fund for the Roberts family. About thirty Amish attended Roberts's funeral; Roberts's wife Marie was invited to the funeral of one of the Amish girls.

This moving story, like Dirk Willem's tale, is one of a compassion that overcomes instinctive reactions. How natural it would have been for the traumatized Amish community, especially parents of the girls, to blame Marie for failing to act on signs that her husband was losing his grip on reality, or Roberts's parents for raising a son capable of murdering innocent young girls. But this deeply faith-shaped community, steeped in the Gospels, met a horrific deed with a compassionate response. Their grief at losing their children was no less intense than any other community's would have been, but their faith would not let them blame others or ignore the profound sorrow of the families Roberts was part of. By God's grace, love of their own spilt over into love of others in an astonishingly Christ-like way.

Not everyone in the Anabaptist family would respond to human tragedy like this in the same way. Natural instincts can only rarely be kept on a short leash consistently. All Anabaptists, however, would feel the tug of the Amish example on their hearts and hope that faced with similar heartbreak they too would have the faith and grace to show compassion to their enemies. At the very least, the Amish would remind them that apathy in the face of the suffering of their neighbours – near or far, friends or foes – is not an option for followers of Jesus, for those who love God. The imitation of Christ to which Anabaptists feel called is in the first instance the imitation of his mercy and love.

CHAPTER 20

Passions and the Disciplines of Compassion: Christian Orthodoxy on the Spiritual Life

DAVID J. GOA

'WHAT I DO, I would not. What I would, I do not.'[1] Why is it that so often we human beings fail to act out of our own centre? Rather, we react to what is before us out of previous experiences, forgotten struggles or idealized hopes and dreams. What is uppermost in our mind or heart frames and colours how we see what is coming to greet us. Our mind has prepared the ground for what we assume is before us and our passions, our suffering, shape how we react. We fail to be present to what is. Old patterns are called forth, fill the space and bracket new possibilities, spontaneity, actual engagement. Of all the creatures in the world, at least as far as we know, we human beings are the only ones who have the capacity to *not* live our own life. We live the moment based on the landscape of yesterday or our dreams of tomorrow. 'What I do, I would not. What I would, I do not.' This diagnosis of our spiritual disease dates from the foundations of the Christian tradition.

The central challenge to the spiritual life of human beings is not acquiring virtue, not even the virtue of compassion. The central challenge is our passions,[2] our suffering, our illusions, our stepping out of life, our 'missing of the mark.'[3] So, it is not surprising that we have a story called, 'The Passion'[4] at the centre of the Gospel. Odd, how such an awful story of the killing of the best of human beings, an innocent man, comes to be seen as a divine revelation, indeed, the 'good news' at the very heart of human nature and what holds the world together. The passion story of Jesus Christ anchors all Orthodox spiritual discipline. It is a haunting, tragic, and liberating narrative.

It is a narrative of him who we see as the fullest expression of human nature and all we really know of God. His life, acts, and teachings reveal to us the 'Word of life', unveiling for us our deepest nature. It invites us to the recovery of our nature through emptying ourselves of our passions so we may be present to what is given in each encounter in the life of the world. It is the disciplines of self-emptying[5] that opens, nurtures, and enlarge our capacity to be present without desire or fear. In that presence our heart and mind are attentive to the passions of others, to their suffering. Co-suffering love, compassion, bubbles up when our own struggles, our passions, are no longer front and centre.

Confession as Self-emptying

Many years ago when I first began my field research on the liturgical life of the Orthodox Church I witnessed a young man bow and place his head on a Gospel Book that graced a side altar. This was his final preparation for ordination. A fresco icon of the crucifixion of Jesus Christ flanked by the two thieves covered the wall in front of him. If he had looked up he would stare into the dark pit underneath the cross. He would be looking at a skull and cross-bones, looking into the face of death. Tradition has it that Golgotha was the burial place of Adam and Eve, the burial place of the human nature. Holy tradition has it that the blood of Jesus Christ flows down onto the bones and, as the icon of the Anastasis,[6] the Resurrection, unveils, calls forth Adam and Eve from the grave. The Passion and Resurrection of Jesus Christ restore human nature.

A priest in full vestments moves beside him and places his *epitrachelion* (stole), the insignia of holy office, over the head of the penitent. He leans down and whispers in his ear. I, of course, did not hear what he said or what the penitent spoke as he knelt there for the better part of an hour. Later I asked the priest what he had spoken. He told me that he assured the young man of God's enduring love, that there was no sin that God had not already forgiven, and that he was free to speak whatever was on his heart. He then gave a meditation of the icon of the Crucifixion and the two thieves. He asked: 'Which thief are you? Are you the one on the left, who, even when he was dying refused to recognize his situation and simply cursed the Giver of Life? Or, are you the one on the right who recognized he was in death's grip and turns to the Lover of the World saying, 'I know why I am here, that I am dying. Remember me today in your Kingdom.'

These words echoed the following day in the Sunday liturgy. As the priest is praying the Eucharistic prayer over the gifts of bread and wine, and calling on the Holy Spirit to make them the body and blood of Jesus Christ, he is joined by the faithful in a prayer that includes the following: 'Of thy mystical supper, O Son of God, accept me this day as a partaker; For I will not speak of the mystery to thine enemies, nor will I give thee a kiss like Judas; but like the thief I will acknowledge thee: Remember me, O lord, in thy Kingdom.'[7]

'Remember' is not about memory. We often confuse the two. Rather it is an expression of the human heart to resurrect from what has cut one off from life. And, death in Orthodox theology is not the same as mortality. Death is a spiritual condition, being possessed by passions in ways that remove one from the presence of life. The priest went on to tell me that he asked the young man what it was that was getting between him and the life of the world, the fullness of life that is the Presence of the Kingdom.

Some years later the practice of confession became part of my spiritual discipline. My liturgical family chants the Vesper Liturgy on Saturday evening after sunset in candlelight. Since light comes out of darkness, Orthodoxy, as with the Jewish tradition, has its first service of the Sabbath on Saturday night. As we chant the Psalms some of the faithful are prompted to move forward to the side altar, bend their head down to the Gospel Book and, as with the young man, engage the discipline of confession in the hope of healing. This liturgical family has people from many different walks of life. I sometimes think it includes the whole 'ship of fools', the brilliant and ignorant, pleasant and boorish, arrogant and humble, those with words and those who have yet to find a language that speaks their heart. One of the faithful is a man of national reputation. He has a style I have slowly learned to appreciate and, I have often thought, his politics is beyond the pale. I had grown to a modest appreciation of him although his politics continued to stick in my craw. I remember the evening I first saw him slowly make his way to the side altar and bend his head. We were chanting Psalm 141:

With my voice unto the Lord have I cried, with my voice unto the Lord have I made supplication.
I will pour out before him my supplication, mine affliction before Him will I declare.
When my spirit was fainting within me, then Thou knewest my paths.
In this way wherein I have walked they hid for me a snare.
I looked upon my right hand, and beheld, and there was none that did know me.
Flight hath failed me, and there is none that watcheth out for my soul.
I have cried unto Thee, O Lord; I said: Thou art my hope, my portion art Thou in the land of the living.
Attend unto my supplication, for I am brought very low.
Deliver me from them that persecute me, for they are stronger than I.
Bring my soul out of prison that I may confess Thy Name.
The righteous shall wait patiently for me until Thou shalt reward me.[8]

As he slowly rose from his confession, received the priest's blessing and wiped a tear from his eye my heart was filled with warmth and I wanted only to embrace him and ask his forgiveness for the 'snares' I had set for him, for not knowing him in his deep humanity. I had cared more about his politics than for his soul.

In the early Christian community the spiritual discipline of confession was public. Speaking of one's passions to the whole community became too much for many to bear and elevated shame in ways that damaged instead of healed. In the Roman Catholic tradition, this situation led to private confession with a priest. In Orthodoxy, however, it simply came to be shaped as I have described since part of the discipline of the public act of confession in the midst of worship deepens our compassion for each other by strengthening our recognition of the common human struggle.

The spiritual discipline of confession is cradled in the whole of the liturgical life. The Liturgy of Saint John Chrysostom is the large common prayer of the Church, itself a discipline for the healing of the mind and heart and of our relationship to self, others, and the life of the world.[9] The most common word in Chrysostom's liturgy that continues to be used in its original Greek form is *kyrieeleison*, 'Lord have mercy'. It is a short repeated prayer that punctuates all the cries of the human heart that makes up the public work that is the churches' prayer. We first encounter it in the *Apostolic Constitutions* (*c.* 375). But, of course, it is much older with deep roots in the Hebrew Bible. The writers of the Greek New Testament, particularly the Apostle Paul, were steeped in the Psalms where the Hebrew word *hesed* is ubiquitous. It means 'steadfast love' and is usually translated with the English word 'mercy'. In every Divine Liturgy *kyrieeleison*, is chanted at least forty, fifty, a hundred times. The root Greek word is *eleos*, the name of the olive tree. This should not surprise us since olive oil was the primary ointment in the ancient world. It purifies, aids healing, and ultimately makes the scare tissue of wounds supple again. The Orthodox sensibility is one of healing. God is the 'Lover of Humankind' as the Divine Liturgy repeats, the One whose love is steadfast, forgiving, seeking the return of all creation to wholeness.[10]

In Christian Orthodox traditions compassion is not a heroic virtue. Rather it flows naturally from every human heart when the heart and mind are restored, healed of the cumulative sufferings that mark human experience. The spiritual disciplines of a liturgical life anchor the faithful in divine mercy and invite the unspoken passions to surface and the will to open to the 'grace that is everywhere present'. They seek to restore the deepest of human desires, the desire to be present to the gift of our life together in the world and accept the healing of all that stands in the way. And, that is why confessors and spiritual fathers and mothers will often remind the penitent that the sin, the passion, they have confessed is also a gift revealing our human struggle and inviting us to a deeper compassion for others with whom we share such struggles. And when they anoint the penitents forehead with oil it is the oil of gladness healing the wounds so mercy may flow into the life of the world.

Notes

1. These are the words of a great struggler, a Jew with a good Greek education, in the first century of the common era. The Apostle Paul knew this condition in the marrow of his being. In many of his letters he discusses one or another aspect of this disease. Romans 7: 15-20.

2. 'Passion' means 'suffering' in the Orthodox literature on the spiritual life. In the Orthodox understanding of the human nature, human desires are not disordered. Rather, the Fall narrative is a revelation of self-forgetfulness. In Orthodox spiritual theology healing and restoration is the point.
3. 'Missing the mark' connotes an archery term, to miss the target. For Jews, the goal or target of life is life itself, being present to the existence given when we are born into the world.
4. The 'passion narratives' take up a substantial part of the four Gospels, Matthew 26: 30-27: 66; Mark 14: 26-15: 47; Luke 22: 39-23: 56; and, John 18: 1-19: 42. These texts are at play in every Orthodox Liturgy and form the bulk of the liturgies shaping Holy Week leading up to and including Pascha, the Feast of Resurrection.
5. 'Self-emptying' is at the centre of the apophatic theology of the Christian East. See, 'The Spiritual Way', *John Chryssavgis in The Cambridge Companion to Orthodox Christian Theology*, ed. Mary B. Cunningham and Elizabeth Theokritoff (Cambridge: Cambridge University Press, 2008): 150-63
6. Anna D. Kartsonis, *Anastasis*: *The Making of an Image* (Princeton, New Jersey: Princeton University Press, 1986).
7. *The Orthodox Liturgy* (Oxford: Oxford University Press, 1982): 89
8. *A Prayer Book for Orthodox Christians* (Boston, Massachusetts: Holy Transfiguration Monastery, 2005): 36-7.
9. The word 'liturgy' has been used for the church's common prayer since the first century. It is the Greek word for public service or public work. In Orthodox spiritual theology the liturgy is thought to be the prayer, not for personal salvation or the salvation of those who are faithful. Rather, it is the prayer for the healing of the world and preparation of the faithful to engage in the compassionate works of mercy for the life of the world.
10. It is interesting to note that the word 'justice' is only used once in the Orthodox Liturgy and many times in Western liturgies.

CHAPTER 21

Practices of Compassion: The Way of the Heart in Christianity

M. DARROL BRYANT

ON 12 NOVEMBER 2015, Interfaith Grand River, a local interfaith group gathered for its monthly meeting. Around the table we had Buddhists, Hindus, Muslims, Jews, a Bahai and a wide range of Christians (Catholic, Mennonite, Lutheran, Swedenborgian, etc.). A central issue this month, as last, was refugees from war torn Syria. Last month we had heads of the Mennonite Central Committee, the Catholic Diocese, and Lutheran World Service speak about their plans and efforts to sponsor and resettle refugees from Syria here in Canada. Earlier the newly elected Federal Liberals had pledged to settle 25,000 Syrian refugees before the end of the year, and church organizations would be central to making this happen on the ground. Yesterday, another secular refugee organization joined the conversation. It was a striking example of compassion in action.

Compassion has become central to contemporary spiritual/religious discourse. HH the Dalai Lama writes in *The Heart of Compassion* that '... to truly love God, one must demonstrate that love through the action of loving fellow beings in a genuine way, by loving one's neighbor. One might also reflect upon the life of Jesus Christ himself, how he conducted his life, how he worked for the benefit of other sentient beings, and how his actions illustrated a compassionate way of life.'[1] The language of compassion is to be found in secular as well as religious contexts. Dean Ornish, a well-known American medical doctor, writes in *Love & Survival* that 'the ability to feel another's emotions is the essence of compassion'.[2]

We have also recently seen the emergence of Karen Armstrong's Charter of Compassion. It believes that 'a compassionate world is a peaceful world' and 'that a compassionate world is possible when every man, woman, or child treats others as they wish to be treated – with dignity, equity and respect.'[3] This visionary affirmation is a contemporary restatement of the wisdom/golden rule of the great religions.

'Compassion' in the World Religions

Compassion is a term that is found across the world's religious traditions. In the sacred texts of the Buddhist way it is the Sanskrit terms *karuna* and *metta* and in Pali compassion is often linked to *metta* (loving-kindness) and *upekkha* (equanimity). While in Tibet, *chenrezig* is the manifestation of compassion as is *guan yin* in Chinese Buddhism. In Islam there is more than one word for compassion, but the most common is *ar-raHeem* or *raHeem*, it is also one of the 99 names of Allah. All but one Surah of the Koran opens with the phrase 'In the name of Allah, the compassionate, the merciful. ...' In Hinduism, compassion is the translation of the Sanskrit term *karuna* or 'seeking to understand from another's perspective', or *daya*, the virtuous desire to mitigate the sorrows and difficulties of others, and, *anukampa*, 'one's state after having observed and understood the pain and suffering of another.' It is also often said that Vishnu is the Lord of Compassion.

In Judaism, the Hebrew term for compassion is *rahmana*, and one source says 'the feeling of a parent for a child'. Yahweh is the 'Father of Compassion.' In the Jain tradition, *ahimsa* or non-violence is understood as 'compassion for all living things'. In Christian scripture God is, like the longer Jewish tradition, called the 'Father of Compassion' (2 Cor. 1: 3-5) and the Koine Greek term for compassion in the New Testament is *splagchnizomai.* The term means 'to be moved in one's bowels, hence to be moved with compassion, for the bowels were thought to be the seat of love and pity.' And in Chinese one translation of compassion is *tongqing* but there are other characters as well that mean: to sympathize with or for, kindness, and real affection.[4] While this quick survey of the meanings of the English word compassion points to something shared across tradition, it should also alert us to the fact that the term compassion has its unique and different meanings in the many traditions and streams of global spirituality.[5]

Compassion in the Christian New Testament

The Koine Greek term for compassion (*splagchnizomai*) occurs but 12 times in the Synoptic Gospels (Matthew, Mark, & Luke). For example, 'He (Jesus) saw a great throng; and he had compassion on them, and healed the sick' Mt. 14: 14. Then there are Jesus' parables of the Prodigal Son – a story of the son who squanders his inheritance and is embraced when he returns to his father – and the Good Samaritan – the story of the injured person who is passed-by by religious folks but is cared for by the outcaste Samaritan. These parables reflect the compassion of the Heavenly Father (Prodigal Son) and compassion towards the neighbour (Good Samaritan). Here compassion is a disposition or feeling that fuels acts of kindness and mercy. Compassion, in the Christian traditions, is a form of love and empathy aroused within us when we are confronted with those who suffer or are vulnerable. In medieval Christianity compassion was understood as co-suffering, mirroring the suffering of Jesus on the cross.

Even Jesus' death on the cross by Roman authorities is regarded in the New Testament as an act of compassionate love, one that lays down his life for the other. As we read in I Jn 3:16 'By this we know love, that he laid down his life for us, and we ought to lay down our lives for the brethren.' And I Jn 4: 7 'Beloved, let us love one another, for love is of God, and he who loves is born of God and knows God … for God is love.' It is human acts of compassionate love that reflect and embody the Father of Compassion. And it is compassionate love that is a 'many splendored thing'.

That compassionate love is to be extended to all is clear in this teaching of Jesus that concludes:

> Lord, when did we see thee hungry and feed thee, or thirsty and give thee drink? And when did we see thee a stranger and welcome thee, or naked and clothe thee? And when did we see thee sick or in prison and visit thee? ...
>
> And the King will answer: 'Truly, I say to you, as you did it to one of the least of these my brethren, you did it to me.' Mt. 25: 37-40

And we find these words of Paul, the Apostle to the Gentiles, in his letter to the Christians in Corinth that are suffering persecution:

> Praise be to the God and Father of our Lord Jesus Christ, the Father of Compassion and the God of all comfort, who comforts us in all our troubles, so that we can comfort those in any trouble or affliction, with the comfort with which we ourselves are comforted by God. For as we share abundantly in Christ's suffering, so through Christ we share abundantly in comfort too. 2 Cor. 1: 3-5

Now we want to explore some practices of compassionate love found in the Christian traditions.

Institutionalized Compassionate the Lutheran World Federation/WCC

In 1969-70 I worked for the Lutheran World Federation (LWF) in Geneva, Switzerland, an 'interconnected communion of Lutheran churches' around the world. It is housed in a wing of the building that also houses the World Council of Churches (WCC). A major part of the LWF is Lutheran World Service (LWS). Earlier it was called Lutheran World Relief, but its name change reflects changing understandings of how Christians relate to the global 'other'. It is an expression of 'faith active in love'. It is, says LWS, the way 'we care and show compassion for those who are in need'. It works with communities across the globe to support education, health care, and sustainable development. It is not limited to other Lutherans or Christians, but is assisting communities in need throughout the Third World. Here compassionate love is expressed in and through an institutional agency.

While in Geneva I also became aware of SODEPAX or the joint Vatican/World Council of Church's Commission on Society, Development, & Peace. Founded following Vatican II, it is celebrating its 50th anniversary in 2015. While the Catholic Church is not a member of the WCC it has been, from the beginning, part of SODEPAX. It both cultivates an intra-Christian ecumenism and urges joint programmes in global societies for development, justice and peace.

Today most of the Christian world focuses on sustainable

development, education, health care, and community building in its outreach programmes, rather than conversion. This shift from conversion to compassionate love grows out of the heart of Christianity.

These are practices of compassionate love within institutionalized Christian traditions.

Cultivating Compassion: Ways Within

Compassionate love also needs to be cultivated in the hearts of Christians. Two practices that have emerged in contemporary Catholic circles are based in 'Centering Prayer'. In the first instance, this led to the 'World Community for Christian Meditation', around the Benedictine John Main (1926-82) and Brother Lawrence Freeman, OSB.[6] The second is linked to Fr. Thomas Keating (1924-) who, together with Fr. M. Basil Pennington founded Contemplative Outreach.

John Main learned meditation from Swami Satyananda while stationed in Malaysia in the 1950s. Main had been born in London, and studied law in Ireland. He became a Benedictine monk in 1959 and continued the practice of meditation together with a *mantra* or *prayer-phrase*. While in the USA in the early 1970s, Main encountered the teachings of John Cassian (360-450 CE) one of the Egyptian Fathers. He found that Cassian taught a form of prayer that was identical with his practice of meditation. Together with Brother Laurence Freeman he established a monastery in Montreal where they taught Christian meditation. Main's teaching was simple: 'sit still and upright for 20-30 minutes, close your eyes, and recite a prayer-phrase (mantra)...preferably *maranatha* (come, Lord). They founded the World Community of Christian Meditation. They understood meditation as 'a way of friendship and compassion' that 'builds bridges of the Spirit between peoples of different faith'. Sometimes they describe their practice as 'contemplative prayer', 'a listening and being' that 'aims at union with the indwelling Spirit of God'. The movement has become global and is widely practiced among Catholics, but has also reached into the Protestant world.

Fr. Thomas Keating is a Trappist and a Catholic priest.[7] During the 1960s and 1970s he was at St. Joseph's Abbey in Spencer,

Massachusetts. While there he encountered a fellow Trappist, Fr. William Meninger. Father Meninger had read the *Cloud of Unknowing*, a fourteenth century spiritual classic. It taught a way of contemplative prayer that Father Meninger called Centering Prayer, a method that cultivated an interior silence that was centred in God. Fr. Thomas Keating and Fr. M. Basil Pennington also contributed to the emergence of Centering Prayer, and in the 1980s established Contemplative Outreach (CO). CO saw Centering Prayer as a simple method that leads into contemplation. As they write on their website: Centering Prayer is 'a method of silent prayer that prepares us to receive the gift of contemplative prayer'. And it was the reviving of Christian contemplative practice that Contemplative Outreach sought to bring to lay Catholics as well as to the religious. They have also welcomed Protestant and Orthodox Christians as well as people from other traditions.

Contemplative Outreach gives these four steps to begin: (1) Sit comfortably, with eyes closed, relax and quiet yourself. Be in love and faith. (2) Choose a sacred word that best supports your sincere intention to be in the Lord's presence and open to his divine action within. (3) Let the word be gently present as a symbol of your intention to be in the Lord's presence and open to his divine action within you – Keating recommends keeping the word in silence. (4) Whenever you become aware of anything (thoughts, feelings, perceptions, etc.) simply return to your sacred word. Although contemplation unfolds in interior silence, Keating feels that 'it fosters a communion with the indwelling Trinity, Father, Son, & Holy Spirit.' Moreover, contemplative prayer 'builds communities of faith and bonds members together in mutual friendship and love.'

These are but two examples in Catholic Christianity that cultivate compassion. When I turned to Protestant Christianity in relation to prayer and meditation, I found the following:

> Compassion is a feeling deep within ourselves – a quivering of the heart – and it is also a way of acting – being affected by others and moving on their behalf. Buddha and Jesus are the most well-known exemplars of compassion, and it is the central ethical virtue in the two religions. . . .
>
> The spiritual practice of compassion is often likened to opening the heart. First, allow yourself to feel the suffering in the world, including your own. Don't turn away from pain, move towards it with caring. Go into situations

where people are hurting, identify with your neighbors in distress. Then expand the circle of your compassion to include other creatures, nature and the inanimate world.[8]

There are now many groups across the Christian world that practice forms of prayer, meditation, and spirituality that have been influenced by the global interfaith movement and especially the emphasis on mindfulness in the Buddhist traditions and yoga in the Hindu traditions.

Conclusion

I want to conclude with a brief mention of the Orthodox tradition of the 'Jesus Prayer'. The Apostle Paul writing to the Thessalonians urged them to 'Always seek to do good to one another and to all. Rejoice always, pray without ceasing, and give thanks in all circumstances.' It has long puzzled Christians how they might 'pray without ceasing'. It is in *The Way of a Pilgrim* that we encounter a Russian Orthodox layman who heard the reading from scripture about 'praying ceaselessly'.[9] He then went to a hermit monk (*staret*) who instructed him as follows:

'Sit down in silence, lower your head, shut your eyes, breathe out gently, and imagine yourself looking into your own heart. As you breathe out say, 'Lord Jesus Christ, have mercy on me.' Say it moving your lips gently, or simply say it in your mind. Try to put all other thoughts aside. Be calm, be patient, and repeat the process very frequently.'[10]

The pilgrim continued on his way. He repeated this phrase as he walked 6,000 times a day. This went on for some weeks, until he doubled the number to 12,000 times a day. He began to notice how these repetitions were not only in concert with his steps, but also with his breathing. Every inhalation and exhalation, now in silence and internally, these words/these sounds echoed in his mind. His very breathing had become his prayer.

He also read his Bible and his *Philokalia*, a volume of spiritual teachings that included the words of people like St. Simeon, St. Gregory of Sinai, Ignatius, Peter the Damascene, and Gregory Palamas. He continued his walk across the Russian steppes, meeting people now and then.

What he noticed was that his practice of prayer was affecting the way he regarded those he encountered. Now he felt more compassion for those he met. He felt closer to them. He felt a love for them that he had not known before.

It was a practice of compassion.

Notes

1. HH the Dalai Lama, *The Heart of Compassion: A Dalai Lama Reader* (Delhi: Full Circle, 1997), p. 148.
2. Dean Ornish, *Love & Survival* (New York: HarperCollins, 1998), p. 109.
3. The Charter of Compassion can be found on the internet.
4. These meanings of compassion in diverse languages can be found by consulting English-Arabic dictionaries and resources on the internet. The etymology of the English term compassion come from the Latin *compati* or *compassio* meaning 'suffer with' or 'co-suffering' and from old French sympathy, pity. The Latin term compassion is from the Greek *sympatheia* (sympathy), but came to mean the 'response to the suffering of others that motivates a desire to help'.
5. During the discussion of my paper in Hyderabad, I recalled that there are three Greek terms that are found in the New Testament and simply translated into English as 'love'. Those are the following terms: *agape* or self-giving, unconditional love, divine love, *eros* or desire, intimate love and *philia* or brotherly love, friendship, love between equals.
6. See John Main, *The Way of Unknowing* (Bangalore: Indian Institute of Spirituality, 2003).
7. See Thomas Keating, *Open Mind, Open Heart* (New York: Continuum, 1986). In the mid-1980s I participated in an interfaith gathering at Snowmass, Colorado, led by Father Keating. See 'Meeting in Snowmass: Some Dynamics of Interfaith Meeting', in John Miller, ed., *Interfaith Dialogue: Four Approaches* (Waterloo: Department of Religious Studies, 1986), pp. 1-20.
8. See Christianity – Protestant at www.spirituality&practice.com
9. See *The Way of a Pilgrim & The Pilgrim Continues His Way*, trans. R.M. French (San Francisco: HarperSanFrancisco, 1991).
10. For this quote from the *Way of the Pilgrim* see www.hermitary.com/articles/pilgrim.html

PART VII

PRACTICES OF COMPASSION IN DIVERSE SETTINGS

CHAPTER 22

Awareness, Art and Service

ZULEIKHA

We do not serve ideologies, we serve people.

POPE FRANCIS, 2015

EXCEPTIONALLY CURIOUS ABOUT the longing of the human spirit to find home here on earth, I began to explore ancient spiritual and movement technologies of the sacred. Having practiced and been given permission to study in various traditions, I found my way into what could be referred to as the presence in essence, or for that matter, the essence in presence.

I grew up in the San Francisco Bay Area, a centre for cultural interchange and artistic innovation. As a young girl, in a musical family, I studied Western classical music, played piano and silver flute throughout my education, practicing the arts of avant-garde dance and 'natural movement'. I was drawn from a young age to ancient methodologies of the sacred, including Chinese therapeutic health exercises inside the martial arts, and Balinese dance. I attended the Ali Akbar College of Music, which was the first classical Indian music college in the West. There I began to learn and practice the art of *kathak* dance, which includes an extensive study of rhythm, melody, and ancient wisdom stories from the legends of the sacred texts of India. We studied from *The Natya Shastra*, or the text of the Theater of the Divine, exploring the portrayal of characters, male and female, animals, and nature. Learning in this beautiful form gave me the foundation for understanding emotions and feelings; not only their portrayal in movement arts, but also how these are ways that human beings travel in the course of life. Later, I studied with the Afghan music maestro, Ustad Hashim Chishti, a *tabla* master and gifted teacher in the arts of north Indian classical music, which reached up through north India, Pakistan, and Afghanistan. This art form includes singing, instrumental arts and rhythm.

To this day, I sing every morning and compose my own songs, based in poetry and sacred phrases of the mystics of different traditions. I have created several CDs, and groups of women and children around the world sing some of these songs.

As my practice of movement art forms and sacred traditions deepened, I became aware of many striking commonalities among world cultures. Realizing that underlying these creative modalities is a unified field inside of expression, which helps to enliven inherent awareness of the links between sound, movement, breath, and emotion as they are felt and expressed through the body, I thus began to discover a root system of movement that touched upon physical and emotional wellbeing. This system became the foundation for the 'Core Wellness & Movement Arts' work I have been doing with women, girls, children and families worldwide.

I liked the way that all root cultures kept what was to be remembered: in stories. I began to call myself a 'Storydancer', and have been using story with dance to express wisdom teachings of the traditions through which I have moved.

Through my work as Artist-in-Residence in the USA, and on the New Mexico Governor's Council of Health and Fitness, I came to create a set of exercises that is simple to learn, and as some have said 'profound in scope', called 'Take a Minute ™ for your Life Core Wellness Exercises.' I now use this series of movements in many world communities as doorways to open from trauma and constriction into relief, resilience and self-care.

My own personal health story has played a critical role in developing this deep feeling and innovative approach to wellness. Years ago, coming out of an unfortunate operation, I became very ill. In the surprising way dysfunction can sometimes appear, I found myself, one morning, unable to stand up, and could only crawl. After enduring a long series of medical explorations and alternative trials that led nowhere, I met an extraordinary physician of Eastern and Western medical modalities who understood the nature of my illness. Though it took years of many kinds of treatment and medicines, I have been restored to good health.

To remain healthy, as I moved through many other crises and obstacles, I began to explore the inner workings of physical, mental, emotional and devotional being. Through this process of what I jokingly referred to as 'inner movement research', I developed a practice I now call the 'BodyListening© MAP (Movement Arts Practice).'

BodyListening© is an internally focused Movement Awareness Practice, where participants learn to be held by the floor and by the surrounding space, and to *listen to the way the body feels like moving* versus *trying to move in various ways.* It is a dynamic process, wherein participants can explore the freedom of movement and spirited embodiment that becomes possible with sufficient support. Spontaneous exploration of movement can bring about a great inner awareness and a feeling of spaciousness. When people feel at home in the body and spacious at the same time, the heart expands. The heart is the home of Love, the wellspring that can bring uplifting inspiration, or as Rumi says, 'the place of the Placeless'. The outcome is one of constant awareness without speculation.

These movement techniques of awareness are integral in my performances, as well, which weave together dance, storytelling, music, poetry and humour. I have performed for audiences worldwide, and for mystics in many traditions: Zen priests, Tibetan Lamas and Rinpoches, Sufi Sheikhs, Pirs and Murshids, Rabbis, and members of many liturgical communities of the world. I have danced and told stories for Native communities and performed in schools for children worldwide. Reflecting on the art of embodiment, I like to remember Lalla, the Kashmiri mystic poet, as she gives us the instruction to 'dance with nothing on but air'. When we move in the nakedness of our souls, a lightness of being comes into play, and essence meets expression in this body. All traditions of reverence are practiced here, in this body. The Sufis, as well as mystics in the Tibetan, Vedic, Chinese, and nature-based traditions, have always developed the use of dance, walk, breath and spiritual practice as inroads to the expression of what some call 'a real human being'.

I perform in my own one-woman shows, as well as collaborate with many gifted world musicians. I have worked for many years with the well-known American poet and translator of Rumi, Coleman

ZULEIKHA IN RUMI CONCERT 2015
© KATIE JOHNSON

ZULEIKHA WITH CHILDREN AT SEELAMPUR SUPPORT CLASSES, HOPE PROJECT

ZULEIKHA AT HOPE PROJECT HEALTH CLINIC USING SKY LISTENING, ONE OF HER TAM EXERCISES

ZULEIKHA AT A CANSUPPORT HOME VISIT USING RTHEP©

Barks. Together we perform with musicians to create a landscape of poetry, music, dance, story and humor based in the poetry of the renowned mystic, Jelaluddin Rumi.

Applying my Take A Minute™ Core Wellness and BodyListening© MAP as ways of working in the midst of trauma, I started The Storydancer Project, a non-profit international artistic health resource organization, which facilitates programmes with survivors and offenders of domestic abuse, children of marginalized communities, and girls and women oppressed by political injustice and human trafficking. Using the vehicle of The Storydancer Project, or TSP, I teach and train community leaders, nurses, doctors, psychologists and educators to use Core Wellness movements to prevent burn-out, rekindle enthusiasm and inspire daily practices of self-care that ripple outward to enliven entire communities. I also work to bring relief to palliative care cancer patients and their families, using an offshoot of Take A Minute™ that I have developed over many years of working with palliative cancer patients and home care teams in the slums of Delhi. These exercises have come to be known as The Relaxation Therapeutic Health Exercise Program© (RTHEP©). RTHEP© is being implemented by home health care teams throughout the slums and villages in and surrounding Delhi, India, impacting over 8,000 people yearly. I have received several awards for humanitarian efforts, including the Images and Visions of Hope Media Award of Appreciation for 'infusing the art of dance with the gifts of healing, understanding and love of life through … outstanding work in the world promoting positive personal and social change'.

For me, spirit and feeling are intimately connected. I have spent the majority of my life exploring movement from the point of view of feeling, and inviting others to do the same. I like to refer to the unique nature of our sensate, physical selves as a doorway to awareness of spirit and an attitude of reverence for life: After all, the human body is like a miraculous spacesuit designed perfectly for Planet Earth.

Each of our bodies is unique, encoded with an exclusive set of fingerprints. Some traditions say that the whorls on the fingerprints are a sign of the breath breathed into each of us. In these times, everyone is going so fast that we often don't remember to take a breath. The word 'breath' comes from the Latin word, *spiritus*, or spirit. When the heart expands with the breath, gratitude for life becomes present. I feel that these principles in my work reach to the very heart of what it is to be human – to the best in us that longs to unite this spirit with this body in this moment.

I am a dancer in this unusual adventure we call life. There is no accounting for how we each move through it, and that is what we do – we *move* through our lives.

I believe if people will 'Take A Minute' now and then throughout the day, our nervous systems will be able to relax amidst the chaos of modern technology, and we can have the opportunity to feel the connections we long for, bringing awareness of the essence of depth into our everyday existence.

In this way we can feel our connection in the world community, and be of service in the joy we feel. One of my great mentors always has said, 'Do Good and Be Good, it will take up most of your time.'

I like to say, 'Joy with movement brings healing, and inside Love there is room for everything.'

CHAPTER 23

Compassion as 'Living for the Sake of Others'

THOMAS WALSH

THE UNIVERSAL PEACE FEDERATION (UPF), a network of individuals and organizations, works to build a world of lasting peace. At its Inaugural Assembly in September 2005, its Founder, Rev. Sun Myung Moon, wrote out a motto, 'True Love is the guiding principle of the Universal Peace Federation.' UPF, rooted in the spiritual vision of its Founder, affirms five core principles:

There is one universal origin and essence, called by many and various names, such as God, Allah, Yahweh, the ultimate reality.
The family is the school of love and peace.
Human beings are not merely biological beings; we are also spiritual and moral beings.
Dialogue and cooperation among religions are necessary for peace.
By practicing true love we can establish healthy, productive, harmonious and prosperous relationships.

The practice of 'true love' is characterized by unselfishness, 'living for the sake of others'. The ideal of true love is similar to the concept and practice of *compassion* which is widely affirmed by the world's religions, being highlighted in sacred scriptures of virtually all traditions.

Consider, for example, the following passages, taken from an anthology of sacred scriptures.[1]

Oh good man! Compassion acts as parent to all beings. The parent is compassion. Know that compassion is the *Tathagata*. O good man! Compassion is the Buddha nature of all beings. Such a Buddha nature is long overshadowed by illusions. That is why being cannot see. The Buddha nature is compassion. Compassion is the *Tathagata*. *Buddhism*, *Mahaparinivana Sutra* 259.[2]

'Make your mosque of compassion, your prayer mat of sincerity; your Quran of honest and legitimate earning. Be modesty your circumcision, noble conduct your Ramadan fast; thus shall you be a true Muslim. Make good deeds your Kaba; truth your preceptor; Good action your creed and daily prayers. Make your rosary of what pleases God: Thus will you be honored at the last reckoning' (Sikhism, *Adi Granth, Var Majh*).[3]

'What sort of religion can it be without compassion? You need to show compassion to all living beings. Compassion is the root of all religious faiths' (Hinduism, *Basavanna, Vadana* 247).[4]

'Have benevolence toward all living beings, joy at the sight of the virtuous, compassion and sympathy for the afflicted, and tolerance toward the indolent and the ill-behaved' (Jainism, *Tatvarthasutra* 7.11).[5]

'Even though it be the home of someone who has managed for long to avoid misfortune, we gods will not enter into the dwelling of a person with perverse disposition. Even though it be a dwelling where a man be in mourning for father and mother, if he be a man of compassion, we deities will enter in there' (Shintoism, *Oracle of Kasuga*).[6]

'Those of fallen nature are receptacles of compassion from those whose nature is great' (Nagarjuna, Buddhism, *Precious Garland*, 331-7).[7]

Praise be to the God and Father of our Lord Jesus Christ, the Father of compassion and the God of all comfort, who comforts us in all our troubles, so that we can comfort those in any trouble with the comfort we ourselves receive from God. For just as we share abundantly in the sufferings of Christ, so also our comfort abounds through Christ. If we are distressed, it is for your comfort and salvation; if we are comforted, it is for your comfort, which produces in you patient endurance of the same sufferings we suffer. And our hope for you is firm, because we know that just as you share in our sufferings, so also you share in our comfort (Christianity, *New Testament*, II *Corinthians* 1:3).

As these quotations indicate, the concept of compassion is a universal value, a common ground found in all religions, and moral systems.

I want to underscore three aspects of compassion.

Compassion Originates in God

The concept of true love, as compassion, is not merely a human virtue, but rather it describes a core characteristic of ultimate reality, or God, the Origin and Source of all that is. The essence of God's nature is true love, a desire and an intentionality to establish harmonious, cooperative, productive relationships, with others and with all things, thereby generating and multiplying joy.

True Love does not function or express itself effectively, and all too often destructively, when divorced from its origin, when the agent is separated from the source of true love and compassion. UPF's Founder teaches that, 'The universe was created by investing, based on love for the sake of others. Hence, when a person lives for the sake of others, he aligns himself with the original activity of creation, and thus brings himself into oneness with God.'[8] In other words, compassion is a trait of the ultimate, the Heavenly Parent.

Human compassion or the human capacity for compassion derives from our origin, God. The capacity to practice compassion is linked to the capacity to suffer, to understand suffering, not merely as some abstract concept, but rather to identify with the suffering of others and to not only wish that it were otherwise, but to engage with the other in ways that are aimed at liberation.

Closely associated with the concept of care for others and solidarity in the suffering of others, the concept of compassion may also extend to and apply to our relationship with ultimate reality. Just as ultimate reality, or God, understands and has compassion for human suffering, it is also the case that the compassion, or true love of God is such that the suffering of humanity is not felt as mere pity, as might an entirely self-sufficient God of aseity.

God, too, suffers. Thus, compassion extends not only to our neighbour, but also to God. We are to be compassionate toward our neighbour, as Jesus taught in the parable of the Good Samaritan, and we are to be compassionate toward God. In other words, there is a natural reciprocity that is part of the fabric of the universe, including God's nature.

Moreover, compassion extends to those who have departed, and who dwell in the spiritual world, some at peace, but others still tormented by lives misspent, wasted or weighed down by injustices received or administered.

Compassion is a Relational Virtue

True love, as compassion, does not exist autonomously or independently. It is fundamentally a virtue that has meaning and value in relationship to others. Thus, the ideal is not independence, but interdependence; our personal relationship to the ultimate origin is an essential condition that allows true love and compassion to be awakened and strengthened within us.

True Love aims to produce reciprocity that is not essentially 'rights' oriented or 'justice' oriented, but compassion oriented, living for the sake of the other, for the well-being of the other. Action that aims to create understanding, respect, growth, cooperative interactivity, such action is an expression of true love, and compassion.

In this respect true love or compassion transforms justice. Such practices as criminal justice, for example, may be approximations of compassion, applicable in a world where compassion is lacking.[9]

True Love recognizes that need for the differentiation and balance among complementary, mutually valued entities, like the husband and wife, the young and the old, the teacher and the student, the mind and the body. Compassion understands and expresses itself with an understanding of the need for balance, mutual respect, while recognizing the other as a 'thou', to use Martin Buber's well-known concept.[10]

Like other cardinal virtues – courage, temperance, justice, prudence – or theological virtues – faith, hope, love – compassion is partly given to us as a gift and partly cultivated over time through practice and habit formation. It is part of our nature, just as it may be said to be a part of the natural world, and at play at the micro and macrocosmic levels. It may be seen within the world of animals, in their parental care, their interactive bonds and friendships, as well as protective tendencies.

Compassion as Virtue: The Role of Family

Within the realm of human agency, compassion may be described as a virtue. Virtues are human strengths and qualities of character that are developed within social contexts, or communities that uphold, affirm, and support the cultivation of virtues. Sometimes the desire to cultivate virtue may lead one to adopt a particular lifestyle or discipline, or to join an intentional community, where instruction, as well as interaction with master teachers may occur, along with the benefits of a supportive culture and social framework.

One of the most widespread, if not universal contexts for virtue development is the family. The care of mothers and fathers for their children may be the primal, most natural, and more powerful form of compassion, in terms of the impact on the child. Compassionless parenting brings harm to children. Abuse creates a tendency toward abusiveness in the victims of the abuse. This is a sad irony. Whereas, true love within a family engenders true love and compassion in the children, which in turn impacts the wider society in a positive ways.

Conclusion

Compassion has universal relevance. As we experience and observe the world around us, we cannot escape the reality of widespread suffering due to the lack of love, the lack of compassion. The expansion of the practice of true love and compassion in individuals, marriages, families, neighbourhoods, civic institutions, places of work and worship, is a necessary foundation for the transformation of our world and the achievement of lasting peace.

Notes

1. *World Scripture: An Anthology of Sacred Texts* (New York: Universal Peace Federation, 1985). During the first Assembly of the World's Religions, sponsored by the International Religious Foundation, a project entitled 'World Scripture' was initiated, featuring a collection of passages from sacred scriptures from the world's religions. The idea of compassion is represented widely in the selected passages.
2. Ibid., p. 89.
3. Ibid., p. 615.
4. Ibid., p. 684.
5. Ibid.
6. Ibid., p. 685.
7. Ibid., p. 761.
8. Andrew Wilson, ed., *World Scriptures and the Teachings of Sun Myung Moon* (New York: Universal Peace Federation, 2011), p. 664.
9. See Reinhold Niebuhr, *Love and Justice: Selections from the Shorter Writings of Reinhold Niebuhr*, ed. D.B. Robertson (Westminster: John Knox Press, 1957).
10. See Martin Buber, *I and Thou* (Touchstone: New York, 1970).

CHAPTER 24

Interspirituality and the Practice of Compassion

KURT JOHNSON, SWAMI SHRADDHANANDA AND YANNI MANIATES

> The real challenge for you, Wayne, is to be *a monk in the world*, a *sannyasi* who lives in the midst of society, at the very heart of things.
>
> BEDE GRIFFITHS TO WAYNE TEASDALE
> (*A Monk in the World*, xxii)

ANYONE WHO KNOWS 'interspirituality' – or the legacy of Br. Wayne Teasdale who coined the word right on the cusp of this new millennium – knows that within a year of publishing his now classic book *The Mystic Heart: Discovering a Universal Spirituality in the World's Religions*[1] [*MH*]. Teasdale finalized his next volume, *A Monk in the World: Cultivating a Spiritual Life*[2] [*MW*]. Although delayed in publication until 2002 because of Teasdale's failing health, it became one of the foundational books on what is now called sacred activism. Thousands, if not millions, of people have been influenced by these two iconic books – sometimes not knowing which to call their favourite. In the end most join them as 'bookends', seeing them as framing the grand 'yin-yang' of Being and Doing.

Teasdale himself came from a lineage of major foundational teachers across the Western monastic traditions who began the joining of Eastern and Western spirituality just as post-World War global civilization was entering what is now widely called the Integral Age. This widely influential group – Teasdale, Thomas Merton, Bede Griffiths, Raimon Pannikar and Thomas Keating (all but Pannikar were Christian contemplative monastics) are often called 'the big five' of Western monasticism for their bringing to Western consciousness the non-duality – the Oneness – which was the perennial hallmark of the world's great Eastern traditions.

But it was not to be left at that. Merton, as early as 1973, had written *Contemplation in a World of Action*, Panikkar(1984) had written *The Monk as a Universal Archetype*, Griffiths had travelled the world in his latter years speaking on consciousness and the new physics, and Keating brought the world's traditions into an active three decade dialogue resulting in *The Common Heart* (2006), which included the 'Nine Points of Agreement' among the world's religions. These, and Teasdale's 'Nine Elements of a Universal Spirituality', saw spirituality and the active world as inextricably engaged. Indeed, over half of the 'Points' and the 'Elements' have to do with human behaviour and the action of compassion, love, kindness, nurturing and co-creation in the wider day to day world. For these pioneer interspiritual visionaries, compassion and practice, contemplation and action were one and the same.

All this intertwining was not by accident. Teasdale, profoundly influenced by his four elders in this group of five, himself had ended up in the doctoral programme in theology co-founded by the world's seminal 'Eco-Theologian', Fr. Thomas Berry. Berry, following on the vision of Jesuit cosmologist Teilhard de Chardin in writings from 1988-2009, had declared the dawning 'Ecological Age'. Thusly, eco-consciousness, eco-ministry and care of Gaia/ Mother Earth became inextricably part of the interspiritual mandate as well.

Teasdale himself was an activist both on the street and across global governmental agencies – especially for the causes of the Tibetan people (working closely with his friend His Holiness the Dalai Lama), global freedom of religion in general, and of care of the earth which he called 'a sacred duty' [*MW*, 231]. In *A Monk in the World*, his now classic book on the spiritual life and sacred activism,Teasdale joined these visions in sections elaborating 'From Withdrawal to Engagement', 'The Outer and Inner Monk', 'The Community of Nature', 'Nature's Symbolism','The Struggle to Promote Change', 'The World as Community', and 'The World as Testing Ground' among many others.

Contemporary Elements for a Practice of Compassion

The three of us join in writing this piece because like the pioneers above who inspire us, we are similarly inextricably linked. All of us are apart of Interspirituality.com, the global website that now joins over one hundred associations and networks advancing interspirituality, now in its wider variety of forms, from 'multiple belonging' to spiritual but not religious, global or universal spirituality, trans-traditional or world-centric spirituality, and many more. We are also founders or leaders of The Community of The Mystic Heart (CMH), founded originally as Br. Teasdale's 'Universal Order of Sannyasa'. In his vision of such a 'Universal Order', Teasdale further transformed the role of the ancient Sannyas, or renunciate. 'In our time', he said, 'with its special needs, we require a spirituality of intense involvement and radical engagement with the world. It is in the real world that people live their busy lives, and it is in the real world that the wisdom of the monks [Sannyas] must be …' [*MW*, xxiii].

Swami Shraddhananda is the lineage holder and preceptor for the sannyas component of CMH and Johnson and Maniates work with a host of others, including another former close friend of Teasdale, Jeffrey Genung, in a formative experiment of virtual community about the mission of 'Monks in the World', so named by Swami Shraddhananda who considers Teasdale's second book to be a foundational text in the world of Interspiritual Studies alongside *The Mystic Heart*. The entire vision and work of these organizations is about compassion *in practice*, the being *and* doing or, as the East's great Heart Sutra states, the joining of the Wisdom with the Skilful Means of action.

This allows us to underline four emphases herein, with the fourth requiring a more detailed elaboration. This is because it concerns the *most* contemporary of elements – how geographically far-flung spiritual communities might utilize modern technology to help sustain their communities and socially engaged actions. The first three are these:

- The vision of inner and outer practice of compassion
- The practice of compassion through spiritual community
- The practice of compassion in the wider world of politics and policy

The fourth is this:

- An exploration of new possibilities that enable people globally to connect and build local and virtual communities by leveraging mobile, web and virtual technologies. In this context we want to use this opportunity to address 'The Practice of Compassion' by discussing concrete directions, actions, activities, and programmes which can illustrate and further promote the skilful joining of contemplative consciousness and sacred activist practice – from the meditation room or cushion to the complex arenas of social and political policy. Fortunately today, the inextricable interconnection of both Doing and Being are widely understood across the world's spiritual traditions. Both are needed and the challenge is how to skilfully connect them. This is what Teasdale called the joining of heart, head and hands [*MH*, 29-30]. Today is truly a time for a dynamic co-creation across diverse arenas that can lead to actual and tangible transformative change at a global level.

The Sannyas and 'Monk in the World' Today – A Path for the Practice of Compassion

Just as the Christian contemplatives known as 'the big five' – Griffiths (1906-93), Merton (1915-68), Panikkar (1918-2010), Keating (1923-), and Teasdale (1945-2004) – were making headway teaching the West to think perennially, so they were being influenced by a group of Asians who were no less intent on showing us how to bridge the gap between Doing and Being.

We could say, in fact, that Paramahansa Yogananda came to Los Angeles in the 1920s to help further what Swami Vivekananda began at the first Parliament of the World's Religions in 1893; that is, Yogananda came to guide the Good Ship USA in its love affair with yoga which continues to this day, from scores of yoga studios open worldwide with yogis who practice varying forms of Interspirituality, to a huge international yoga festival in India with people attending from all parts of the globe. Indeed, 2014 saw the declaration of an 'International Yoga Day' by the United Nations.

We could also say that Shunyu Suzuki Roshi arrived in San Francisco in the 1950s to open conversations about 'beginner's mind' – 'mindfulness' finding its way out of the zendo in the 1980s and into medical circles. The 1950s also saw the birth of Transcendental Meditation, the brainchild of Maharishi Mahesh Yogi who taught the Beatles how to meditate.

In the same generation, *c.* 1970, Baba Muktananda appeared in

Manhattan to announce that he intended to conduct a 'Meditation Revolution', and ChogyamTrungpa Rinpoche showed up from Tibet, by way of Scotland, with the possibility of 'enlightened society' on his mind.

The merger of East and West gave rise to a global situation which almost necessitated the creation of an Interspiritual order of monastics. After three trips to India, Teasdale embraced the task laid out for him by Griffiths, who told him to head back to Chicago and carve out a place for himself as a monk in the world.

Teasdale's vision for an Interspiritual order manifested originally as the Universal Order of Sannyasa. The name was changed to The Community of The Mystic Heart [CMH] when a member of the Ramakrishna order objected to Teasdale's free-wheeling use of the term, Sannyasa. In the early years, about 300 people joined CMH which promoted Teasdale's concept of Interspirituality perhaps more than it worked to establish an order of monastics.

Fast forward to 2013: Swami Shraddhananda, having taken formal Sannyas in the Saraswati order of monastics, one of four maths established by Shri Shankaracharya in eighth century India, approached Teasdale's friend Dr. Kurt Johnson about anchoring CMH at her ashram in Kentucky. Johnson's Interspiritual Dialogue Board said yes, so Teasdale's photo now hangs beside Fr. Bede's and a host of other Indian and Tibetan teachers in Unmani, the meditation hall at Boat Dock Road Retreat.[3]

Swami Shraddhananda is intent on creating the Interspiritual order that Teasdale envisioned when he returned from taking Sannyas in India. Members of the order who take full Sannyas will be expected to honour vows of brahmacharya, or celibacy, spend time living in community at Slate Branch Ashram, and offer service to help develop ashram hours and rituals.

'Full Sannyas' is not for everyone, so it is possible to take 'lay Sannyas' in CMH, or choose to join the latest incarnation of CMH, 'Monks in the World [MITW]'. Whichever version or degree of monasticism a candidate chooses, the emphasis in CMH is on compassion in action. CMH, and by extension, MITW are devoted to fostering dharma, or sacred purpose, and discipline in a world driven by consumerism, greed, and disrespect for the earth.

CMH hosted its first retreat 29 April-1 May 2016 in Kentucky on 'The 9 Elements of Mature Interspirituality' from Teasdale's book, *The Mystic Heart.* In the 9 Elements, Teasdale clearly outlines a path of compassion in action. He makes a case for maintaining a strong sense of ethics, and for practicing simplicity, a monastic virtue dating back to the Middle Ages, refurbished by Thomas Merton in the 1960s as 'voluntary simplicity.'

In a culture in which self-hatred is rampant, individuals stand to benefit by first learning compassion for themselves and their families before trying to save the world. Otherwise, the bodhisattva ideal is likely to fall short of Mahayana Buddhism's intentions for it. Imagine what a world we might live in if everyone worked for everyone else's well-being. Selfishness would have no choice but to evaporate.

Both members of CMH, whether full of lay sannyasins, and MITW may carry their compassion into the world by working on concrete projects designed to help human beings and the planet. Swami Shraddhananda is particularly interested in affiliating with Swami Chidanand's Global WASH Alliance which seeks to clean up the Ganges River and provide better sanitation for the Indian people. She would like to see members of the order spend time volunteering in hospitals like St. Jude's that treat cancer in children. *Seva*, or selfless service, in the organic garden and orchard at Slate Branch Ashram is always welcome too, as a way to enhance CMH's affiliation with the 'From Self Care to Earth Care' programme.

Just as CMH and MITW members write their own 'Personal Covenants' which work in tandem with Teasdale's 9 Elements,[4] so CMH members may propose independent projects they wish to undertake in the world. Even better when monks elect to work together in teams, to be 'intertwined', as are the three writers of this essay. Working in a collective helps monks to deepen their compassion for each other. As Pema Chodron has suggested, ashrams and monasteries are fertile places for conflicts to brew – and for monks to work them out together.

Following her presentation entitled 'A Short Seminar about Killing' for the Parliament of the World's Religions 2015 in Salt Lake City, Swami Shraddhananda began offering workshops to help people deal with the aftermath of domestic and international terrorism. Her book entitled *A Short Book about Killing*, which pays tribute to the Polish filmmaker Krzysztof Kieslowski's 'A Short Film about Killing', was published early in 2016 by The Sacred Feet Publishing Imprint.

Wayne Teasdale notes throughout his chapter entitled 'Spiritual Friendship' in *A Monk in the World* that monasticism offers excellent opportunities for fostering the compassion inherent in camaraderie. As the eminent theologian Paul Tillich wrote, we must first find the 'courage to be' as individuals and then find the courage to be as part of a group, of a 'we'.

Monastics across traditions historically have risked 'falling from grace' to support various initiatives ranging from helping slaves escape to harbouring radical feminists who were viewed as threats to the patriarchal hierarchy. 'The personal is the political' – a truly non-dual statement! If we apply this statement from 1970s feminism to the practice of compassion in action, then surely we can say it is just as monastic to march on Washington or Beijing as it is to meditate in a cave solo.

'Virtual Communities' of Practice and Compassion – Are they Possible Today?

One of the challenges of the emerging 'Interspiritual Age' is that persons who have recognized the value of a trans-traditional spirituality and regularly use more than one – often many – practices from many and various spiritual traditions are geographically scattered. Right now, only in certain population or cultural hubs are large communities of 'Interspirituals' able to regularly and personally share their spiritual lives and practices.

The reason for this demography is that, across all the world's religions, traditions are being lived out at what integral and developmental writers call 'different levels of development'. The use of trans-traditional practices, common to 'interspirituals' arises because they are experiencing religion at a pluralistic or integral level of development. If they were practicing religion, let's say, at a more 'magic-mythic, literalist' level, they would more likely be tied to the specific practices of one tradition. This is just a matter of what is happening in cultural evolution as the world goes global and multicultural – a process that is inevitably unfolding.

Thus today, in step with the advent of highly versatile interactive internet resources, many are experimenting with how 'community' may be maintained, across the miles, with the aid of the worldwide web. The Community of The Mystic Heart is beginning an experiment in this area in cooperation with another early colleague of Br. Wayne Teasdale, Jeffrey Genung, who has created www.contemplativelife.org.

When Br. Teasdale introduced his vision of the Interspiritual Age in *The Mystic Heart*, he said it would unfold because 'of a new set of historical circumstances' [*MH*, 4]. Certainly the internet is one of these! Even in the world of news and political influence alone, the so-called 'blogosphere' has already revolutionized how people worldwide access, and act on, information. This brings new reality to Teasdale's statement below about the relationship of spirituality and community at a global level, and the role of those who are leading modalities of the practice of compassion:

> Spirituality, finally, is awareness and sensitivity, and sensitivity is itself awareness-in-action. It is this quality that we most require in our time and in the ages to come, but it is a quality refined only in the mystic heart, in the steady cultivation of compassion and love that risks all for the sake of others. It is these resources that we desperately need as we build the civilization with a heart, a universal society capable of embracing all that is, putting it to service in the transformation of the world. May the mystics lead the way to this rebirth of the human community that will harmonize itself with the cosmos and finally make peace with all beings. (BR. WAYNE TEASDALE)[5]

Many people today are starving for a new vision, a new paradigm – a vision that is not rigid and hierarchical, but one in which women and well as men are free to explore their humanity and their divinity. How people connect with others and the earth in inspired and compassionate ways is central to this new vision

New Community and Global Change

Because of the evolutionary shift identified by Br. Teasdale, there are significant changes happening today in the depth and breadth of what can be taught, and the media through which these teachings can occur. Traditionally, we are used to recognizing 'transmission' of the dharma through spiritual teachers, the written word, and also the sangha or community. But today we add to this the burgeoning electronic media of the internet, CD's, DVD's, interactive 'chat' and blogging, Skype and many, many more. At numerous spiritual education institutions there has been a shift in the last few years to having far more on-line students than students who are attending in person, even if they live locally.

No matter what the medium, people seem to long for 'awakening', along with a 'calling' that urges them to share their newfound sense of compassionate connection/vision with others. The latter, a 'growing up', if you like, involves their desire to share the riches of their personal experiences with others instead of just keeping it to themselves. Today, many become 'teachers' in their own right and, by doing so, they have begun to build communities as well. The internet social media are full of 'Groups', ranging anywhere from a few dozen to hundreds, that identify themselves as such communities.

Overall, for better or worse, the internet is awash with 'spiritual/ metaphysical' websites and online publications and programmes. All of this is an indication of what is happening evolutionarily on both the subtle and external worldwide realms. And this is bringing a recognizable surge to what is commonly called today 'engaged spirituality' or 'social-' and 'sacred- activist' spirituality. With the 'new set of historical circumstances' Teasdale referred to, people are engaging to try to 'ramp it up' to the level of global change. The new, emergent 'unity consciousness' is wanting to link global challenges such as climate change, resource scarcity, social inequity, ethnocentric-based violence and war, to the possibilities of global structural shift. We need look no further than Pope Francis's 2015 encyclical *Laudato Si'* – 'On the Care of Our Common Home' – to see the comprehensiveness, and suddenness, of these emergences. All of this indicates an evolution in both the subtle and external realms worldwide.

A major inspiration from Br. Teasdale is for us to make it our work to help people connect the random dots of insight and inspiration they have received into a coherent vision. Then they can see where they themselves can fit into the bigger picture being revealed and then they can contribute to the evolutionary impetus unfolding. We believe that the current burgeoning of the desire to create real and fruitful community in the context of the practice of compassion – and what that implies at a global level – is one of these major emergences. We are happy to be part of communities and worldwide discussions designed to advance tangible models and experiments. Ours is described in more detail below.

Tangible Development of Internet-aided Community

Nearly all spiritual communities whose visions stem from emergent holistic, integral, or interspiritual world-views are by nature geographically far-flung. This was acknowledged as far back as 2000 when Paul Ray and Sherry Anderson wrote the classic book *The Cultural Creatives*.[6] They acknowledged that, even then, some 30 per cent of the world holding such forward looking views had more in common with each other, across the miles, than with many of their closest neighbours at home. But how can such persons step-up to sustained and ongoing commitments to personal spiritual practice and far-flung community involvement when a natural tendency (what philosopher Ken Wilber calls 'states' *versus* 'stages') is for short-term, initially compelling, inspirations to rapidly fade over time?

We don't yet know the extent to which internet-aided community can be widely successful and sustained. But it is clear that the possibilities are one main attribution of the Internet Age. Sufi Mystic and Jungian psychologist Dr. Llewellyn Vaughan-Lee points this out in a recent video of his welcoming remarks to a Silicon Valley conference on consciousness and technology.[7]

As we have planned CMH's internet-aided vision, these are the aspects we have emphasized in our web-platform design:

- Creating an intuitive and elegantly designed digital platform to enable users to cut through the constant distractions of today's busy world and easily find practices and build community both locally and virtually.
- Developing a truly universal, and interspiritual digital hub, bringing the myriads of contemplative practices under one umbrella, and

enabling people, communities and practice leaders to connect and work together in an open and highly collaborative environment.

- Creating a virtual and real-time digital framework that enables practice leaders, contemplative activists and communities to become self-sustaining by sharing valuable teaching and content.
- Developing a global virtual community consisting of 'communities of practice'. This 'community of communities' will serve as a hub uniting contemplatives from all walks of life. This includes the great spiritual traditions, mindfulness movement, contemplative movement, indigenous traditions, new thought movement and other contemporary forms of this movement arising in science and technology.

To this end we are creating the 'pilot' for Community of The Mystic Heart though the Contemplative Life website. CMH members will develop and provide the site's vision and content. Content and activity will be structured to serve and enhance the Community's current five 'Kinds of Membership' and, for each group, there will be interactive modalities, from forums and blogging to joining members in creating initiatives, courses, gatherings, events, and so on, each possibly aided by podcasting, live video streaming, video archival sharing, and the like. In turn, it is hoped that these activities will support and further expand the frequency and meaningfulness of the Community's in-person and real-time activities, such as short-term gatherings for community-wide inspiration and sharing, longer enterprises like residential retreats, to offer spiritual teachings and practices, and tours and nitty-gritty projects of service. In 2015-16, through associated networks, several CMH members and leaders created teaching tours as well as book signings.[8] Of course, we do not know the ultimate result, but we do know that the natural gaps created by the daily realities of geographically far-flung communities offer opportunities for Interspiritual advancement.

Conclusion

When combined, the four emphases used to frame this article's view of 'The Practice of Compassion' offer both a diagnosis and a vision for Interspiritual people to meet today's challenging times with grace and skill. The four emphases are these: the vision of inner and outer practice, the practice of compassion through spiritual community, the practice of compassion in the wider world of politics and policy, and today's exciting possibilities of invigorating communities and practices of compassion through Internet platforms and Internet communities.

If the world were ever in need of new models, now is one of those times – brought about by what Br. Wayne Teasdale called 'a new set of historical circumstances'. Employing modern developmental history theory, Johnson and Ord, in their follow-up book on Br. Teasdale's Interspiritual vision (*The Coming Interspiritual Age*) emphasized that every historical paradigm shift is followed by a perilous period of experimentation. This period distinguishes and determines the socio-cultural processes and structures that reflect the vision and values of the emerging paradigm. During this experimental period some innovations will work better than others, some may not work at all, and some that work may even engender collateral damage from the transitional conditions that they create. This process is common to all evolution.[9]

In a world of 'uncharted frontiers', conclude Johnson and Ord, 'mature collective discussion from multiple perspectives is so important as the holistic age unfolds'. Thus, it is fitting that the four emphases used in framing this article parallel those also used in social activism and community organizing work. Moving from being a 'circle of dialogue' to being a 'circle of influence', any evolutionary enterprise must ultimately become a 'system of influence.' According to Johnson and Ord, this is how all 'evolutions and revolutions' have functioned, and by extension, how compassion in an Interspiritual context makes itself felt in the merger of Being and Doing.

Notes

1. Wayne Teasdale, *The Mystic Heart: Discovering a Universal Spirituality in the World's Religions* (Novato CA: New World Library, 1999).
2. Wayne Teasdale, *A Monk in the World* (Novato CA: New World Library, 2002).
3 See www.communityofthemysticheart.org and http://www.jonesfoundation.net/node/41.
4. See http://communityofthemysticheart.org/membership.

5. Words from Brother Wayne at the founding of the Universal Order of Sannyasa, 9 January 2010 (http://multiplex.isdna.org/sannyasa.htm).
6. Paul H., Ray and Sherry R. Anderson, *The Cultural Creatives* (New York: Broadway Books, 2001).
7. Video from 'Consciousness, Technology and the Future' conference (Contemplative Alliance): https://vimeo.com/144390164.
8. See www.selfcaretoearthcare.com [Features], www.thecominginterspiritualage.com [*Initiatives*] and *Anchor* magazine, 2015 (4 [fall/winter]), pp. 32-5.
9. Kurt Johnson and Robert David Ord, *The Coming Interspiritual Age* (Vancouver CN: Namaste Publishing, 2013). Sections 'Building and Living Interspirituality', 'Paradoxes and Ironies of a World Awakening' and 'Appendix 1' based on Integral and Spiral Dynamics theory.

PART VIII

A POETIC ENDING

CHAPTER 25

Importance of Compassion for Mahayana Meditation

GESHE LHABU THUNDUP

Compassion fulfills all desires.

Compassion alone is seen as a seed that brings
your mind to enlightenment.

Compassion is like water and fertilizer that
helps to develop the merit
and wisdom to gain full enlightenment.

Until the end of cyclic existence,
compassion never lands you in the extreme of solitary peace
but encourages one to lead all sentient beings through teaching
to full enlightenment.

And at the end, it is like the ripening of
fruit for the wellbeing of all sentient beings.

As the rain makes all crops grow,
So Buddha guides all the sentient beings out of cyclic existence
through his great compassion.

In a nut shell,
all mankind has compassion from birth.
But due to ignorance,
we fail to see the path that will widen and expand compassion.

Therefore, we distinguish all of mankind into three categories:
hostile, friendly, and middling.

Buddha stated (1) that we are our own enemy
and (2) that we are also our own master.

This is really true.

Compassion is the origin of all sorts of happiness.
Compassion with wisdom is essential.
Compassion and wisdom are complementary.
Compassion is like a very honest person and wisdom is
like the very able person.

Depending on the level of wisdom
there are different dimensions or levels of compassion.

There is compassion which is motivated by an
awareness of the ultimate nature of reality,
by the impermanent nature of existence,
and by the suffering of other sentient beings.

These compassions are distinguished only in the
terms of the objects of focus.
Yet these three types of compassion share the same essence:
They all wish to free beings from suffering.

If you join compassion with wisdom
then
the result becomes very effective.

The most important lineage of meditation for
cultivating the great compassion are:
a warm heart
and an awareness of suffering of other sentient beings.

Compassion alone will not work
unless it is joined with a sense of caring
and a resolute intention.

People in modern society are full of distress.
Yet they lack courage to face their own hatred and anger.

Out of the billions of people in the world,
some are attracted to religion,
but many, increasingly, are not.
In such circumstances, we need a secular ethic.
One that is more relevant and acceptable to modern people.

Nevertheless, we must bear in the mind that we are all
connected with each other.

This is basic to our understanding of humanity;
it is the way to widen compassion beyond religion.

This is called the interdependent nature of reality
or relation between cause and effect.

Our entire happiness is somehow dependent on
the actions of others
either directly
or indirectly.

The rule and connection between cause and effect is
a kind of constant rule and does not change.
For instance, negative emotions like hatred and hostility
lead to undesirable consequences,
and bring distress and frustration of mind.

On the other hand,
a sense of caring and patience leads to positive consequences,
and bring about calmness and a presence of mind.

From the Buddhist view point:
compassion is the wish to free all beings from suffering.

Suffering is broadly divided into three categories:
suffering of suffering,
suffering of change,
and the all-pervasive suffering of condition.

The suffering of suffering is painful suffering.

And the suffering of change is due to the fact
that what is pleasant is not eternal
but bound to change.

All pervasive suffering is the most subtle suffering.
It is inherent

in the very nature of the five contaminated aggregates*
but it is not apparent when
or why it arises.
Nevertheless, it is still the cause of suffering.

That is why Lord Buddha says:
on the needle point of cyclic existence
there is never any happiness.

*The five aggregates: A person of the desire realm or form realm has five aggregates: the aggregates of form, feeling, discrimination, compositional factors, and consciousness.

Contributors

SEYED MOSTAFA AZMAYESH is a scholar and researcher in the fields of spirituality and Gnosticism. He studied Theology at the Sorbonne, History of Law at the Pantheon in Paris and comparative science of Islam and Christianity at the University of Lyon. After completing his academic career he continued his research in religions, philosophy and scientific subjects. He is a renowned Sufi master and a strong advocate for human rights globally, having spoken on a number of occasions at various United Nations human rights conferences and in the European Parliament. He has published numerous books.

M. DARROL BRYANT is the founding Director of the Centre for Dialogue & Spirituality in the World's Religions at Renison University College/University of Waterloo, Waterloo, Ontario, Canada. From 1973 until 2007 he taught at Renison University College and retired as a Distinguished Professor Emeritus. The author/editor of more than 25 volumes including *God: The Contemporary Discussion, Religion in a New Key*; *Muslim-Christian Dialogue: Promise and Problems* and most recently a three volume series on *Ways of the Spirit: Celebrating Dialogue, Diversity and Spirituality*; *Ways of the Spirit: Voices of Women*, and *Ways of the Spirit: Persons, Communities, Spiritualities*. In 2017, he published his 750 page *Guide to Religion in the Modern World*. He has been engaged in the dialogue of religions since the late 1970s and has been in India more than 20 times.

SWAMI CHIDANANDA has been a teacher of Vedanta for three decades. He has been an active speaker and writer in India and North America. In the mid-1990s he was stationed in San Jose, California, for five years. He has been on the Board of the Krishnamurti Foundation India. Many of his former students are now Swamis across the world. He addressed the Interfaith Conference in Rome that celebrated the 50th anniversary of *Nostra Aetate*, a document of Vatican II on the Church's Relation to the Non-Christian Religions. While there he received the blessings of Pope Francis.

ROBERT CHODOS grew up in the Jewish community of Montreal, Quebec. He is a writer, editor, and translator. A long-time member of the Reform Jewish congregation in Waterloo, Ontario, where he is a lay service leader and bar/bat mitzvah tutor. He is a founding member of Interfaith Grand River and participates in a number of study groups, both Jewish and interfaith. In the course of his interfaith involvement, he has been the editor of a Jesuit magazine, lit Chanukah candles in a mosque, co-led a bar mitzvah service with a Unitarian minister, and said the mourner's kaddish in front of an altar to the goddess Brighid.

BRENDAN OZAWA-DE SILVA is an Associate Professor of Psychology in the Department of Positive Human Development and Social Change at Life University in Marietta, Georgia, USA. He is also the Director of the Chillon Project and the Associate Director of the Center for Compassion, Integrity and Social Ethics. He has published numerous articles on secular ethics and the scientific study of meditation. He has also brought compassion training to various groups including school children, foster children, and prison populations.

MOHAMMED FAYYAZUDDIN is an Islamic scholar. He graduated from Jamia Darussalam in Oomerabad, Tamil Nadu, India. Well versed in Islamic studies and Arabic, he has lectured on peace, interfaith harmony, and Islam in Nepal, India, and the U.A.E. A disciple of Maulana Wahiduddin Khan, he is currently the zonal manager of Goodword Books, Delhi. Goodword Books has published more than 200 books in Urdu and English on Islam, peace and global harmony. Among those volumes is Maulana Wahiduddin Khan's *The Prophet of Peace: Teachings of the Prophet Muhammad*, and *The True Jihad: The Concept of Peace, Tolerance and Non-violence in Islam*. Their website can be accessed at www.goodwordbooks.com and www.cpsglobal.org

MARY PAT FISHER is an American author of many college textbooks on religion and on art, including *Living Religions* (bestselling textbook on the world's religions), *Women in Religion, Living Religions: A Brief Introduction*, and three editions of *An Anthology of Living Religions.*

Since 1991 Mary has been living as a volunteer in Gobind Sadan, a unique living interfaith programme with its central community on the outskirts of New Delhi. Her work includes hospitality for visitors, praying for people, education for children, and managing practical aspects of the community such as farming, dairy, water, electricity, maintenance, and gardening.

VIC FROESE is Library Director at Canadian Mennonite University in Winnipeg, Manitoba, where he has worked since 2000. Apart from a Master of Library and Information Science degree, he has a PhD in theology from the University of St. Michael's College in Toronto. He has published a book on Schleiermacher's early ethical work, *On the Highest Good*, and he currently serves as the general editor of *Direction: A Mennonite Brethren Forum*. He resides in Steinbach, Manitoba, and is an active member of the Steinbach Mennonite Brethren Church.

DAVID J. GOA teaches religious studies and theology, leads workshops and seminars on the demanding issues of religion and public life. He was the founding director of the Chester Ronning Centre for the Study of Religion and Public Life at the Augustana Campus of the University of Alberta. Earlier he built the programme for the study of culture at the Royal Alberta Museum. It was based on field research in the full range of religious communities including Hindu, Buddhist, Sikh, Jewish, Muslim and Christian communities in Canada. Recently he has also worked with the Muslim and Christian communities in Syria and Turkey. He was the chief curator of a major international exhibition in the year 2000 titled, *Anno Domini: Jesus Through the Centuries* and the recent internet based exhibition, *U Encounter*. He has published widely on tradition and modernity, most recently *The Christian Responsibility to Muslims* (2015).

JAMES GOLLNICK is Professor Emeritus of Psychology of Religion at St. Paul's University College, University of Waterloo, Ontario, Canada. He was educated at Marquette University (Milwaukee) and Die Freie Universitaet (Berlin), and received his M.A. and Ph.D. from St. Michael's College, University of Toronto and certification from the International Gestalt Association at the Gestalt Institute of Toronto. He is the author of several books, including *Dreams in the Psychology of Religion* (1987); *Religion and Spirituality in the Life Cycle* (2005); and *The Spiritual, Social, and Scientific Meanings of Dreams* (2013).

KURT JOHNSON, co-author of *The Coming Interspiritual Age*, is well known internationally as a scientist, comparative religionist, social activist and former monastic. With a PhD in evolution, ecology, and comparative biology, he was associated for twenty years with the American Museum of Natural History and teaches at the One Spirit Interfaith Seminary in New York City. He is co-author also of *Nabokov's Blues* (a 10 Best Books in Science, 2000), *Fine Lines* (Yale University Press, 2016, on scientific and artistic genius) and *Ethics, Spiritual Values, and the New UN Development Agenda*.

MAULANA WAHIDUDDIN KHAN is an eminent Islamic scholar who was born in 1925 in Azamgarh, India. The Maulana has worked to interpret, reinterpret and redefine an Islam that is relevant to contemporary times. He has not only dedicated his life to understanding his faith but is also a very keen proponent of the ideology of peace. He advocates dialogue with the representatives of all religions and the cultivation of the middle ground that can yield peace. The Maulana has authored over 200 books on the teachings of Islam, prophetic wisdom, spirituality and peaceful co-existence. His writings have been used in universities across the world. In a recent book, *The 500 Most Influential Muslims of 2009*, published by Georgetown University, the Maulana has been named as 'Islam's Spiritual Ambassador to the World.'

ANNE C. KLEIN (RIGZIN DROLMA) is a professor of Religious Studies at Rice University and a founding director and resident teacher of Dawn Mountain Tibetan Buddhist Temple Center and Dawn Mountain Research Institute in Houston, Texas. She is the author of many books including *Meeting the Great Bliss Queen: Buddhists, Feminists, and the Art of the Self* and with Geshe Tenzin Wangyal Rinpoche, *Unbounded Wholeness: Dzogchen, Bon, and the Logic of the Nonconceptual.*

YANNI MANIATES (www.insideoutjourneys.com), MS, is Director of Eco-Ministry, Forum 21; Event coordinator, The Interspiritual Network; Co-editor, *The Eco-Activist Newsletter*; Editor, 'Steering Toward the Omega Point: Roundtables 2, 3 and 4;' and Curator, Self-Care to Earth-Care. In the 1980s he was the Director of a large organization that hosted many major international, interfaith, ecumenical conferences. Also, he was the Director of a medium sized publishing company in NYC for five years and has been teaching Meditation, Intuitive Development and Hermetic and Perennial Wisdom teachings for nearly thirty years. The primary focus of his work has been to help people experience the 'still, small voice within' or as he prefers to call it, 'The Embrace.' He is the author of six mini-books on Meditation and Intuition and three Meditation CDs.

M.P. MATHAI is a leading Gandhian scholar. He was born, educated, and taught in Kerala, India. A Ph.D. from Mahatma Gandhi University, he also served there as a Professor of Gandhian Studies. Following the publication of *Mahatma Gandhi's Worldview,* Professor Mathai was invited to lecture across the USA, in England, Indonesia and in Mexico. He is also a noted Gandhian activist and a member of the Gandhian Peace Foundation in New Delhi. He currently serves as the Director of the Gandhian Studies Programme at Gujarat Vidyapath University in Ahmedabad.

WANGCHUK NEGI is a Professor of Indian Buddhist Philosophy at the Central University of Tibetan Studies in Sarnath/Varanasi, India. He holds a Ph.D. in Tibetan Buddhism and has taught in Australia, the USA, and Japan. He sits on many Boards and Committees. He has published five books including *What is Buddhism? Dhammapada Commentary in Hindi,* and *Vajrayana Darshan Mimansa*, and more than 45 scholarly articles. He has presented papers at 40 conferences across the world. At the meeting in Hyderabad he was universally known as the 'Smiling Buddha.'

TASHI PALJOR was born in Lahul Valley in Himachal Pradesh, India. He received primary education in local schools. After securing a Sanskrit diploma in 1963, he continued his studies in Varanasi and received his Ph.D. in 1968 from Sampurnananda Sanskrit

University, Varanasi. Dr. Paljor then taught Sanskrit and Tibetan literature in various academic institutions. He held the position of Principal at the Central Institute of Buddhist Studies, Leh, Ladakh from 1979 to 2006. He continues to contribute scholarly and experiential papers to different seminars and conferences.

IDRISA PANDIT is the Director of Studies in Islam, an interdisciplinary programme at the University of Waterloo. She received her PhD from the University of Illinois, Urbana-Champaign. Her current teaching and research interests include: Islam in North America, inter-religious Dialogue, gender and faith, conflict resolution, and peace building. Idrisa is also the founder of Muslim Social Services of Kitchener, Waterloo. Currently she is undertaking two research projects – children and mothers of war in conflict ridden Kashmir, and role of faith/interfaith agencies in settlement of newcomers to Canada. She has received several awards for combining her scholarship and community activism.

SUDHAMAHI REGUNATHAN was the Vice Chancellor, Jain Vishva Bharati University in Ladnun and is currently the member-secretary of the Foundation for Understanding Religions and Enlightened Citizenship. She has authored books on the religion of the tribals of North-East India and on the fundamentals of Jainism. She has translated many books by Acharya Mahapragya into English and edited magazines and books, notably on sacred music. Her most recent publications are a translation, *Rishabhayan: The Story of the First King* (2014), *The Colours of Desire on the Canvas of Restraint: The Jaina Way* (2015), and retold stories in a compilation titled *Life is A Story* (2016). She now lives in Delhi.

SWAMI SHRADDHANANDA (AKA REV. DR. SONJA JONES) is a member of the Saraswati Order of Monastics. She serves as the Spiritual Director of Slate Branch Ashram, Head of Sacred Feet Publishing, and Preceptor for the Community of the Mystic Heart. She is the author of numerous books including *Jesus was a Shaktipat Guru* and *A Short Book about Killing*. She holds a doctorate from Emory University, has lectured on six continents, taught for two decades at Allegheny College, and eleven years in the Honor Program at the University of Kentucky.

SHIV TALWAR was educated in civil engineering in India, the USA and Canada. He taught engineering in India and Canada. He retired early to establish the Spiritual Heritage Education Network Inc. (SHEN at http://spiritualeducationeducation.org) with the purpose of helping integrate diversity with education in the core spirituality of humanity. Shiv's education in human values and spirituality began informally in India on early morning walks with his parents. This introduction was followed by excellent courses in high school. He remains beholden to his spiritual mentor, the late Swami Vishwatma Bawra who still continues to enrich his life and shape his values.

VEN. OLANDE ANANDA THERA was born in Amsterdam and studied economic-sociology at the University of Amsterdam. He was ordained in Sri Lanka, practiced meditation at the Kanduboda Meditation Centre before receiving his higher ordination in 1977. He has been a Resident Teacher at Rockhill International Meditation Centre near Kandy (1979-84) and the Buddhist Delegate to Inter-religious Living Dialogue in Europe, Japan, Pakistan, and many other countries (1982-present). He has given retreats in Germany, South Africa, Ladakh, Indonesia and Australia, and served as Abbot of Kottawa Nagaranya, and a resident teacher at Pagode Vanh Hanh Vietnamese Temple in Holland. He has been actively involved with Buddha's Light International Association, the International Network of Engaged Buddhists and the Network of Western Buddhist Teachers Conference. He is the resident meditation teacher at the Pagoda Meditation Centre, Nugegoda, Sri Lanka.

GESHE LHABU THUNDUP was born in the Tehor region of Tibet in 1937. He received his basic education at the Dhargye Monastery in Kham and later in Drepung Monastery in Lhasa. He further studied Buddhist philosophy in India, first in the Buxa Lama Camp and then at Varanasi, and received his Acharya Degree in 1975. He served as a reader at the Central Institute of Buddhist Studies in Leh Ladhak from 1981 to 2001. In 1989, he received his Geshe Lharampa Degree from the Gelukpa University. He taught Buddhism in various institutions both within India and abroad and continues his teaching activities at Drepung Monastery in the Karnataka state of India.

LAMA DOBOOM TULKU was born in the Kham region of Tibet in 1941 and recognized as the reincarnation of the previous Doboom Tulku at the age of two. At the age of 12, he joined Drepung Monastery in Central Tibet and studied Buddhist Philosophy. He came to India in 1959, and lived in a monastic camp in West Bengal to continue his studies. At the Central Institute of Higher Tibetan Studies then under the auspices of Sanskrit University, Varanasi, he studied Buddhist Philosophy and received a Geshe-Archarya degree in 1972. He was awarded an honorary doctorate degree in Buddhist Studies by the Mahachulalongkorn Buddhist University of Bangkok in 1999. From 1972 until March 2011, he worked in various academic, cultural and administrative institutions of His Holiness the Dalai Lama. He pursued a millennium project of World Festival of Sacred Music which became a worldwide event with festivals at over a dozen venues in different continents. He is currently engaged in inter-religious and cross-cultural activities through art and culture, as the Founder Managing Trustee of World Buddhist Culture Trust (www.wbct.org).

THOMAS WALSH is the President of the Universal Peace Federation and Secretary General of the Sunhak Peace Prize Foundation. He has a Ph.D. from Vanderbilt University and been a teacher, author, and editor specializing in areas of interfaith relations, religion and peace, philosophy and social theory. He is Vice Chair of the International Council of the *World Association of Non-Governmental Organizations* and on the board of directions of the *International Coalition for Religious Freedom.* He is Executive Editor of *Dialogue and Alliance.* He has contributed to and edited more than twenty books related to interfaith relations, peacebuilding and on the United Nations including *Renewing the United Nations and Building a Culture of Peace* and *The Millennium Declaration of the United Nations: A Response from Civil Society.*

ZULEIKHA is an international performer and educator whose work inspires dynamic creativity and rejuvenation through the profound art of movement. Renowned for her global work with women, children and families, 'storydance' performances, innovative classes, and collaborations celebrating the poetry of Rumi, she is also the creator of *Take a Minute*, a dynamic self-care exercise programme to increase vitality and resilience. Founder/executive director of The Storydancer Project, a non-profit organization that serves girls, women, children and families facing challenging life circumstances, Zuleikha is a recipient of numerous awards for her outstanding work in the world promoting positive personal and social change.

Index